PHANTOM LADIES
The New Edition

ANDREW GREEN
Edited and Enlarged by ALAN MURDIE

Published 2024 by arima publishing

www.arimapublishing.co.uk

ISBN 978 1 84549 830 6

© Alan Murdie & Estate of Andrew Green 2024

All rights reserved

This book is copyright. Subject to statutory exception and to provisions of relevant collective licensing agreements, no part of this publication may be reproduced, stored in a retrieval system, or transmitted in any form or by any means, without the prior written permission of the author.

This book is sold subject to the conditions that it shall not, by way of trade or otherwise, be lent, re-sold, hired out, or otherwise circulated without the publisher's prior consent in any form of binding or cover other than that which it is published and without a similar condition including this condition being imposed on the subsequent purchaser.

arima publishing
ASK House, Northgate Avenue
Bury St Edmunds, Suffolk IP32 6BB
t: (+44) 01284 700321

www.arimapublishing.com

CONTENTS

Introduction to the New Edition (2024) 1
by Alan Murdie

Acknowledgements 5

Part One 7
by Andrew Green

Preface (1977) 9

Acknowledgements 11

List of Illustrations 13

Classification 14

A County-by-County Guide to Phantom Ladies in the UK 15

Further Reading/References 126

Part Two: Exploring Aspects of Phantom Ladies 127
by Alan Murdie

Chapter One
Phantom Ladies from the perspective of psychical research 129

Chapter Two
Human Issues and Impacts 145

Chapter Three
Investigating Ghosts 159

Chapter Four
White Ladies and Phantom Ladies – one and the same? Or different altogether? ... 177

Appendix 195

Index 197

INTRODUCTION TO THE NEW EDITION

By Alan Murdie

I am pleased to introduce this new edition of *Phantom Ladies.*

When originally published in 1977, it was described by its author Andrew Green (1927-2004) as an 'alphabetical, county by county guide to hauntings in Great Britain, with the accent on cases which have involved women'.

In doing so, it provided the first book exclusively devoted to haunted sites around the UK where the ghost is reputed to be female. In addition to showing how the traditional categories of ghostly ladies, 'such as nuns and unhappy lovers, form the majority of cases' the book also acknowledged '…there are many others, including barmaids, aristocrats, mothers with their babies, and even a highwaywoman'.

The collection also affirmed a conclusion being reached in the 1970s that reports of ghosts and hauntings no longer emerged mostly from the customary ancient castles and monasteries but were also being reliably reported from a wide range of modern and often mundane premises, such as 'golf clubhouses, multi-storey carparks, industrial estates and pubs'.[1]

Forty-six years on, these patterns of haunting experiences continue, which prompts this new and enlarged edition of *Phantom Ladies*. It is also hoped it will fulfil a number of other aims.

The first is to acquaint a new generation of psychical researchers, scholars and serious ghost hunters with the book itself, and more widely with the work and ideas of Andrew Green who, for nearly sixty years, was amongst the most active ghost hunters in the UK. Variously described as "Britain's Spectre Inspector" and "our leading Ghost Buster" by the press, Green conducted practical investigations and research into the paranormal from 1944 onwards until shortly before his death in May 2004. Over this period, he personally investigated many hundreds of haunted sites and wrote numerous books and articles. Working in the field he adopted the approach pioneered by the Society for Psychical Research in 1882 of gathering accounts of ghostly phenomena from witnesses and did much to encourage the use of equipment in practical investigations conducted from a scientific perspective.

Green catalogued the results from his first thirty years of ghost research in a series of books appearing in the decade 1970-1980, three of which were conceived as gazetteers and were national in scope. The first of these, *Our Haunted Kingdom* published in 1973, comprised a nationwide survey of hauntings with examples from every county and totalling over 300 haunted locations, all of which had reported manifestations in the previous 25 years. Seven years later he was easily able to fill a similar volume, *Ghosts of Today* (1980) containing a collection of a further 400 contemporary examples.[2]

In the course of gathering this material, Green noticed a large number of reports of hauntings being attributed to specifically female ghosts or claims of manifestations which were considered to be evidence of a haunting female presence. Finding himself with so many accounts of ghostly women, he thought these were worthy of a volume to themselves. A number had been personally investigated by him or he had learned first-hand details from witnesses to manifestations. With others, drawn from documentary sources, he generally maintained his restriction on only including sites where phenomena had been reported in the previous quarter of century.

The result was *Phantom Ladies* which takes a gender-specific and national gazetteer approach in the hope of advancing further investigation.

To encourage and inspire such research anew from a scientific perspective is a secondary aim of this re-issue. Analysis of the evidence from the perspective of psychical research indicates such experiences are spread across four of the five senses, with witnesses variously seeing female apparitions, hearing what they interpret as the sounds of a ghostly woman, experiencing touches ascribed to phantom ladies or perceiving a strange smell or scent which they consider connected with a specifically feminine rather than masculine ghost. However, these experiences may engage postulated paranormal senses, collectively known as 'psi' abilities. In other cases, there may be a sense of an intangible feeling of a presence which carries the impression of being female in nature. With some sightings the ghost is identified as a once-living woman known to be associated with the location.

In the remainder, which is the bulk, she is presumed to be a once living woman, now deceased. Often the identity of the phantom lady remains unknown, with only folklore and hearsay providing clues to whom she once was or might have been. With some there may be no back story or tradition at all.

Green had a number of theories of what lay behind these experiences, considering that any of a number of possible causes were at work, many potentially involving the misinterpretation of natural stimuli or auto-suggestion and imagination.

Others he considered paranormal in nature. On what ghosts – whether male or female – might potentially represent in terms of survival and life after death, Green himself took a materialist position and rejected spiritual interpretations. He did not believe in spirits of the dead, but rather that human beings were capable of creating an energy that transmitted information and which could be picked up by sensitive people and experienced as a ghost. He believed this energy was typically generated by people undergoing stress and postulated that it was likely to be electromagnetic in nature. After the death of the person this energy might persist, being fixed at a location and be experienced as a ghost, eventually fading with time. Those hauntings which were paranormal in nature he linked with postulated abilities of telepathy, clairvoyance, precognition and psychokinesis (the power of the mind to influence matter) all of which have been studied in parapsychology laboratories in many countries since the 1930s.

Green continued to endorse these theories up until his own death in 2004. He hoped that by espousing a scientific and rationalist approach to ghostly phenomena this would also help dispel some of the superstition surrounding psychic phenomena and reduce the alarm, fear and distress that hauntings sometimes engender for those experiencing them.

Whatever their nature, Phantom Ladies as detailed in this work continue to be reported into the 21st century, including the persistence of ghostly phenomena at a number of sites in this book, providing a further justification for this new edition.

If ghostly ladies do indeed haunt then it is entirely possible that a number of these sites remain active today and provide opportunities for investigation, utilising methods not available at the time of original publication.

Accordingly, it is hoped that with its gazetteer and a county-by-county approach with accompanying details of road and rail links it will provide a practical guide for all those seriously interested in investigating such cases afresh and inform research that may already be underway.

Whilst it is recognised that *Phantom Ladies* is in no way an exhaustive study, being very much a much a survey of its time, it is nonetheless hoped that republication may succeed in bridging the gulf which is discernible between much ghost research before and after the year 2000 with the rise of the internet.

Research in parapsychology has progressed and gained greater academic recognition, with departments established at several British Universities since 1985 but there has been relatively little progress with ghosts. Whereas the growth of experimental work in laboratories has allowed some standardisation of paranormal research, often taking a statistical approach to postulated abilities such as telepathy, clairvoyance and precognition (labelled together under the general term of 'psi') this has not been possible with spontaneous cases such as hauntings and poltergeist activity which occur outside controlled conditions.

Research into hauntings has been for many years in the hands of a small number of independent investigators, each with his/her own methods, perspectives and sets of findings. Psychical research itself lacks any testable explanatory theory or common paradigm for approaching ghost reports. Furthermore, too many cases of alleged ghost sightings and haunted houses end up as 'one-off' investigations with no follow-ups or further study.

This problem is compounded when, in the natural course of things these researchers die leaving no successors. Decades may then pass without anyone recording anything further in permanent form, and with the original research being forgotten. The fact that it has taken over four decades to bring *Phantom Ladies* and the material within back into print and circulation aptly illustrates exactly this problem. Often it may be years before anyone returns to a particular location to see if activity is still being reported in the same way. Hence the need to bring 'old' material back to wider attention.

Knowing Andrew Green myself and having the privilege of mutually sharing research with him up until his death, I know he welcomed fresh analysis and study of the material he accumulated and sought to encourage the application of technological advances to research. Benefitting as I did from many discussions with him on aspects of paranormal phenomena and enjoying unique access to his original notes and other materials which he accumulated from the late 1940s enables me to include some additional material to accompany the 1977 text.

Like all sciences, Green considered all findings and theories in psychical research should be considered provisional, to be altered, corrected and expanded as the field progresses in time. No cases were ever considered permanently closed.

Consequently, this new edition consists of two parts, expanding upon Green's original text written from his home near Robertsbridge in Sussex where he lived permanently with his wife Norah up until his death.

Part one consists of the original gazetteer of haunted sites contained in *Phantom Ladies* as it was written by Andrew Green himself and with his entries on each site virtually unaltered. Obviously, the fact that phenomena were being reported in the past does not mean these sites are still haunted today; equally there are some where hauntings continue unabated.

Wherever further information has come to light, I have provided details in additional 'Editor's Notes' expanding on the entry and encompassing new information. Some of this is drawn from Andrew Green's archives, including information he received after the book went into print in 1977. The rest has been gathered by myself from a range of other and more recent sources.

Following on from the gazetteer, part two of this book attempts a deeper examination of the ghostly phenomena covered, applying some of Green's own insights along with the views of other psychical researchers.

Analysis of reports indicates certain repeating patterns in the data which I seek to examine in four new chapters by myself. The first chapter considers some discernible and recurrent patterns with phenomena found with accounts in the book and an outline of major theories, including some of Green's own ideas on the formation of apparitions.

The second new chapter analyses yet further and recurrent features in reports including personal meanings attaching to some female apparitions and the various impacts upon witnesses who have experienced them.

The third chapter then aims at providing advice on the conduct of practical investigations for the interested reader (and would-be ghost hunter) including some pointers as to how he or she may go about it. This is best read in conjunction with other serious texts published in this field, including guides issued by the Society for Psychical Research and the second and updated version of Green's own *Ghost Hunting: A Practical Guide* published in 2016.

It is a hoped this may encourage new investigations at sites where appropriate permission can be obtained, utilising techniques and methods developed into the

21st century. At the most basic level new it may be possible to verify, corroborate or correct the information originally published by Green in 1977 as well as discover if manifestations have continued or have ceased. With some others naturalistic explanations may have emerged. It will be appreciated that with some sites, access arrangements have altered over the years, some premises have been closed down or even demolished. So, when it comes to seeking new access checks need to be undertaken by any investigator and the most up-to-date information obtained.

The concluding chapter examines the challenges posed by 'White Lady' apparitions. In the course of this book, it became apparent that these emerge as a distinct sub-class of Phantom Lady report, distinguishable from more routine reports of manifestations typically associated with haunted premises. Because of their sporadic nature these apparitions pose major problems in terms of both explanatory theories and in practice for investigators seeking to study them. Widely reported at diverse locations in the UK, they appear not only in the British Isles but represent a possibly global phenomenon, one hitherto addressed by folklorists, Jungian psychoanalysts and esoteric writers.

It is hard to fit these appearances of phantom females dressed in white (or typically monochrome attire) into existing paradigms of psychical research (though this does not mean ones cannot be developed). Whilst Green would not personally have endorsed some of the ideas I raise, equally he would not have discouraged serious research and speculation about the nature of these ghost sightings and would readily have accepted that our existing knowledge is far from complete.

Finally, let me say in recent years there has been a cultural fashion for labelling the 1970s and early 1980s as the time of a 'haunted generation' exposed to troubling and unsettling media imagery and motifs which reflected wider political and social strains. With republication of *Phantom Ladies* I hope this book will demonstrate that the Britain of the 1970s was also literally haunted, with so many reports of ghostly activity being received.

For this new edition, I have retained all of Green's original 1977 acknowledgements, together with his list of sources. Entries marked with an asterisk were personally investigated by him. At the time of original publication, the fashion was against popular ghost books containing extensive bibliographies of references. However, with my additional chapters I have included a set of references for each one.

Acknowledgements: I would like to thank the following for helpful information and suggestions: Nigel Bundy, Claire Davy (also for help with proof reading), Chantal Warren-Jones for help with indexing, John Fraser and the late Mr Tom Perrott, long-time chairman of the Ghost Club, for assistance with references to particular sites; Mr Philip Hutchinson for information relating to Guildford; Chantal Warren-Jones, Dr Urszula Wolski and to Nexus 24 Ltd, Edinburgh for digital assistance with the text. In the years since Andrew Green's death, I have also benefitted greatly from help and assistance from many people who knew him, including his late widow Norah Green, his step-son Paul Cawthorne and his friends and neighbours Jackie Spriggs and Trish and Roger Jones, to all of whom I express my grateful thanks. I would also like to thank the following individuals for help at various stages, including Kathy Gearing, Rita Leek, Dave Gordon, Robert Halliday, members of the Spontaneous Cases Committee of the Society for Psychical Research and the late Philip Paul and the late Guy Playfair.

[1] Andrew Green, on the original dust-binding to the first edition

[2] *Our Haunted Kingdom* (1973) Wolfe Publishing and *Ghosts of Today* (1980) Kaye & Ward.

PART ONE

A County-by-County Guide to Phantom Ladies in the UK

PREFACE (1977)

By Andrew Green

It has always interested me that the majority of ghosts reported in Britain consist of phantom ladies, though it is not really surprising when one realises that there are fewer men in the country and always have been. Women are also more likely to report hauntings, presumably because men are more reluctant to expose themselves to unjustified ridicule or scorn.

Some of the misconceptions regarding ghosts will, I hope, be dispelled by this selection of cases, for it will be realised that phantoms can be seen by anyone at any time of the day and anywhere associated with humans, including a public telephone box.

All the cases documented herein have been experienced within the last 25 years, it being felt that older incidents are less likely to be certifiably authentic. One question which frequently arises is how does one gauge whether a sighting is genuine? In my view the initial basic need is to assess the characters of the witnesses and the rationality of the information that they provide. Perhaps it is because of these criteria that some of the better known or more publicised hauntings have been omitted. Because poltergeist activity relates solely to individuals and not property, all such cases have been left out.

Unfortunately, I have never had the pleasure of seeing a female phantom, unless it was the ghost of poor little Nan Tuck in Buxted, Sussex which I saw late one evening a few years ago, but should any reader know of any genuine modern haunting I would be only too pleased to receive details. Meanwhile I hope you will enjoy this collection of Britain's female phantoms, but if you meet one, do be polite.

Andrew Green
Robertsbridge

ACKNOWLEDGEMENTS

To all those kind people who have helped me compile this selection of ghost stories through writing detailed experiences, lending me their personal notes, supplying valuable material, carrying out searches or spending valuable time discussing phenomena, may I offer my sincere thanks.

In particular I would like to acknowledge the great assistance provided by the following: Cicely Botley of Tunbridge Wells, D. T. Brett of Bramshill, Edwin Chapman, contributor to Radio Leicester, Stephen Clarke of Gwent, Fred Cook of Basingstoke, Mrs. Anne Deane of Cranbrook, Kevin Desmond of London, Colin Dwyer of Batley, John Fennelly of Enfield Newspapers, Robert Glenton of *The Sunday Express*, Goodliffe Estates of New Romney, Dr. J. R. A. Gray of Bolton Museums, Michael Jack of Folkestone, Barry King of DPRG, Dagenham, Walter Libby of Robertsbridge, Alfred Mills of Holyhead, Anglesey, Irene Newton of Cranbrook, Miss Roper of Littlestone and H. Slatter of Plymouth.

I am also indebted to the following authors and relevant publishers for allowing me to quote from their books: Anthony Hippisley Coxe (*Haunted Britain*) Pan Books, Jack Hallam (*Ghost Tour and Haunted Inns of England*) Wolfe Publishing, Winifred I. Hayward (article) *Country Life*, Rodney Legg and Tom Perott (*Ghosts of Dorset, Devon & Somerset*) Dorset Publishing, John V. Mitchell (*Ghosts of an Ancient City*) Cerealis Press of York, Robert Neumann (*Plague House Papers*) Hutchinson, Diana Norman and Tom Corbett (*Stately Ghosts of England*) Frederick Muller, James Turner (*Ghosts of the South West and Sometimes into England*) David & Charles and Cassell, Kathleen Wiltshire (*Ghosts & Legends of the Wiltshire Countryside*) Compton Russell; Wolfe Publishing and David & Charles for allowing me to use extracts from my own books (*Ghosts of the South East* and *Our Haunted Kingdom*) and to all those other authors and writers who have produced such interesting material mentioned in the bibliography or the relevant text.

My special thanks are offered to Janet Gaskell of Littlestone, Dick Godden of Folkestone and Valerie Kent of Broadstairs for their considerable assistance in providing greatly appreciated help with some of the Kent cases, Eddie Pratt of Caterham for his valued assistance with some London and Surrey cases, to Mary Fraser of St. Leonards for the help with my photographic requirements and to Mike Jacobs of St. Leonards. I am particularly indebted to Colin Smith of Birmingham for, without his vital assistance in providing so much valuable material, this collection would be sadly lacking in details of cases in the Midlands. And to Deidre Borner of Whyteleafe for again setting her typewriter on fire for my benefit, deciphering my scribble and putting some of it into sense. Also to Marian Williams of Robertsbridge for the greatly appreciated assistance and overall encouragement.

The illustration for Bramshill House is Crown copyright and reproduced with permission of the Controller of Her Majesty's Stationery Office.

LIST OF ILLUSTRATIONS

The Police College, Bramshill House, Hartley Wintney, Hampshire 36

Old Soar Manor, Plaxtol, Kent 53

St. Nicholas Church in Pluckley, Kent 54

Boston Manor House, Brentford 65

Roundshaw Estate, Croydon, London 66

The Chapel of Rycote House, near Oxford 76

Church of St Lawrence, Ludlow, Salop 77

Wray Farm, Reigate, Surrey 87

Shovells, All Saints Street, Hastings, Kent 91

Pevensey Castle, Pevensey, Sussex 93

Pashley Manor, Ticehurst, Sussex 95

Maxstoke Castle, Coleshill, Birmingham 102

St. Nicholas Church, Curdworth, near Birmingham 105

Ripley Castle, near Harrogate, Yorkshire 112

Theatre Royal, York 115

Muchalls Castle, Stonehaven, Grampian Region 119

CLASSIFICATION

* Indicates a personal visit or experience by the author or the witnesses have been interviewed by him.

OP Open to the Public -

OPA Open by Appointment-only

PP Private Property – at normal hours or implies free access. It would be wise to check opening times of properties before visiting the sites classified as such. In some cases this classification refers to clubs or semiprivate residences, so check first. Do please respect.

A COUNTY-BY-COUNTY GUIDE TO PHANTOM LADIES IN THE UK

AVON

Garricks Head Hotel, OP
Shaw Close,
Bath *On A4/A36 – Nearest Station – Bath.*

There seem to be many weird noises heard in this popular hotel, which adjoins the Theatre Royal, ranging from 'knocks on a bedroom door' to a 'rumbling laugh'. Most of the phenomena are associated with Beau Nash who is supposed to have run a gaming house here in the olden days. One of the ladies in this case hanged herself in a bedroom after her lover was killed in a duel, but she has not been seen for some time. The other ghostly girl has been witnessed fairly recently as a 'grey shape' which wafts out of the window in a room situated above the main bar.

This 'shape of the Grey Lady' has also been spotted sitting in a box of the theatre, but no-one knows her story. Some wit suggested she was a 'blithe spirit of the pub.'

BEDFORDSHIRE

Chicksands Priory,* PP
Clophill.

It is a pity that so many interesting establishments are closed to the public because they are owned by the Ministry of Defence or some other Government authority. One such building is this ancient Priory founded by Countess Rohese in 1150, which now forms part of the Officers' Mess for the USAAF and RAF personnel. Captain Kennett of the USAAF was kind enough to provide me with a wealth of material for another case book on which I was working in 1972, and among the records is the statement that 'in the 1960s a figure of a woman dressed in black was seen disappearing through a wall in the picture gallery adjoining the King James's Room.' The apparition had long hair covering most of its features, which would hardly match the description of the nun which, legend has it, haunts the Priory. She is supposed to be a nun named Berta Rosata who fell in love with a canon and was put to death on the discovery of her pregnancy. Admittedly there were 'naughty goings on' in the house of religion, for Dr. Richard Layton, writing to Cromwell in 1534, stated that on a visit he discovered 'two of the said nunnes not barren', one of them having been made pregnant by a 'serving man' and the other by 'a superior'. A romantic but completely inaccurate tale has been created to account for the plaque set over one of the windows in a wall of the remaining cloister which refers to 'Berta Rosata'. "This is an obvious invention of the late 18th century," says an expert historian. "There is no need to feel that the nun ever existed." Yet someone haunts the Priory, or rather two – or is it three women?

A member of the female staff saw a "fascinating woman dressed in white glide past me. I saw the long white train as she moved and heard the rustle of the dress." This was at 10 o'clock in the evening, also in the picture gallery. In 1954 a Flight Lieutenant woke up at 3.45 am, switched on the light and saw "a woman with a ruddy face and untidy hair, wearing a dark dress with a white lace collar." The figure moved to the foot of the bed and vanished. Three years later, in March, another officer reported a phantom "of a middle-aged woman dressed in what we associate with a nun's head-dress." Perhaps when the Priory is released for civilian use it might be possible to find out a bit more about the ghostly women of Chicksands.

Editor's Note: Chicksands Base returned to British military control in the 1990s. The absence or disguising of facial features occurs in many apparitional accounts. Since early in the 21st century investigations have been continued by Damien O'Dell and the Anglia Paranormal Investigation Society who have conducted monitoring of the site since an investigation at Christmas 2005. Damien O'Dell of Anglia Paranormal Investigation Society (APIS) considers that that "Chicksands has multiple hauntings of every description. There's the prioress who haunts the place, kids who run around in the kitchen, and a monk who was spotted three times during our investigation. "Three different teams on three separate occasions all said the same thing, that they'd seen a monk. "They couldn't see its face but could see its hood, and it glided noiselessly through the priory, on one occasion floating through a wall." He adds: "We'd all of course heard of the supposed hauntings at Chicksands and had researched it a lot before, but I don't think we were prepared for what some of our team saw." His research has led to an entire book *Chicksands Priory – England's Most Haunted House* published in November 2022.

Wilden, OP
Near Bedford. *Off B660 – Nearest Station – Bedford.*
One day in 1973 I was travelling back to Bedford from a visit to Kimbolton Castle, an interesting Tudor manor house, and decided to call in at a nearby pub before proceeding further. Standing in the bar I started chatting to one of the other customers. We got on to the subject of ghosts and it was with some surprise that I learnt that he had seen one the previous week on the road between Wilden and Ravensden. What had astonished him was that it had been during the afternoon for, like so many witnesses, he thought that apparitions only appeared at night. The gentleman described her quite well. "She was an old woman, all in black, with a long skirt practically down to the ground," he said. "She was walking slowly along the path beside the road and as I passed her, I gave her a glance. Blimey, if looks could kill, I wouldn't be here mate. If I believed in witches, she was one. But up till then I didn't believe in ghosts either. Anyway I turned back and there she was, gone, just vanished."

He had been so upset by the incident that he had called into another nearby pub for a 'pick me up' and learnt that the old woman he had seen is well known in the village as the ghost of a witch, but who she was originally is anyone's guess. It was also surprising to the publican involved for it seems that she had not been seen for a long time. So, she's back!

Skefco Ltd, PP,
Leagrave Road,
Luton

Late in 1972 when the canteen of this well-known engineering factory was being modernised and refurbished, the stock controller, Mrs. Dora Rouget, was working in the storeroom checking the supplies when she sensed someone behind her. Thinking it was one of the girl workers, she turned to enquire how she could assist but was surprised and puzzled by seeing, not one of her colleagues, but a "white form" in front of her. As she gazed at the shape it faded away. A few weeks later Mrs. Tina Tyrell, a control clerk, saw "a peculiar figure" walk into the cloakroom. Intrigued, she looked inside the room but found no-one there. Discussing the incident later with other members of the staff, she learnt that it was not the first time that the shape had been seen. Some witnesses described it as that of a woman wearing white overalls and boots. To those who had seen the apparition clearly it appeared to be identical – at least in clothing – to that of a cook who had died in the building some nine years earlier.

BUCKINGHAMSHIRE

Claydon House, OP
Middle Claydon
Near Winslow.   *Off A413 – Nearest Station – Aylesbury (13 miles)*

One of the most interesting parts of this National Trust property is the Florence Nightingale Museum, her bedroom and sitting room. The manor house itself was built in the 16th century and added to in the 18th century by the second Earl of Verney. However, about a hundred years later, parts were demolished and a new south front added. The 'lady with the lamp' was a sister of Lady Verney and frequently stayed here. There is a magnificent carved ceiling in the Gothic Room and, for the enthusiastic collector of chinoiserie, a vast display of Chinese objet d'art in the adjoining room.

A legend of Claydon is that Sir Edmund Verney, refusing to part with the King's Standard at Edgehill, was killed and his hand hacked off so that the Roundheads could take the colours. The knight's hand was recognised by a signet ring and buried in the grounds of Claydon but his body was never discovered and haunts the manor. A figure that is not legendary, however, is that of the 'grey lady' seen recently in the Rose Room and near Miss Nightingale's bedroom. Antony Hippisley Coxe asks in his *Haunted Britain* could it be that of Florence herself? There certainly seems no reason why it shouldn't be.

CAMBRIDGESHIRE

Sawston Hall, PP
Near Cambridge.

To the avid ghost hunter Sawston Hall is nearly as well known as Borley for its hauntings. Practically every book on the subject refers to the phantom of Queen Mary I being seen in the room where she slept. But more convincing are the reports of the 'grey lady' who sometimes glides through the Tapestry Room and, it seems, rattles the door catches. She was once seen in the grounds but this still did not help to identify the female.

Editor's Note: The first resident of the house to report paranormal activity was Clare Eyre-Huddleston who married Captain Reginald Eyre-Huddleston in 1930. She heard a spinet (a keyboard instrument popular during Tudor times) playing in the building. Her friends heard it too, although Reginald did not. Clare obviously had a sensitive musical ear: there was a harpsichord in the Hall, but she insisted the tone was lighter, and that she heard it when she knew the harpsichord was not being played. In about 1960 the *Cambridge Evening News* quoted the cook, Mrs. Fuller, who had seen a silent ghost drifting in and out of one room. The British Travel and Holidays Association sponsored Candy Scott, a model, to sleep in the *Tapestry Room*, which was said to be a particular focus of ghostly activity. Candy saw nothing but felt icy winds and heard noises including doors opening and closing, which convinced her that the hall was haunted. In 1984 *Cambridge Evening News* reporter Carmel Fitzsimons stayed at Sawston Hall for a Halloween feature and although she saw no ghosts, she slept badly and caught flu.

Harston, OP
Near Cambridge. *Off A10 – Nearest Station – Cambridge*

On the road between the villages of Harston and Haslingfield there is a bridge over the River Cam and here, it is said, will be seen a spectral 'lady in white' jumping into the water. Antony Hippisley Coxe claims that she is more frequently seen gliding towards Mill Road from 'The Queen's Head'. Why is it, one wonders, that many phantoms of both sexes can be found either near water which causes mists, or associated with pubs?

Editor's Note A story, collected in the 1930s, says that a "lady in white" haunted a road bend at Harston between the Queen's Head Pub and Mill Road: two boys are said to have waited for her with a gun and shot at her, only to wound a cow. Another white lady threw herself into the river from the bridge on the road between Harston and Haslingfield. The ghost of a white lady on a bridge at Alconbury, was said to have caused several car crashes. In 1973 the noted Cambridge psychical researcher and vice President of the Society for Psychical Research. Tony Cornell set up infra-red cameras in an attempt to photograph her, but he enjoyed no success.

CHESHIRE
Gawsworth Hall,*
Macclesfield. *OP On A536 – Nearest Station – Macclesfield (4 miles)*

Mr. Raymond Richards told me a few years ago that "the Hall, the Church and the Rectory, all 15th century buildings, have been associated with manifestations at one time or another … but we have come to attach no importance to happenings which occur from time to time. At all events they are all part of the household." Although one of the most recent incidents was that of Monica Richards reporting the perfume of incense in her bedroom which was situated immediately beneath a priests' hole, a ghostly lady "in ancient costume" has also frequently been seen. She is associated with 'the fighting Fittons' who lived here from 1316 to 1662. The house itself, a beautiful half-timbered manor, has been occupied by only five families since Norman times. Mary Fitton, daughter of Sir Edward, was appointed Maid of Honour to Queen Elizabeth, but her career was short lived. It is this young lady who some believe was termed 'The dark lady' by Shakespeare. In 1602 Sir Robert Cecil told the Queen that her Maid of Honour had lost her honour and was pregnant.

Her Majesty, enraged at such effrontery, sent Mary and the Earl of Pembroke, the father of the unborn child, to the Tower 'to dwell awhile'. What happened later is not known, though some claim that 'the dark lady' is the one in 'olden dress' who still frequents the house in which she was born.

CORNWALL
Penfound Manor, PP
Poundstock
Near Bude.

Once open to the public, but now strictly private, this 600-year-old manor is one of the oldest lived-in houses in the country. The owner at the time, Mr. Kenneth Tucker told Diana Norman, author of *Stately Ghosts of England*, in 1963, that he had spent a considerable time trying to discover any documented evidence of the ghost which haunted his home and had found none. Legend however provides the tale that the phantom is that of Kate Penfound, daughter of a Royalist, who fell in love with John Trebarfoot, a Cromwellian, and was shot for this heresy by her father. Because there is no record of Kate there is no reason to think that the story is anything other than mythical, however, it should be noted that many church registers were destroyed by Royalist supporters during the Civil War.

Although neither Mr. Tucker nor his wife saw any sign of Kate, some puzzling incidents occurred whilst they lived in the Manor, including an occasion when one visitor, a sensitive, asked about someone called 'Editha'. Kenneth was surprised because he knew that a house on the site once

belonged to Queen Edith who is referred to in the Domesday Book as 'Eddeva'. Many visitors told the Tuckers about experiences that occurred in previous years. The son of a former tenant admitted that his father and neighbours had frequently seen Kate crossing the Great Hall on her way towards the main stairs.

Chapel Street,* OP
Penzance. *Off A30 – Nearest Station – Penzance*

Only three miles from a 2000-year-old Iron-Age village, tourists find one of the most popular resorts of Cornwall, which enjoys a climate so mild that sub-tropical plants are seen to thrive in the public parks. The local 'high spot' is St. Michael's Mount which local romanticists claim is part of the mythical Kingdom of Lyonesse.

Chapel Street, leading down to the docks from Queen Street, once housed a smallish orchard owned by a Mrs. Elizabeth Baines who, it seems, was rather concerned about the value of the fruit and the risk of losing some of it to thieves, robbers and criminal youngsters. Being rather over-protective, or perhaps just mean, she hired a local fisherman to guard the fruit and provided him with a pistol. One evening, nearing harvesting time, she went to check that the guard was still doing his job. The old man, thinking that she was a thief, didn't bother to call out but simply fired and shot her. Her phantom, wearing a dark cloak and bonnet, has been seen by one or two locals and a few tourists taking an evening exploratory stroll round the town. She has been seen near the top end of the street where she disappears through a wall.

Editor's Note: The story of the ghost of Mrs Baines appears in *Traditions and Hearthside Stories of West Cornwall, Vol. 1* (1870) by William Bottrell which describes occurances which took place after her death, thereby dating the events mentioned here to the second decade of the 19th century. Bottrell states: 'The ghost became so troublesome at last, that no person could be found to occupy the house, where she was all night long tramping about from room to room, slamming the doors, rattling the furniture, and often making a fearful crash amongst glass and crockery. Even when there was no living occupant in the house, persons standing in Chapel Street, often saw through the windows a shadowy form and lights glimmering in the parlours and bedrooms.' These phenomena have a ring of truth to them but it appears that some subsequent disturbances were attributable to a hoax by a local man, a Captain Carthew. Whether he was responsible for all of them or simply imitating them is unclear but he could not be responsible for any more recent reports.

CUMBRIA

Lorton Hall,* OPA
Lorton,
Cockermouth. *On B5289 – Nearest Station – Workington (14 miles)*

In September 1972 the Rev. J. A. Woodhead-Keith-Dixon was kind enough to provide me with an interesting letter in which he described the haunting of this 17th century manor house. He told me that 'The Grey Lady' of Lorton Hall, often seen by visitors and once by himself, would seem to be a member of the family living there in the 18th century and who were unfortunate enough to produce a generation of mongoloid children. This family, which died out completely in 1851, was a branch of the Winders, the original owners of the estate and forebears of the current occupier.

The ghost is probably that of Elizabeth, one of the children who was officially only a 'half mongol', but as she grew older her mental state grew worse. The Rev. Dixon believes that she died in her sixties, but because there is no record of her burial in the churchyard this is only conjecture. "We have a grave in the garden," he says, "always supposed to be that of the Grey Lady. I have a plan eventually to exhume this and take any remains to the churchyard." The reason for her exclusion from the normal burial place is that the vicar refused to allow lunatics to be buried in consecrated ground.

"The appearances of the ghost are always connected with the full moon and the opening and closing of doors between 5 and 7.30 in the morning." The Rev. Dixon was lucky in actually witnessing the apparition himself, for her arrival was at the unexpected time of 9.20 am. "I thought it was my wife coming downstairs, as the sounds were of feminine footsteps, and I went towards the library door to speak to her.

All I saw was a grey, gauzy figure carrying a lighted candle, completely ignoring me and going on down the corridor. I recovered quickly enough to get down the corridor in time to see the figure pass through the dining room window, where the front door used to be when she lived there. I never really believed the stories until then but I am now quite convinced of their truth." In July 1974 I received written confirmation that other people had experienced hauntings. This came from Mrs. Yvonne Irena Todd who now lives in Field Broughton, but she produced a different version of the tale – or perhaps information of another ghost which shares the Hall with Elizabeth. Mrs. Todd understood that the phenomena she experienced many years before the current owner purchased the manor, when it was an hotel, was caused by Rose Dixon.

With the enthusiasm of a fascinated teenager, she insisted on being allowed to sleep in the haunted bedroom "in the hope that something would happen." After some time she was rewarded. According to the information Mrs. Todd was given, Rose, a beautiful young girl, had a lover who was badly wounded in a battle. He had suffered a severe injury to the head and was kept under lock and key in the tower room of Lorton Hall but, appalled by this treatment, Rose had brought him to her room so that she could care for him. A maid was taken into their confidence and she would leave a door open for the couple to wander in the grounds at night. One night the couple failed to return and they were both found dead on a little stone seat set into the wall. The legend claims that Rose would sit on the stone and play on a harp to her lover. One night Mrs. Todd was woken at "about 3 o'clock by what felt like someone touching my forehead very lightly."

Unable to account for the incident, she tried to get back to sleep but noticed that her little dog, which was allowed to sleep on a chair in the same room, was foaming at the mouth. "As I lay there," she says, "I suddenly heard the sound of a harp playing and, although frightened, I forced myself to listen for about a quarter of an hour. Then the door to my parents' room started to open and close and they got up several times to close it."

During one of her numerous visits to the hotel Mrs. Todd also heard a mysterious rustling in her bedroom. On the same day she was told that one of the owners saw a dark figure standing by the grave of Elizabeth and was so scared by the apparition that she ran to her car, intending to drive away. Her terror was so great, however, that she crashed, fortunately without being injured.

Levens Hall,* OP
Near Kendal.   *On A6 – Nearest Station – Kendal (5 miles)*

Well known as an expert on harpsichords, Mr. Robin Bagot, the owner of this Tudor House, recently had the dubious honour of being one of the 61 per cent of living phantoms. His ghost was seen and described by Dom Julian Stonor as "standing by one of the harpsichords illuminated by what seemed to be electric light." At the time the rest of the house was in darkness due to a power cut and Mr. Bagot himself was in Whitehaven, some 40 miles away. Since including the case of the haunting of Levens Hall in *'Our Haunted Kingdom'* I have had the pleasure of speaking to the owner's wife during the radio programme 'Late Night Extra' with John Dunn. Mrs. Bagot told of the phantom black dog which frequently rushes down the staircase, disconcerting visitors about to ascend. The animal was also seen by Dom Stonor when he met Mrs. Bagot shopping in the village in 1958. He thought it was a normal animal and only asked her about it later in the afternoon when having tea with her at Levens Hall. "It's nearly always with me," she said, "but I didn't know it was with me in the village today."

In 1973 two groups of visitors saw a ghostly 'Pink Lady' and two members of one party saw the black dog which continues to appear with monotonous regularity. The lady in pink is often observed gliding across the hall and sometimes in the garden. The better-known phantom is that of 'The Grey Lady' last seen in 1972 on Levens Bridge. She is thought to be the ghost of a gypsy who was turned away when begging for food from the owners of the Hall several hundred years ago.

The legend is that she cursed the family, saying that no son should inherit the house until the River Kent ceased to flow and a white fawn was born. To ensure that the curse was broken however, fate took a hand by arranging for the birth of Alan Bagot when the river was frozen and a white deer was seen shortly afterwards in the herd kept on the estate. In 1971 the 'Grey Lady' was seen standing on a narrow bridge leading to the house and a nasty accident was averted only by the skill of the astonished car driver.

Editor's Note: In April 1998 the magazine *History Today* reported Hal Bagot, who took over from his father in 1975, stated that, as a girl his sister Liza had been upset by the unexplained figure of 'a woman in a straw hat, boots and a heavy skirt' vanish through a stable wall ('One home Ground: Levens Hall, Cumbria: History of a famous English estate' in *History Today* Vol 48 No.4 1 April 1998 p.62)

DERBYSHIRE

Denleen Separates Ltd., PP
Primrose Street,
Ilkeston.

For over a century this building has housed workers of various types but it is only during the last few years that several have commented on the sound of footsteps climbing the stairs to the top floor, yet no one has been seen to account for the noise. One morning in 1972, says the *Ilkeston Advertiser*, Linda Skeath, a young machinist, was the first to arrive for work and on switching on the light in the main machine room, saw the figure of a woman wearing a long, grey dress running silently across the room toward the staircase. Linda had no time then to fully realise that the face of the mysterious visitor was "blurred" for, thinking that the woman was a thief or a burglar, she chased the figure across the room.

On reaching the top of the stairs, however, she realised that the woman had vanished and that the front door on the ground floor of the building was still firmly closed. Unknown to Linda at the time, this was not the first occasion that the phantom had been seen, for she had been witnessed by a former colleague some six months earlier in the same room. Unfortunately no one has any clue as to the identity of the ghost, but the popular belief is that she was a cleaner who died there many years ago.

The Lady in Grey (Restaurant) (Closed)
Wilne Lane,
Shardlow *On A6 – Nearest Station – Long Eaton (3 miles)*

There are not many restaurants actually named after a resident ghost, but the owners obviously feel that it adds interest (if not a potential service charge or entertainment tax if you see the phantom). There seems to be some doubt as to whether she is still active. The owner, Mr. M. Morton, says that when this lovely old house was privately owned about 18 years ago the previous owner told his wife that he had seen the wraith of the ghost, one Jeanette Soarsby, who glided from one front room, across a landing and into another room. The witness was at the other end of the landing at the time. She was certainly seen by more than one person and on more than one occasion. She is a young lady wearing Victorian clothing and is believed to have died in her twenties.

Editor's Note: The Lady in Grey closed as a restaurant and as of January 2021 the building was unfortunately standing derelict awaiting further development.

DEVON

Shute School, OPA
Shute,
Near Axminster.　　　*On B31 61 (off A373) – Nearest Station – Axminster 10 miles)*
Shute House, a girls' school built in the 1800's, shares the estate with Shute Barton which was built in the mediaeval era. Although it is the school which accommodates 'The Grey Lady', who has her own 'Lady Walk' among a cluster of trees, the phantom belongs to the older property.

Shute Barton, at one time owned by the father of Lady Jane Grey, was forfeited to the Crown and Queen Mary gave it to Sir William Petre. Despite the strong support for Cromwell in the surrounding countryside, Shute was an island of Royalist sympathy and the locals believe it was at this time that the original 'Grey Lady' – a Lady Pole – met her fate.

"She was hanged from a tree in the grove," is the oft given story, "which withered and died." One Saturday sports day the phantom was seen walking near the playing field, which is bordered by 'The Walk', and mistaken for "some strange woman" by a member of the school staff. "She is walking up and down as if she owns the place," she said to one of the mistresses.

Some time later one of the school children said that she had seen the same figure whilst glancing through a dormitory window.

Some parents have also enquired as to the identity of the 'woman in grey' who refuses to answer questions.

Berry Pomeroy Castle,* OP
Berry Pomeroy.　　　　　　　　　　　　*On A 381 – Nearest Station – Totnes*
Keith Fordyce, in a conversation before a BBC radio interview a couple of years ago, told me an amusing tale slightly connected with the haunting here and involving his youngest daughter. Reports of an apparition and the sounds of a baby crying in the grounds of this ruined castle extend back for over 50 years.

The belief is that the noises come from the ghostly child of a 13th century Pomeroy woman who suffered an incestuous relationship with her father. The figure of the mother (and maybe it is that of Margaret Pomeroy starved to death by her sister Eleanor in mediaeval days) has been seen occasionally near the gatehouse, wearing a long blue cape with a hood. One of the few photographs of the ghosts of the castle taken by visitors near St. Margaret's Tower, shows the profile of a young woman, but this only adds to the mystery of the phantom's identity.

Over the last few years numerous people have told me that the most overpowering atmosphere of dread, of horror and of absolute desolation surrounds the arches near the gatehouse. One friend, Edward Pratt, said that he was nearly overcome, the atmosphere was so intense and powerful. But as to the legend which claims that if you see the phantom of Margaret Pomeroy walking the ramparts, you'll be dead in a year, you can take it from me that it's rubbish.

Editor's Note: I first visited Berry Pomeroy Castle in February 1988 and spoke with a local man whose teenage son had been frightened by something he had seen in the ruins but was unable to trace any first-hand witnesses. The site continues to attract ghost hunters, a number of whom have made extravagant claims detailed in Peter Underwood's *Nights in Haunted Houses* (1994) but these have not been independently verified.

Chardstock Church, OP
Chardstock. *Off A358 – Nearest Station – Axminster (8 miles)*
Within a stone's throw of Somerset and Dorset lies this quiet little Devon village, by-passed by tourists on their way from Chard to Axminster. Only about two miles from the haunted Forde Abbey, Chardstock was once owned by the Diocese of Salisbury, but who the ghost is that frequents the churchyard here nobody knows. She appears as such a 'vague little creature' that there is difficulty in establishing that the phantom is even that of a female. However, witnesses claim that she is, and is wearing a "greyish dress". She has been seen coming from the vicarage and simply fades away when nearing the church.

Clothes Shop, OP
High Street,
Exeter. *Off A38 – Nearest Station – Exeter*
The chief city of the South West offers a jarring mixture of ancient and modern architecture, mainly due to a severe bombing raid during World War II, but enough remains of the old city for it to interest and intrigue tourists, casual visitors and even residents.

Exeter is situated on a Celtic ridgeway and the High Street marks the original route used by tribes some 2000 years ago. The Romans built walls round the City and remnants of a Norman castle can still be found in Rougemont Gardens.

Claimed to be the oldest municipal building in the country is the mediaeval Guildhall, complete with creepy dungeons, which adjoins the basement of this haunted boutique. It is on this lower floor that several members of the staff have seen the ghostly figure of a raven-haired young girl.

The Exeter Express reported in February 1973 that Mr. Peter Rouse, manager of the shop, went to the store beneath the sale room to replenish the stock and was mystified to see some of the clothing on the racks swinging about, as if someone were hiding among the garments. Unable to find a reason, he took a friend to examine the room and saw the head of a girl gliding towards him and his colleague. As the phantom neared the couple, it vanished.

Miss Gillian Davis, one of the sales assistants, saw the complete figure of the spectre in the same area, but again it faded away when only a few feet from the witness.

Because of the location, it is believed that the apparition is that of a victim of some horrible crime committed "on the other side of the wall" a couple of hundred years ago. The wall itself is a comparatively modern addition to the general structure, which certainly implies that the old dungeons once encompassed the present basement.

Chambercombe Manor, OP
Ilfracombe. *Off A399 – Nearest Station – Barnstaple (14 miles)*

At first glance this ancient property is perhaps a little disappointing, for the outward appearance somewhat belies the fact that it was constructed in the 14th century. The existence of the manor house and farm is recorded in the Domesday Book and it has been known by the various names

of Champernowne, Champernon's Wyke and Champernon. It is the oldest occupied manor in north Devon and is surrounded by two acres of gardens. Admittedly it is a small manor, but it does contain a private oratory with some interesting Tudor and Jacobean furniture.

Secret rooms have always intrigued me and I can never understand owners who disinterestedly state "oh yes, there is a sealed room behind the chimney," or "we found a priest's hole in the bedroom but have never opened it up."

It was at Chambercombe in 1865, according to James Turner in *Ghosts of the South West* (David and Charles) that a secret room was accidentally discovered containing a four-poster bed, with its rotting curtains still drawn. One can perhaps imagine the trepidation with which the tenant drew back the dust-covered cloth and the sudden horror of seeing a skeleton lying on the bed. It was that of a young female, later buried in the local churchyard.

Adding to the romance and mystery was the fact that a tunnel was recently exposed leading from the adjoining Manor Farm to the Hele beach. There seems to be strong evidence that Lady Jane Grey visited and slept in the manor and because of this one of the rooms now bears her name. A coat of arms was recently discovered over the fireplace in the room, but so far, the family which is associated with it has not been identified. Perhaps it is that of the Champerons, the Bonvilles or the Greys, for all owned the property at varying times.

Unfortunately for the seeker of visual ghosts the phantom has not been seen, but she is often heard walking the corridors to the Chapel and to the cobbled courtyard. As one might expect, "weird sounds" also issue from the former secret room, now visible through a small window between two bedrooms.

Romantics believe the ghost is that of a titled woman who came to visit relatives at Chambercombe. Her ship was wrecked and smugglers dragged her through the underground passage to the tiny room where she was robbed and left to die of starvation. Another belief is that she was Kate Oatway, whose father was noted for his smuggling and wrecking activities in the 1700s. But this fails to explain how she came to be walled up.

There is even another possibility. Was she an unfaithful wife of a former owner murdered by her outraged husband? Unless the current occupiers find another secret room, which could provide the answer we will never know.

Pussycat Club,* (Closed)
Palace Theatre,
Union Street,
Plymouth   *On A38 – Nearest Station – Plymouth*

Formed from the original Circle bar of the old theatre, this nightclub retains a ghost known affectionately as 'Mary'. She is frequently seen near a permanently locked room and was observed as recently as March 1976.

One of the partners of the club is Mr. H. Slatter, who was kind enough to provide me with the information about this genuine and modern haunting. Although he admits that he has not seen 'Mary' himself, in 1974 when locking up the club at 2.20 am with his partner Mr. T. Woodman and a Mrs. Judy Davies, he was astounded to see the lights of the 'fruit machine' suddenly come on for no reason.

The building itself, he admitted, is really creepy at night but as to who 'Mary' is, "Well," he said, "there are three stories. Take your choice. She is an artiste who was having an affair with an actor and her husband shot her; she had a broken love affair and hanged herself, or in the 1890's a fire in the theatre occurred when there were five people inside and only four bodies were recovered."

One thing that is quite clear is that 'Mary', whoever she is, still haunts. There are literally dozens of people who have seen her or felt her presence, and all within the last three or four years.

Editor's Note: The Long Bar is now closed, having also operated as a strip club and escort bar at various stages in its commercial history, roles which may have contributed to the sense of a troubled feminine presence at the property.

Corfe Castle.* OP   *On A351 – Nearest Station – Wareham (6 miles)*

There was something about the ancient village here that I found a little sad and overpowering. Perhaps it was the steadily pouring rain which was responsible. Unfortunately neither my colleague nor myself saw the vague figure of a headless woman who is sometimes seen on the pathway leading to the crumbling gateway of the castle or, according to a statement in 1967 by John Seager, near the bridge on Corfe Hill.

She was seen again in 1971 and again the story was circulated that she has something to do with the manor house a few yards away, from which a tunnel leads to the castle.

The romantics, however, like to think that she is in some way connected with the cruel Elfrida who murdered her stepson, King Edward, in 978. Personally, I should imagine that the connection with the Manor is likely to be more accurate, for during the Civil War the village and the dominating castle were strongly attacked by the Parliamentarians.

It was only due to an unpleasant case of treachery that the castle was taken. Can one not imagine what the outraged Royalist supporters and Lady Banks, who defended the fort, felt towards the traitor, even though it happened to be a woman of the village under stress?

Longham Road, OP
Longham. *On A348 – Nearest Station – Bournemouth (6 miles)*
It is here on the A348 that the ghostly lady of the river Stour is seen at a variety of sites near Langham.

In November 1971 Mrs. Jorgenson of Kinson was quoted by *the Bournemouth Evening Echo* as saying that the young son of a publican in Langham was found to be terrified of the "lady in a long white dress" that he had seen in the garden. Another reader from Langham confirmed that this was no imagined creature resulting from too much television watching, for his neighbour had also seen the lady "in a long white dress and wearing a bonnet" whilst he was burning rubbish in his garden one evening.

But in *Ghosts of Dorset, Devon & Somerset* by Legg, Collier and Perrott (Dorset Publishing Company), it is pointed out that an identical ghost had also inhabited a cottage adjoining the Wimborne Road. This 'old lady' whose description matches that of the figure seen between Longham and Kinson was identified as a Mrs. Gridger who had died many years before.

I personally do not think it surprising that an old soul would wander about a bit in the evenings even though her appearances seem to be limited to the Autumn.

Royal Lion Hotel, OP
Broad Street,
Lyme Regis. *On A3070/A 3052 – Nearest Station – Axminster (6 miles)*
'Open all the year round and with one room with a four-poster bed' is how the guide books describe this popular hotel at the bottom end of the town, situated a few yards from the sea. Nothing is said, though, of the ghost reported by *Bridport News* in 1973.

Nearly opposite the hotel is the old courthouse and museum equipped with ancient dungeons which, it is said, continue under the road and run beneath the Royal Lion. It was in the courtyard of the house of justice that public hangings were carried out in mediaeval times and no doubt

many smugglers saw the last light of day while kicking at the end of a rope and finally swaying in rhythm to the sound of the nearby waves.

Probably there was at least one victim of the hangings who had some relative waiting in a nearby house to learn of the death of her lover and perhaps it is she who has been heard by several people, moaning through the night somewhere in the upper floor of the hotel.

Two girls have seen a shape "like drifting mist" in the dining room, where members of the hotel staff have also heard the sound of footsteps when the room was empty. A "cold chilly sensation" has been experienced and the manager reported that on one occasion he heard the sound of an invisible entity approaching him near the dining room. Sounds of an organ playing have also been claimed, but when a sceptic suggested that this was the wind or the nearby stream in one of the tunnels or exposed cavities beneath the hotel, a musician replied, "Oh no, that's an organ, but being badly played."

Angel Inn,* (Closed)
Coombe Street,
Lyme Regis.   *On A 35 – Nearest Station – Axminster (6 miles)*

Sometime in 1926 Mrs. Langton, the proprietress of this attractive old pub realised that because her daughter had become an alcoholic there was nothing else to do but to leave. Strongly resentful of this situation she told all and sundry that "no one will do as well as I did" and, according to a Mrs. Clarke, those words came true.

Twelve licensees have tried to break the 'curse' and only in recent times does this seem to have been achieved.

Mrs. Langton herself could have been taken for Queen Victoria as far as looks and dress were concerned so there is never any doubt as to her identity when seen in the town or elsewhere, but why she haunts the pub is not clear except that the circumstances suggest she so hated having to leave that she decided not to.

The young son of one of the proprietors was scared at seeing the old lady coming out from a cupboard in what had been her daughter's bedroom one evening and on another occasion his brother saw the phantom bending over the bed with a 'very sad expression'. Might I suggest that the apparition was merely repeating what she had done so many times earlier when her daughter lay in a bed on the same spot?

Mrs. Clarke herself, who lives only a few yards away from the pub, told me that when doing a bit of cleaning she had more than once heard footsteps in the empty room.

Another witness to the ghost was a man suffering from an incurable disease who was staying at the pub. He saw the old woman bending over him and thought at first it was the phantom of Queen Victoria until being told of Mrs. Langton the following morning.

In a nearby fish and chip shop I learnt from the owner that he had been offered the licence of the Angel but had been a little scared by a particular incident and had declined the offer. One day, when helping his father, he opened a cupboard and "something just glided straight out at me. I ran." He was unable to describe what it was, but it was obviously far more frightening than the ghostly little girl he has seen in his shop. "My wife has seen her too and so have a couple of customers. She looks about 12 years old." But "she causes no trouble. We've only seen her a couple of times recently. She glides out of the kitchen."

Editor's Note. This venue closed as a pub in 2016.

DURHAM

Lord Crewe Arms,* OP
Blanchland,
Near Consett. *Off B2678 – Nearest Station – Newcastle-on-Tyne (23 miles)*

'A small and golden place' is how Robert Glenton describes the tiny hamlet of Blanchland in an article published in the Sunday Express. 'Every single building around its ancient square is made and roofed of sandy millstone. Just a single hint of sunlight and it glows.'

In 1165 it was a monastery and most of the village still is. Part of this religious community, founded by White Canons, was sold on the dissolution. The guest house and kitchen became a manor house and eventually the Lord Crewe Arms. The remainder was turned into private establishments.

The ghost which haunts the hotel is understood to be that of Dorothy Forster. Jack Hallam, in his *Haunted Inns of England* (Wolfe), provides an excellent case history of recent incidents, but it was in March 1975 that Robert Glenton experienced a puzzling occurrence in his bedroom.

"Half asleep in the middle of the night I could see a grey, amorphous shape somewhere around the foot of the bed. Then I discovered I had forgotten to open my eyes and when I did the shape disappeared." How did he know where the shape was, one could ask? However, he continues. "But what had awakened me in the first place? It had been a sort of rattling as though a string of beads or a delicate chain had dropped on to the polished floorboards surrounding the edge of the carpet. It was only in the morning that I realised that the room had a wall-to-wall carpet."

Not perhaps a spine-chilling experience, but one that puzzled the writer and just another case to be added to the file of weird incidents.

An earlier case was that of Hazel Jones of Canada who wrote in December 1968 issue of *In Britain* that she felt a presence in her bedroom and a "thump at the bottom of the bed" and minutes later "a muffled knock at our door. Four raps by a gloved hand." Shortly afterwards a chambermaid, having completed tidying up, turned round for a last-minute check and was astounded to find that the neat fresh linen on the bed had been pulled apart and was "now heaped in disarray." But the girl had been alone.

The unseen but 'felt' phantom is believed to be that of the sister of Thomas Forster, one of the plotters of the 1715 rebellion. Thomas was imprisoned, but thanks to Dorothy he escaped and was hidden in a secret room before being smuggled to Europe.

Another version, adding to the confusion of the identity of the lady in question, is that the ghost is of Dorothy Forster's aunt, but why either should continue to frequent a particular bedroom and other areas is anyone's guess. She was seen in the village square by a vicar and, according to a previous manager of the hotel, "a large number of other people."

Mr. Ingle, the resident manager in February 1976, said that "unfortunately there have been no recent phenomena" but, perhaps tomorrow . . . ?

ESSEX

Woolston Hall Country Club, OPA
Chigwell. *Off A 113 – Nearest Station – Chigwell (Central Line)*

Mr. Barry King, research co-ordinator of the Dagenham Paranormal Research Group, was kind enough to provide me with information relating to 'Agnes', the uninvited house guest of this select country club. Depending on the sensitivity of the witness, she has been seen as "just a haze," or "an indistinct figure of a young girl with a very sad face, wearing typical 17th century clothing."

Tony Fleming, a member of the staff, confirms that "many people have seen what looks like a puff of smoke" near the stairway. A common feature in paranormal occurrences is a very rapid drop in temperature and this sudden chill is always experienced before the appearance of 'Agnes'.

One of the witnesses of the 'hazy lady' is Jose Gonzalez, the head waiter, who has frequently seen 'Agnes' standing on the stairs and, although he is unafraid of the phantom, he prefers not to stay nearby for long.

The belief is that the female is the daughter of the Scott family, owners of the manor and Sheriffs of the area in the 17th century. To account for her remaining in her original home, the story is told of her suffering a broken love affair and jumping from a bedroom window, breaking her neck. Legend has it that she is buried somewhere in the grounds.

Valence House, OP
Valence Park,
Dagenham. *Off A 13 – Nearest Station – Dagenham (District Line)*

Containing the world's largest housing estate, designed for 90,000 people, Dagenham also has this pleasant park to offset the heavy industrial and commercial aspect of the area.

The manor house of Valence, standing in its own grounds with an attractive lake, is used in part as a borough library and as the haunt of Agnes de Valence, believed to be the victim of a murder in the 14th century.

Although the deputy borough librarian, Les Carson, has experienced nothing unusual, there are several people who have seen the figure of a woman in the park near the building.

Mr. King, of the Dagenham Paranormal Research Group, feels that the evidence is inconclusive but there are, he tells me, at least two people who witnessed the phantom during 1975. One young lad, walking through the grounds early one winter morning, received the shock of his life on seeing the clear figure of a woman with what looked like a dagger in her back.

De Laches, OPA
Cold Norton,
Latchingdon.　　　　　　　　*On B1013 – Nearest Station – Wickford (7 miles)*

Although Mrs. Barry told me in March 1976 that there is no further information about the ghost which haunts her 15th century home, it is fairly safe to assume that the phantom is still active.

There is no doubt that domesticated animals (cats, dogs, and horses) are far more receptive to 'atmosphere' than their human owners and it is in the De Laches farmhouse that striking evidence of this can be seen. At the doorway of a bedroom cats and dogs bristle, spit and run, some of them howling with fright.

The apparition itself, normally seen only in the very early hours of the morning, takes the form of a young female who stands watching the occupants of the bed.

She wears a 19th century style dress and many of the witnesses who have seen her are, rather surprisingly, inexplicably frightened by her appearance.

Rochford Hall, OPA
Rochford.　　　　　　　　*On B1013 – Nearest Station – Rochford*

Yet another house where that much travelled Anne Boleyn is supposed to have been born and now haunts, Rochford Hall is currently the clubhouse of a rather exclusive golf club and certainly houses a ghost of a 'woman in white' though it is extremely doubtful that it is of Anne.

The figure, a mere shape of a woman, is normally seen near the stairway and more frequently in the grounds, flitting about rather vaguely until it suddenly vanishes. The favourite story is that she is seen at Christmas time and certainly in Victorian times poachers would not go anywhere near the Hall over the festive period.

GLOUCESTERSHIRE

Sudeley Castle, OP
Winchcombe,
Cheltenham.　　　　　　　　*On A46 – Nearest Station – Cheltenham (6 miles)*

Originally dating from the 12th century, this magnificent home of royalty holds many relics, souvenirs and treasures within its walls. A beautiful Elizabethan Garden is one of the main highlights, for the castle was at one time the home of Katherine Parr, the last wife of Henry VIII, and she must often have admired the plants and shrubs here, and perhaps even chatted to a gardener as he trimmed the 15 feet high double yew hedge.

Sudeley, often visited by Queen Elizabeth I and used as a fortress by Charles I during the Civil War, now offers a fascinating glimpse into the days of Queen Victoria through its Emma Dent collection of photographs, letters and autographs.

A unique historical form of entertainment recalling the castle's past in colour, light and sound is also offered to visitors, as is a glimpse of Janet, the late housekeeper. Although the owner, her family and the present resident staff have all failed to see Janet, a former secretary describes her experience one August morning in 1971.

"When I saw her," she writes, "she was in Katherine Parr's nursery, but did not give me the slightest feeling of fear. I thought she was a real person until she vanished as I approached her." The witness not only described the figure to the owner and two of the estate workers, who recognised the phantom from the details, but was able to recall what she was wearing.

"She dressed in the clothes she habitually wore at work, a white blouse, long skirt to her ankles in faded pink and white cotton, white stockings and shoes and a mob cap."

There is no doubt as to the identity of the phantom. "She was Janet, who was the housekeeper here. She came from Scotland and lived with her friend, also a Scot, in Laundry Cottage in Rushley Lane." Providing an excellent reason for the haunting, the letter continues, "She loved the castle dearly and knew every nook and cranny of it. When I saw her, she was busy dusting".

The letter writer is not the only witness, for Janet has also been seen by members of the public coming out of the needlework bedroom, standing in the main bedroom and coming out of the Rupert Room.

The most recent incident occurred early in 1975, shortly after the castle was opened for the season. There are reports of a phantom lady having been seen in the garden as well, but as there is no accurate description of her it need not be Janet.

Joanna Jansen, the current secretary to the owner, Mr. E. Dent-Brickhurst, who was kind enough to supply the details given above, admits that there have been no sightings since last year, but chairs have been found to have moved by themselves in the recently enlarged restaurant. As she suggests, perhaps Janet does not approve.

Swan Pool, OP
Newland Road,
Redbrook.   *On B4231 – Nearest Station – Chepstow (10 miles)*

Practically on the border line between Gloucester and Gwent lies this tiny hamlet cradled by the beautiful Wye Valley. Just above it is the haunted Swan Pool, associated with several mythical spectres including but not limited to the ghosts of a tall woman, a young child and a black dog.

There are but few people who have seen the trio lately, though the cries of the baby have been heard from some yards away. The original tale was that the phantom of the lady, wearing a white gown, would slowly rise from the pool carrying the tiny infant in her arms. A few reports of the incident even claimed that the apparition was covered with green weed, but I think this is hardly likely. If a ghost can walk through a door it is hardly physical enough to carry a weedy shroud, is it?

The legend to account for the haunting is that the woman, the child and the dog are all victims of a multi-killing in the 18th century.

GREATER MANCHESTER

Hall-i'-th'-Wood, OP
Bolton. *On A 676 – Nearest Station – Bolton*

Now a museum owned by the Bolton Metropolitan Borough, this half-timbered Manor House dates from the late 15th century. A great-grandson of the builder, Lawrence Brownlow, added several rooms at the north west corner in 1591 but overspent and had to sell the property to
Christopher Norris.

It was this new owner who was appointed administrator of the estates confiscated from Royalist families.

Years later Alexander Norris demolished the west side of the building and constructed a new and more elaborate wing on the south west side. This could account for the fact that one of the three ghosts, "seen by many visitors" according to Dr. J. R. A. Gray, the Principal Officer, disappears through the wall in the position of a doorway which no longer exists since the building was extended. The figure is that of a 'small man dressed in green with a lace tunic, breeches and buckled shoes, carrying a sack over his shoulder'.

The building eventually became derelict but in 1900 the Viscount Leverhulme restored it, presented it to the Bolton Corporation and included a large collection of the original furniture to provide an interesting folk museum. It must have been about the time that the gift was being arranged that some catastrophe occurred, for seen on the upstairs landing has been the phantom of a tall man wearing a black suit and winged collar.

But several witnesses enquire about the little old lady who is seen in the kitchen area. A charming old soul, she wears a black dress with lace around the neck and at the cuffs. It is pleasant and reassuring to visitors that none of the phantoms who still inhabit the Hall ever frightens anybody. As for the woman in the kitchen, she just "fits in with the surroundings".

New Avenue, OP
Chadderton,
Oldham. *On A663/A 669 – Nearest Station – Oldham Mumps (tram stop)*

Claimed to be a regular visitor to the industrial estate in New Avenue, built on the site of Birchen Bower, is the ghost of Madam Hannah Beswick. She was ultimately buried in Harpurhey Cemetery, Manchester, on 22nd July 1868, though by then her well preserved body had been displayed at the Natural History Museum in Manchester for some 33 years. Somewhat irrationally her ghostly appearances are supposed to be made every seven years on the date that she was buried and not of her death, which occurred at Cheetwood Old Hall in 1758.

Probably it was because of her eccentricity and seeing her brother being nearly buried alive that she left instructions for her body to be embalmed. This was carried out by a Dr. Charles White who placed her remains in a glass-fronted coffin kept in the summerhouse at Cheetwood. Later the doctor decided to remove Hannah to his own home at the top of King Street, Manchester, on a site now occupied by the town hall.

Recently the case of the haunting of 'The Manchester Mummy', as Hannah is known, has been studied by Mr. Harry Harvey of Oldham who has written an interesting report on his findings. He tells of the author Thomas de Quincey, a close friend of Dr. White, being shown the mummy, which was housed in an old grandfather clock case. It seems that the doctor would amuse himself, and shock a few patients, by suddenly opening the clock face to reveal Hannah's ancient features.

Discounting the belief relating to 22nd July, the Oldham *Chronicle* reported on 24th April 1956 that several nightshift workers at the Ferranti Works in Chadderton had witnessed 'a shadowy figure at one end of the transformer department'. The ghostly female shape was pointed out to other members of the work force, but it vanished when anyone neared it.

The woman was initially seen by three men, but during the course of the next few days no less than 35 workers had either seen or heard the phantom which was, at times, accompanied by poltergeist activity. Switches and lights would be turned on or off and tools would be moved.

Many people became convinced that the ghost is that of Hannah, as the factory was constructed on the site of the Birchen Bower estate which was, years ago, known to be haunted by Madam Beswick. It was here that she lived with her brother John who, despite local ideas, did not serve in the rebellious army of Charles Stuart in 1745.

On referring to a recent report from Colin Smith I learn that Hannah was seen in February 1968 "hovering some two feet from the ground" in front of the workers' entrance to the Ferranti factory. "She was old, but quite tall and wearing a long brown frock," said the witness, a driver for British Road Services.

Colin spoke to a representative of Ferranti's in July 1972 and was told that the ghost had been seen in the canteen there. The description given matched that provided by the driver but with the added comment, "she looked like an old-fashioned school marm."

It seems, though, that she does not limit her activities to Ferranti, for occasionally reports are made of her being seen in other parts of the industrial estate.

HAMPSHIRE

Wherwell Priory, PP
Near Andover.
The area where traces of the ancient priory can still be seen near the Church of St. Peter and Holy Cross is the site of a haunting by a pair of phantom nuns carrying candles. They are, however, only witnessed at twilight during winter months.

The village was a thriving community in the Saxon era and the religious house was founded by Queen Elfrida as a penance. Unfortunately the cause of the haunting is not known, but it may well be associated with the days when the priory was used as a seminary.

Before the priory was dissolved in 1538 a fork-tailed winged monster, a cockatrice, was said to have hatched from an egg in one of the cellars. When it matured it would fly around the village catching and eating young children, or so it is said. No doubt mothers in those days had to scare disobedient youngsters with some sort of tale they couldn't threaten to turn off the television.

However, the monster was disposed of by a courageous young man named Greenno relative as far as I know in response to a reward of four acres of land. A metal portrayal of the creature can be seen in the Andover Museum.

The Police College, Bramshill House, Hartley Wintney, Hampshire, haunted by a beautiful young girl with auburn ringlets. *Dept. of the Environment. Crown copyright, reproduced with permission of the Controller of Her Majesty's Stationery Office.*

Police College,* PP
Bramshill House,
Hartley Wintney,
Basingstoke. *Junction of A 30/B3011 – Nearest Station – Winchfield (2 miles)*
This well-known police college, with a resident population of 500, is open to applicants for training and promotion to senior executive positions within the force. It lies only a few miles from the equally renowned Royal Military Academy at Camberley in Surrey.

The information concerning both the building and the haunting of the College has been kindly supplied by Mr. F. Cook, the Police College engineer who actually saw the ghost, and Mr. W. Libby, secretary of the College from 1959 to 1963.

The site of the house was mentioned in the *Domesday Book*, but sometime in the 14th century Sir John Foxley constructed a manor home for himself and evidence of this can still be seen in the walls of the basement and cellars. Early in the 1600's this building was demolished when a Lord Zouche took over the site and between 1605 and 1612 the present pink brick home was built for the Roman Catholic family. Incorporated into the structure was a chapel and a priests' hole situated in the mezzanine floor close to what is now a lavatory.

Mr. Libby told me that the entrance to the hidey hole "is about two feet square and it is possible to drop into the cavity created between two walls." The aperture would then be covered by a trapdoor set in the floorboards.

There is a belief that Lord Zouche had intended to present the house to the then Prince of Wales, but for some reason it proved to be unacceptable.

In 1690 Sir John Cope purchased Bramshill, where his family were to live for over 250 years. It was some time in the 1930's that a daughter of the family, then about twelve years of age, wrote in a diary of family incidents and included the first mention of 'the ghost'. "Late this evening," she wrote, "a strange but kind and beautiful lady appeared, bending over my bed. I don't know who it was, but she was so lovely."

A Roman Catholic chapel on the ground floor was probably demolished during the Copes' occupation. In 1863 the rector of Eversley, two miles from Bramshill, published his sixth book which became as popular as his fourth work, *Westward Ho!* for this man of the church was Charles Kingsley, author of *The Water Babies*. It may be remembered that Tom, in The Water Babies, would often peer through the gates of a large house and it is this building which has been identified as Bramshill.

The Copes left in 1935 when Lord Brockett purchased the house, but only 18 years later he left it to the nation and the Department of the Environment took over the control of the property. A few months later Bramshill became a Police College.

How Bramshill became associated with the legend of the Mistletoe Bough is not known. The story is that of a new bride, playing hide and seek during the wedding breakfast ceremony, found an old chest in an attic and, climbing in, the lid automatically locked and she suffocated. Hundreds of years later the chest was discovered and opened to reveal the skeleton in wedding clothes. Every time the Mistletoe Bough seeds her ghost walks.

There are at least three, possibly more, homes claiming that they house 'The Mistletoe Bough chest', one of these being Marwell Hall near Owlesbury in Hampshire, some 30 miles south of Bramshill. Certainly Marwell is haunted, but by Lady Jane Seymour for it was here that the secret marriage with Henry VIII took place. Lady Jane's phantom is sometimes accompanied by another woman in white, claimed to be Anne Boleyn.

Admittedly Bramshill has an old chest claimed to be the chest (though it is believed to have originated in Italy) but how it came to be in the College nobody knows. It could have belonged to any or none of the previous owners. There are two haunted spots in the College, one of these being in the Librarian's office near the end of the 147-foot-long library. Here a senior police officer felt an inexplicable and sudden drop in temperature and a member of the academic staff felt an unseen creature which he thought might have been a cat, run over his foot. He also smelled the perfume of 'lily of the valley' at the same time.

Fred Cook, the engineer, told me that in October, during the early 1960s, he actually saw the 'greyish-white figure of the lady' on the stairs near the Protestant chapel on the first floor. A new Roman Catholic chapel was only recently constructed on the assumed site of the original on the ground floor.

Mr. Cook was obviously delighted at seeing the ghost and he said that he wanted to see her again. "She was so beautiful and I saw her for only a few minutes. The only trouble is that dogs are terribly frightened whenever they get near the east end of the building."

Another witness to the haunting, according to Mr. Cook, was a former Queen of Romania who, when staying there and hoping to purchase it as a home, saw the white female gliding along in the Long Gallery now known as the library. This regal lady was also impressed by the beauty of the phantom.

A maintenance engineer in the College, Mr. H. Chalk, has also seen the "very beautiful young lady, walking very sadly along the library. She is about 18 years old," he tells me, "with auburn hair hanging down in ringlets. Her dress is long and old fashioned, sweeping the floor as she walks."

In common with everybody I spoke to about Bramshill, Mr. Chalk "loves this dear old, haunted house." It must have a really enchanting atmosphere.

Editor's Note: The decision to close the Police College was taken in 2012 by the Home Office and it shut for the last time in 2015. Since then there have been plans to convert the site to use for housing but these have been restricted due to legal appeals going up as far as the Court of Appeal in June 2021. Currently, Hart District Council has granted temporary permission for the use of the 106-hectare site (which includes the Grade I Listed house and Grade II historic park and garden and its grounds) for film production until March 2026. Therefore any reports of strange figures in antique or period clothing may well be open to the perfectly mundane explanation that filming is underway.

The Royal Oak,* OP
Langstone Village,
Havant. *On B2149 – Nearest Station – Havant*

"I saw the figure of a woman in white standing in a corner of the bedroom and as I looked, she slowly vanished, just faded into the wall," so Mrs. Spring told me in 1972. "This was in 1969 when I thought I heard someone moving around and assumed it was my young daughter who had been known to sleepwalk. So I got out of bed to lead her back and saw the ghost."

 Who the phantom is nobody knows, but the landlord's wife did suggest that she might be "someone connected with the bakery which existed on the site. Mind you, the place is about 450 years old so it could be anyone I suppose."

Mysterious sounds have been heard in the pub for many years, "like chairs being moved, a sort of scraping noise," and the ghost has been seen by many people. One witness in the summer of 1970 was a guest who had booked to stay for a week but left after only one night. He refused to divulge exactly what he had seen, just that his bedroom was 'haunted'. This was the same room in which the 'woman in white' had appeared to Mrs. Spring.

A neighbour told the landlord that she had seen the ghost when she had stayed there a few years earlier and Colonel Harrison, another local, said that although he had not witnessed anything he was quite convinced that the phantom is genuine.

Scepticism may be aroused after a few months of nonactivity, but Mrs. Spring said that what had dispelled her growing doubt of her own experience was her dog's refusal to be left alone in the room. "And they sense more than we do, don't they?"

Dougalls' Restaurant,* (Closed)
74 High Street,
Ringwood.   *On A 31 – Nearest Station – Christchurch (9 miles)*

The main phenomena experienced in this restaurant in 1973, when it was known as The Four Seasons and managed by the owner Mr. Peter Hill, were of a poltergeist nature. Mugs and cups would be found swinging inexplicably, cutlery disappeared and the sound of crashing pottery was heard. This type of activity continued for some days until a report was unexpectedly made that the mysterious figure of an "old grey-haired woman wearing a greyish dress" had been seen sitting in a rocking chair at the top of the stairs, situated near the kitchen on the first floor.

Much to the consternation of a folk singer who approached the stranger, the lady vanished into thin air.

But this was not an isolated incident, for other members of the restaurant staff saw the woman in grey once or twice a week for a few months during the year. On checking the situation with Mr. Douglas Carr, the new manager, in May 1976, he apologised for not being able to give any further information but explained that he had only just arrived to take over the management. Nevertheless he was quite certain that "the reports are true. I'm a fey Scot", he said, "and believe me it really is cold in that particular corner and there is no explanation for it that I can find." The owner of the restaurant, Mr. Hill, who now runs *The Falmouth Packet*, another popular eating house in the West Country, confirmed the haunting and told me that 'Dougalls' was originally the old stable house of the White Hart Inn next door. The pub was built in the 1600's and "weird things have happened there as well," but mainly just the movement of objects, which is unlikely to be connected with the little old lady but could be associated with the reason for her haunting.

'The lady in grey' has remained quiet for some time now but for how long?

Editor's Note. Since Andrew Green wrote the above, Dougall's has closed and as of 2022 is a Nepalese Restaurant. No further reports of phenomena are currently known, so the haunting may have been fading at the time of the 1976 enquiries.

Ye Olde Seven Stars, OP
Coventry Street,
Kidderminster.   *Off A449 – Nearest Station – Kidderminster*

How it is possible for a ghost to 'call out' I don't know, let alone have it call specific names and more especially the pet nicknames of customers. However, that is the claim made by Mrs. Valerie Pargeter, wife of the licensee of this 18th century pub, built originally as a pair of cottages.

Setting aside the vocal problem there are, or were, four recent witnesses to the phantom lady who haunts the building. A Mrs. Freda Holloway told a local newspaper that after hearing her name being called out, she glanced towards the end of the bar and saw a middle-aged woman dressed in white. "Her clothes," she said, "seemed to be the kind worn at the turn of the century. Suddenly she just vanished."

The mysterious customer was seen several times after that by Mrs. Holloway, but during the evenings.

Following the newspaper report, a Mr. Ray wrote to say that his mother was born in the pub at a time when her father held the licence and brewed his own beer on the premises. This was in the latter half of the last century. Mr. Ray also stated that his mother had seen the ghost, a woman in a large white apron, and believed it was the phantom of someone who had died in tragic circumstances.

The current licensee thinks the ghost is that of a former landlady or barmaid. Colin Smith tells me that he visited the pub in September 1974 and learnt from a Mr. and Mrs. Gray that they saw the ghost "sitting next to us at our table."

The Wicked Lady, OP
Normansland Common,
St. Albans.   *On A5/A6/A 414 – Nearest Station – St. Albans*

No collection of phantom females would be complete without mention of this famous pub, the name of which will remind picture-goers of the film of the same title in which Margaret Lockwood starred. The film was based on the 'Jekyll and Hyde' exploits of Lady Katherine Ferrers who, in the 18th century, would carry out the normal activities of a married Lady in daylight hours but at night become a highwaywoman.

The pub is believed to have been used by her as an illicit meeting place and it is assumed she still haunts an upper room, though she is never seen.

Many people have heard the sobbing cries and weeping of a woman issuing from a room always empty at the time. It would be out of character for Lady Ferrers to cry, for she was too strong-willed, so the crying could be that of a great friend of hers who was with her when she died after being shot. Another point is that Katherine actually died at her home, Markyate Cell, and her ghost has been seen there since the war, riding fiercely across the countryside and in the garden of the house. An intriguing aspect of the tale is that there are rumours of her treasure lying buried somewhere near a well on the estate.

ISLE OF MAN

Castle Rushen,* OP
Castletown, *Junction of A4/A25/A 7*

"The story of the haunting of this castle by a mysterious lady has been going on for many years and will continue for many years to come," said the curator to me in 1972, and he continued, "although I have never seen the ghost, I find it hard to disbelieve all the people who claim to have seen her through the years." Rushen Castle was built in the 12th century with the typical central square tower and ten-foot-thick walls.

Modifications and improvements continued to be made up to the 19th century. Court sittings are still held here and each successive Governor of the island has to take the oath within the castle before assuming his duties. The island has been under the control of Norway and then England, and in 1290 the Earl of Ulster took command of its administration; Scottish control was resumed by the Earl of Moray, but in May 1765 the English Crown finally took possession. Shortly afterwards the castle became a prison and felons were kept in the keep. Many executions were carried out within the grim walls and one of these was of a woman accused of murdering her son.

Antony Hippisley Coxe claims that the mother was innocent, for the boy had died of natural causes. He also states that one of the guides witnessed the figure of a woman in grey standing with a young lad near the drawbridge, but they had not passed the pay box. Members of the Home Guard stationed within the castle walls during the war also experienced the visits of 'the mysterious lady in grey' and a member of the Boys' Brigade camping near the site was so frightened that he had to be given first aid. In August 1960 four lads who impressed the curator with their sincerity handed him a signed statement claiming that they too had seen the woman when the castle was empty and locked.

The description given was that she was dressed in black "with a dead white face, black hands (probably gloves) and something hanging down from the head-dress." The figure appeared at the top of the 86 foot high Eagle Tower. Some years earlier an assistant custodian had seen the woman leading a child from the drawbridge to the dungeon, but he paid little attention to the ghosts at the time thinking the couple were normal visitors. Only later did he realise that the mysterious figures had vanished. The wife of the Warden is yet another witness and she saw the grey lady twice, once near the drawbridge and a few years later in a passage near the dungeon.

Who will be the next to see the lady in grey?

Editor's Note: In reports over the years, the lady ghost seems to have evolved from a rather refined Grey Lady, recognisably human, to a more menacing and shadowy Lady in Black in the last forty years, or even just a diffuse cloud mentioned at the Castle when I visited in 2012.

KENT

Bridge Place Country Club (former) OP (now 'The Pig' restaurant & hotel)
Canterbury Road, Bridge. *On A2 – Nearest Station – Canterbury (3 miles)*

The major causes of hauntings are usually tragic or horrific incidents, mainly because the emotion at the time is heightened to a particular peak of concentration. It is one such case involving, a brutal murder which continues to remind occupants of this Club of earlier days.

The building was originally constructed in 1638 by Sir Arnold Broemens as a manor house, but only a few years later it was badly damaged by the Cromwellians in the Civil War. It remained derelict for some years before being purchased by a local squire who restored it and moved in.

In order to recoup some of the expense involved he was forced to sell it and by 1775 the owner-occupiers were a couple named Taylor. Due to the condition of the building, a major portion of it had to be dismantled and shortly after settling in Mrs. Taylor fell ill and decided to stay with relatives in Scotland in order to assist her recovery. To make such a long journey north in the 18th century under such circumstances seems unusual, but this is not the only peculiar aspect of the tale.

In common with many husbands of that period, the gentleman took the opportunity of enjoying an illicit love affair with one of the more attractive servants, and as a result the object of his attentions, a chamber maid, gave birth to a baby daughter.

Normally in such circumstances the disillusioned mother would be sent packing with her child, though sometimes provided with a 'maintenance allowance'. This could well have happened had it not been for the fact that Taylor lost his nerve on learning that his wife, now fully recovered, was on her way home.

On her return she might have been puzzled as to why one of the maids had left, and despite harbouring suspicions, decided to keep quiet on the subject. However it was later established that murder most foul had been committed, but what had happened to the bodies of the two victims remains a mystery.

In 1967 Mr. Peter Malkin purchased the Club and had to carry out further extensive decorations during which time several dozen Flemish tiles were found surrounding an old fireplace. A few months afterwards he awoke one morning to see the figure of a chambermaid carrying a linen basket glide across the bedroom. "It was most peculiar," he said, "she didn't frighten me. She just put the basket on the floor, turned and vanished, as did the basket." He has since seen the figure three times and is not the only witness, for members of the Club have enquired about "the young woman in old-fashioned clothing who stands at the top of the stairs."

Perhaps giving some clue to the site of the murder and the means of disposing of the bodies, are the pitiful cries of a baby coming from a chimney between the ground and first floors, heard several times both by the proprietor and members of the Club. Although several thorough investigations have been carried out, no explanation for the sounds has been discovered.

Woodside Cottage,* PP
The Vale,
Broadstairs.

Originally built about 250 years ago as a stable/coach house for a nearby farm, this cottage now houses a deputy supervisor of the GPO, his daughter and granddaughter. The current owner, Mrs. Kent, lives in another house a few yards away.

The cottage, which after the departure of two elderly ladies during the war, remained empty for some ten years, was purchased in 1951 and converted from basic accommodation to a charming home.

A few months after moving in, one evening about 9 pm, when her two young children were sleeping, Mrs. Kent heard footsteps overhead on the floor of the original hayloft. Naturally concerned she ran upstairs but found nothing to account for the sounds.

These footsteps have since been heard by at least six people including a 22-year-old daughter and several friends at varying times, the earliest being 7 pm one summer evening. One of the most recent incidents was early in 1976 when the elder daughter heard the noise at 5 am and mistaking it for someone else threw a pillow at the wall with the request to "stop it!" The footsteps stopped.

One of the most interesting factors is that the children have never been frightened by the sounds and have accepted them without question. Also the footsteps are heard as if on bare floorboards whereas the whole of the area is carpeted.

Who the mysterious ghostly visitor is remains a puzzle, but there is a clue for she has been seen and described by a couple of witnesses as a woman with very intense eyes and wearing a long gown. On one occasion she was mistaken for the owner, Mrs. Kent, standing at the opposite end of the building to the site of the noises.

KENT

Chilham Castle Keep,* OPA
Chilham.   *On A252 – Nearest Station – Chilham*

All that remains of an original Norman castle is this octagonal Keep with, in some places, walls 8 feet thick. Despite the creepy dungeons below earth level in which, according to Charles Jardine, 800 prisoners were kept in worse conditions than the Black Hole of Calcutta, the only ghost experienced here is that of a 'mediaeval woman'.

The Keep is opened at weekends to provide mediaeval banquets for groups of tourists. In 1972 one of the young girls acting as a serving wench saw the figure of another woman in clothing of the period approaching the old wall and gateway which abuts the Keep. Assuming that it was one of the more enthusiastic customers she greeted the lady but was shattered when the apparition melted into the wall.

So scared was the young girl that she ran, white and shaking, to the bar in one of the dungeons and had to be given a brandy to calm her nerves. Any doubts as to the sobriety of the witness were dispelled by the claim that she had never tasted alcohol before. Months later two members of another party commented on the glorious dress of "the lady standing by the old wall" and found it difficult to believe that she didn't exist.

In 1974, when a television film unit was using the Keep for location shots of a popular series of a historical nature, one of the actresses thought that she had been pushed by unseen hands down the stairway and certainly suffered a broken ankle as the result of her fall.

Rumours are that a lady friend of one of the owners in the 14th century had been bricked up somewhere in the tower. But whether these rumours relate to the mysterious sounds which emanate from the roof over the ladies' powder room or not will never be established. Dogs are sometimes more receptive to 'atmosphere' than humans and an Alsatian brought to the doorway simply refused to enter but howled with fright and ran downstairs and out into the garden.

Let me hasten to assure readers that I do not normally enter ladies' powder rooms, but for the sake of research I felt that in this case I was justified in doing so and accompanied Mr. Jardine to the comfortably decorated apartment. The room, unfortunately for the customer, was the coldest in the Keep, but whilst we chatted, we suddenly heard sounds similar to those which would result from someone hauling heavy pieces of furniture around, coming from above our heads. We moved rapidly to the roof to find absolutely no cause for the sounds and returned quite mystified. My host, however, assured me that it was not the first time such noises had been heard.

The Pest House,* PP
Frythe Walk,
Cranbrook.

Mr. and Mrs. Deane moved into this unusually named 14th century house in August 1975, attracted by its site, the charm of the building and the peculiar name given to it. Determined to discover some clue to the reason for its title they referred to the library and local residents and found that it was constructed as a 'Pestilence House', a hospital, in 1369 and intended primarily for treating victims of the Plague. In 1379 it had become a private house but in the 17th century was requisitioned for hospitalisation of victims of the second Plague. Bodies of the first catastrophe had been deposited in the cellars which were sealed, but which were re-opened to accommodate the corpses of the second wave of 'pestilence'.

The cellars were re-sealed and the house altered to become two private homes. Cranbrook's first gravedigger lived in one of the cottages.

In the course of her enquiries Mrs. Deane learnt that when Mrs. Irene Newton was baby-sitting for the previous owners in 1970 she had twice seen the figure of "a lovely woman glide from the inglenook fireplace, cross the sitting room and disappear when half way up the stairs".

According to the former owner, Robert Neumann, who wrote his book *The Plague House Papers* (Hutchinson, 1959) in the house, a well-established ghost of the home is that of Theresa Benenden. It is her initials which are carved on the sitting room door, and another small cupboard door in an adjoining room, with six dates between 1770 and 1779. Why Theresa decided to mark the doors in this way is a bit of a mystery. Perhaps it was a childish prank, but the letters are nearly 2 inches long and not easily covered.

At first glance I thought they indicated a growing scale, but realised the dates are haphazard with 1778 at the top and 1779 at the bottom.

Although Mrs. Deane herself has experienced nothing unusual, other than the usual creaks and groans associated with old timbers, her ten-year-old son, William, woke her early one morning by talking to "someone" standing in the doorway of his bedroom, the room which Neumann mentions as being called 'the Ghost Room'. However, it is not associated with Theresa, but another woman, probably the one seen on the ground floor.

The boy was looking directly at "a tall lady" standing beside Mrs. Deane and told his mother that on another occasion a man and a woman standing on the landing had tried to stop him walking down the stairs.

Some sceptical readers may think the lad might have imagined the figures or dreamt them, but he was wide awake and unafraid and his description of the figure in the bedroom matched that given by the baby-sitter.

Edward Deane, the nine-year-old youngster of the family, has seen and heard nothing.

When discussing the case with a Mrs. Newton, an enthusiastic student of local history, I was told that some years ago her son had discovered a tunnel leading from beneath the main inglenook fireplace of the Pest House to a site at Bakers Cross a few hundred yards away. This could suggest that the ghost is that of a young lady who used to keep some illicit appointment with a friend and then secretly travelled back through the hidden passage.

It should not be forgotten that Chancellor Sir John Baker, known as 'Bloody Baker', was very active in Cranbrook conducting a savage persecution of the local anabaptists, and wherever there was religious intolerance, hiding holes and tunnels were constructed to accommodate the victims. Could it have been that centuries ago Bakers Cross was a house associated with the Chancellor which might have been used by him for his notorious womanising? Could it be that the lady in white was one of his victims?

Neumann states that, although he experienced nothing exciting himself, a peculiar tape recording was made by a visitor, in which the words "eight pounds, oh, eight pounds" could be heard. The guest also saw the figure of a woman 'clad in a timeless night garment' bend over her and walk into the second attic, the room in which William Deane saw the lady. Yet another witness saw the woman in a morning gown carrying a candle.

Theresa Benenden was the unmarried daughter of the owner of the house in 1574 and the significance of the 'eight pounds' heard on the recording may be cleared by the fact that she was to have an annuity of that figure. She was paid this amount for five years but payment was then stopped. She petitioned for her rights but failed to achieve justice and committed suicide in the cellar.

Pennis Lane, OP
Fawkham Green. *Off A20 – Nearest Station – Longfield (5 miles)*
Only a few hundred yards away from the famous racing circuit at Brand's Hatch, one finds the small village of Fawkham Green where the phantom of what could be a nun has been seen gliding down Pennis Lane.

Local belief is that she is connected with St. John's Jerusalem a few miles to the north. This establishment is the 13th century headquarters of the Knights Hospitallers of St. John which became incorporated into a house in the 16th century.

The apparition, seen during autumn evenings, could be that of a sister of the order, or a lay woman, a member of a supporting confraternity who would wear the same habit. Whoever, or whatever she is must remain a mystery, but some believe that she is a murder victim of the 1400s.

Savoy Bingo Hall, OPA
Grace Hill,
Folkestone. *Off A20 – Nearest Station – Folkestone Central*
Even so-called 'experts' can be wrong, for I had always believed that to visit a haunted site hoping to see some phenomena was a waste of time. This idea was destroyed when I visited the 'Glebe House' in Folkestone in 1974 (see *Ghosts of the South East,* David and Charles) and when I learnt that Dick Godden, a former student and friend of mine, had seen an apparition at this popular 'Hall of entertainment'.

As a researcher into the paranormal he has been involved in investigating haunted property for some years and one of the most impressive cases is that of the Savoy. I am indebted to him for providing the following information.

The first building on the site was that of a small workman's cottage in 1875, but this was demolished in 1889 to make room for a monumental mason. Then in 1918 came the opening of 'The Electric Cinema', but only ten years later it was destroyed by a disastrous fire. In 1945 a young boy was killed in the rebuilt picture house when an extractor fan fell from the roof during repairs and by 1964, in common with many cinemas, the building was converted to a bingo hall.

By May 1972 several members of the staff and members of the public had been frightened by seeing the apparition of a woman who appeared on the stairs, in the staff room and even walking through the foyer doors, although they were closed at the time.

So concerned was the manager, Mr. George Offen, at the number of staff who were leaving and the continual complaints from Club members that he asked Mr. Godden to investigate the matter. At 11.30 pm on May 25th the first of a series of investigations was held.

Two days later, whilst feeling that he was 'being watched', Dick walked towards the foyer doors and a row of seats suddenly slammed down 'one after another', but it was on May 29th that the investigator was delighted at actually seeing the phantom herself.

Within minutes of the drop in temperature at 1 1.52 pm he saw, standing near an emergency exit on the south side of the hall, the figure of a woman dressed in the style of the 1930's. She was gazing into the centre of the stalls and whilst doing so covered her right eye with her left hand on two occasions. By the time Mr. Godden had reached the balcony the figure had vanished and the temperature rose to its normal 60 degrees.

Two days later a Mrs. Zeuter, the sister of the young lad who had been killed 27 years earlier, was contacted and she produced a photograph of her mother who had been with the boy at the time of his death. It matched that of the ghostly visitor to the hall and when asked if her mother had any unusual mannerisms Mrs. Zeuter told Mr. Godden that she suffered from a weak right eye and frequently wiped it with her left hand.

On June 3rd a group of sympathetic friends joined Mr. Godden in an attempt to eradicate the haunting. Within minutes of arriving a walking stick belonging to a Mr. Downs suddenly levitated from the back of one of the seats, ten rows from where he was sitting, to a height of 8 feet. This was followed by the formation of a 'black shapeless mass' appearing at a corner of the stage, moving along the wall towards the balcony and then fading away. One of the group, Mrs. Ashburn, went to investigate the sound of voices heard to be coming from the balcony but was unable to trace any cause for the noises. A few minutes later the female phantom re-appeared about 50 yards from where the group were sitting and was seen to walk through the centre row of seats, finally disappearing in the aisle.

Theatre Royal,* OPA
Addington Street,
Margate. *Off A28 – Nearest Station – Margate*

In November 1974 it was announced that efforts were to be made to regenerate interest in one of England's oldest active theatres, the Theatre Royal in Margate. Unfortunately for some, the plan was dropped and the establishment, celebrating some 200 years of existence, continues its life as a Bingo Hall. There are over a dozen haunted theatres in Britain but few of them are outside the London area and none can boast of such a variety of phenomena as does this seaside establishment.

Similar in size to London's Strand Theatre, it became the home of a company which had been formed in about 1786 and the working home of a very famous manageress, Miss Sarah Thorne.

Although Miss Sarah was a strong and forthright character, she had gained considerable loyalty and respect through her ability to develop the potential talent in (hitherto) unknown players.

As with a number of theatres, the Royal has been used for many purposes. The first time it ceased to provide entertainment it became a furniture store but was re-opened in 1930. The boom days of the film changed it again, this time into a cinema but as this form of amusement began to lose its appeal it reverted to theatrical performances and more recently to the thrill of bingo.

One of the phantoms of the theatre was originally reported during the latter half of the First World War when the building was used as a store for bedsteads. The ghost then, in 1918, was claimed to be that of the martinet Sarah Thorne, but is it only Sarah who frequents the theatre, for other phenomena have been experienced more recently?

Mr. Harry Jacobs, the proprietor, told me that in 1972 a painter and decorator working in the building at night had experienced several peculiar incidents. He had been so scared by the weird noises that he accidentally knocked a tin of paint all over himself, but it was not really funny. He ran into the street shaking with fear.

When in 1966 Charles Tanner, another decorator, arrived to start work on a Monday night he had heard a soft whispering coming from the stage. He lit numerous matches to pierce the darkness but found no reason or cause for the sounds. Finally he reached the main light switches and started work on a door at the rear of the pit. He tried to dismiss the odd creakings of timber as due to normal shrinkage, but when regular footsteps were heard approaching from the stage and stopped just behind him, he became a little more apprehensive.

However, Charles is a rational character and was determined to find the cause for the sounds and, as calmly as possible, began to check that all the doors were locked. Suddenly the door of the box office banged, but as there was still no-one to be seen and nothing to be found that could account for the noise, he returned to work.

Within seconds of recommencing work on the door in the orchestra pit the sounds of footsteps returned and stopped, as they had done before, immediately behind him. Again he turned round and again there was nothing to see, but a sudden inexplicable 'thump' just in front of the first row of seats alarmed him. It was not just the noise but seeing dust rising from the carpet which added to the weird incident, for no object was found to have caused the noise or the cloud of dust.

Despite these shocks, on Tuesday night of the same week, after checking that all the doors and windows were fastened, Charles put on the auditorium lights and started painting one of the walls near an exit door. He had been working for a couple of minutes when he glanced towards the stage and saw a semi-transparent object about ten inches in diameter and about five feet in height gliding across the floor. He described it later as being surrounded "with a kind of fuzzy halo." The only features were two dim places where eyes would be if it were a face.

The apparition travelled to the middle of the stage and then vanished. Though, as one can expect, somewhat perturbed by this, the painter continued with his work but only a short while later he was disturbed again. Prior to painting the stage area, the two huge curtains had been rolled and placed on the ledge above the lintel. Now one of them began to unroll and descend, slowly and methodically, in a way which suggested the work of a stagehand, but Charles was the only person there. There was no human agency involved.

By now Charles was a little concerned at the prospect of staying more nights in the theatre alone so a sceptical colleague, a David Rogers, volunteered to keep him company. Whisperings from the stage were heard by both men, but when they heard a loud crash in the front row of the dress circle it was the 'unbeliever' who called for the police.

Several hours were spent by the officers of the law in searching the entire building but no explanation or reason could be offered for the noise.

In 1973 another workman, on hearing a loud crash in the front of the stalls, lost his balance when on top of a ladder and was covered in paint as a result.

Other incidents reported, sometimes by the caretaker, include front doors being unbolted by unseen hands, foyer lights being switched on and "an unholy scream" near the front of the stalls.

To account for some of the phenomena there are several legends, the most popular being that the phantom shape seen on the stage was the ghost of Sarah Thorne who was returning to express her disapproval of the changes in the decor.

Another idea offered by Joseph Braddock in his *Haunted Houses* (Batsford) is that an actor, dismissed from the theatrical company, committed suicide by throwing himself into the orchestra pit from the box that he had bought. The claim is that his ghost was seen so often in the box that the management eventually bricked it up.

In an attempt to obtain more information concerning the hauntings, two sensitives visited the theatre. One claimed that she had a 'vision' of Miss Thorne, who had a stern face and frizzy hair and who was annoyed because of the use of reddish-brown paint by the decorators. There was a stain of this colour on her crinoline.

The other medium who visited the theatre was the renowned Ena Twigg who told Alan Whicker (of television fame) that she thought the suicide was connected with gas because of the difficulty she had in breathing.

From the various incidents which have occurred, it certainly seems that two ghosts continued to haunt the Royal Theatre, at least up to 1973.

Sarah Thorne, being the most dominant character, can well be expected to return, though over the years her image seems to have gradually faded.

During the first war her phantom was described as wearing a crinoline and a bonnet, but if the weird oval object seen by Charles Tanner was the fading remains of the good lady it will be surprising if she is ever seen again. But her presence may still be felt.

A comforting thought for the hundreds of bingo players who stream into the old theatre anxious to boost their finances is that the visits, if they are from Sarah, seem to occur only late at night.

Editor's Note: Theatre producer Nick Bromley in his excellent UK survey of haunted theatres and playhouses *Stage Ghosts and Haunted Theatres* (2021) details a number of seemingly paranormal incidents on site, mostly involving low-level poltergeist activity and the sounds of a child crying. In recent years the theatre has come to regularly host ghost hunts and investigations. In 2009 a local theatre group named themselves the Sarah Thorne Theatre Club in honour of the ghost (*Isle of Thanet Gazette* 14 August 2009).

St. Johns Chapel,* PP
High Street,
New Romney.

Mention St. Johns Chapel to residents of New Romney and many will ask where it is or will express complete ignorance of this ancient building, one of the oldest in the county. It is not really surprising for it is partially hidden, though forming an integral part of a shop dealing in second-hand goods.

I am extremely grateful to Miss Roper of Littlestone for providing the historical background of this interesting old establishment. Although frequently referred to as 'The Priory of St. John the Baptist' it is, in fact, only the chapel of the priory founded for regular Augustine canons in 1257 by Sir John Mansal, a Privy Counsellor to Henry III. As a permanent reminder of the priory a site in St. John's Lane is known as 'St. Johns Churchyard' and in July 1929, when foundations were being dug, several skeletons were found and reburied in another graveyard.

The priory was seized in 1410/11 by Henry V and in 1439 Henry VI gave it to All Souls College, but it was used as a hospital until 1495. Miss Roper also points out that on the north wall of the chapel, remains of the piscina, a stone basin in which the chalice used in the service of the Eucharist is rinsed, can be seen and in another room a genuine Tudor fireplace still exists.

It is unfortunate that, like so many ancient and fascinating buildings in Kent, the structure is sadly neglected and rapidly falling into disrepair, but over 350 historic houses were destroyed in Britain during 1975, stressing the overall pattern in the country. There is evidence that there are at least two priests' holes in the Chapel which are associated with the Lollards (followers of John Wycliffe) and constructed to hide some members of the group fleeing from Catholic persecution. When their pursuers departed, the religious dissenters were able to scramble to safety in the Priory through a tunnel. The unfortunate ones who were caught were usually burnt and for this reason many would hide their valuables in their temporary hiding places, usually in chimneys. It may seem ironic that it was partially due to the Lollards that the Reformation was finally achieved.

When the haunting actually started is not known, but it is certainly still current and so many witnesses exist that there can be no doubt as to its authenticity. In the 1960s a woman living in the Chapel claimed to have seen two monks glide through the wall, but it was in the 1970s that the phenomena increased. By then the shop had become established and an assistant going upstairs to get some more furniture to display in the window heard footsteps following him. Upon turning round he saw two women standing on a landing. Another member of the company had also been disturbed at seeing the two silent figures in a doorway at the top of the stairs.

About ten years ago some of the rooms on the first floor were used by a professional consultant who decided to divide one into a waiting area and a surgery. This called for the construction of a plasterboard division, but when it came to painting the new wall problems occurred, for the decorator refused to complete the job having been frightened twice by "something" that glided past him. He also heard the sound of footsteps cross the room when he knew he was the only occupant.

One of the consultant's clients stated in 1975 that she was so frightened by a series of incidents that she fled downstairs. She had arrived early for her appointment at 9.30am and waited outside the office but had the impression that someone was beckoning her from a doorway. On moving nearer the aperture and noticing it was completely boarded up she suddenly "went very cold." When she heard "a thump like someone falling heavily in the room above and faint chattering voices and whispers" she ran.

Another decorator employed to complete some alterations in the basement was also too frightened to finish the work, and a servant girl who worked in the building when it was a private house stated that the servants were so scared by the "mysterious whisperings and chatterings" that they refused to sleep upstairs and would bring their bedding into the kitchen.

Mrs. M. Pollard, an accountant with an office on the first floor, told me that she has heard the "phantom footsteps" so many times that she ignores them. On one occasion she was completely alone in the building with the front door locked when she heard footsteps coming up the stairs to her office. She waited for the client to knock, but heard the sounds continue past her door and along the passage to the end of the corridor. No-one was found and the door was still locked.

On another occasion she heard footsteps walking about in the room over her office and being puzzled, she went to find out what the stranger was doing. The whole floor was empty.

A dog brought in one day by a friend was so obviously disturbed by the atmosphere that it had to be removed.

Another puzzling incident occurred in December 1975 when a Mrs. Gaskell of Littlestone and a friend, working in a room at the end of the first-floor corridor, heard the door close. They turned round to find it still open and yet minutes later when they had completed the work they found the door closed. An unusual case of precognition perhaps?

Another series of incidents was experienced by Mrs. Horton, a sales lady, who has frequently heard the footsteps arid the sound of doors opening and closing even though the only occupant in the creepy old building at the time was herself. Her husband as well as herself has heard some "peculiar dripping sounds, just like a tap," but has been unable to locate the source.

To conclude a 10-week evening course on 'Ghost Hunting' I visited the priory on 9th December 1975 with 13 members of the class and was present when two mysterious tape recordings were made. Both registered peculiar tapping noises similar to the sound of a dripping tap but varied in volume as if the cause of the noise had actually passed the microphone. No other phenomena were noted and as the highest temperature recorded was 46 degrees we all decided at 10.30 pm to return to our warmer homes. Some were convinced that The Priory is haunted not only by footsteps, but tappings and the ghosts of two sinister females. Would they perhaps be the spectres of two victims of religious persecution or one wonders if they are phantoms of a much later period?

Oxney Bottom,* OP
Near Dover.   *A258 – Nearest Station – Dover*
Just about 3 miles north of Dover on the main road to Deal, drivers pass through Oxney Bottom and, it seems, run the risk of colliding with or just missing 'the grey lady' who wafts across the road at a sharp bend beside what looks like the remains of a small quarry. Travelling south from Deal they are given the choice of continuing on the main road or turning along a narrow driveway to a private house.

On the estate and in the wood on the left are the ruins of a church and it is possible that the ghost is in some way connected with the burial ground there.

In 1973 and 1974 a series of fatal accidents occurred at this spot due, it is thought, to the activities of the phantom. Who she is nobody knows, but she was seen one night in 1973 by a group of four young men from an engineering firm in Dover who were anxious to find out the cause of the accidents. She appeared on a hillock at the side of the driveway and glided across the road, nearly causing yet another accident. The lady was described as a tall female figure in a grey dress. The witnesses were so astounded by the sudden appearance of the woman that they were unable to provide more than this somewhat vague description, but one claimed that "her face was very serious, miserable in fact, but it happened so quickly I can't recall any other detail."

Old Soar Manor,* OP
Plaxtol.   *Off A25 via A227 – Nearest Station – Borough Green*
Not very far from the haunted Ightham Mote and only about two miles from Plaxtol village one finds this mediaeval house owned by the National Trust but under the guardianship of the Department of the Environment.

Built of Kentish ragstone and dating from 1290 it consists of only six rooms, three on the ground floor and the others, a garderobe, solar and chapel, on the upper storey. Margaret Wood, in her archaeological guide to the property (HMSO, 1950), describes it as a 'remarkably unspoilt example of a knightly dwelling of the reign of Edward I, and one of the most notable survivors of 13th century domestic architecture'.

Unfortunately the haunting here, though intriguing, is far from impressive.

Little is known of the original inhabitants, although the story is that the mother of William Colepeper, custodian of Leeds Castle, named it Soar (Norman for 'grief'), to perpetuate her own distress at her son's execution by Edward II in 1326.

Eventually it became part of the estate of the Geary family and Mrs. S. L. Cannon gained ownership on the death of Sir William and presented it to the National Trust in 1947.

In 1971 the new caretaker was a little disturbed at being asked whether she knew that the old building was haunted by the ghost of an 18th century dairymaid who committed suicide in the chapel one June because she was pregnant. Her informant, a local resident, continued by telling her that he had frequently seen lights in the empty building at night and a friend had heard the sound of music coming from the chapel.

Old Soar Manor, Plaxtol, Kent, where an eighteenth-century dairymaid still haunts the scene of her death. *Author's collection.*

During the following year a young couple asked about the haunting which they knew existed because of the sudden drop in temperature when they neared the chapel, and the following Sunday another pair of visitors commented on 'the ghostly feeling in the chapel.'

In June 1972 the caretaker herself, when checking the solar before closing up, glanced towards the chapel and saw a long, dark grey cloak hanging on the wall, but when she entered the room the clothing had disappeared. A few days later a clairvoyant saw the phantom of a priest bending over the piscina and on returning in 1974 was affected by the feeling of 'an unhappy presence' on the spiral staircase leading into the solar.

An elderly retired worker who had been employed on the adjoining farm stated that over sixty years ago he used to sleep on the ground floor as a guard against thieves, for the building was used as a store for valuable hay and straw. "Frequently," he said, "I would hear footsteps pacing the floor of the empty room upstairs, but they were light, like a woman's. It was always June when I heard it."

St. Nicholas Church,* OP
Pluckley. *On B2077 (off A20) – Nearest Station – Pluckley*

Whether Pluckley really is the most haunted village in England or not is a matter of personal belief and not just of ghosts. There are various reports listing twelve official ghosts here, others ten, whilst some sceptics state that they are all due to a resident's childish prank, for he claims to have invented every one of the stories.

St. Nicholas Church in Pluckley, Kent, said by some to be the most haunted village in England. *Author's collection.*

I certainly cannot accept the last belief for I have met a couple of rational witnesses to genuine ghosts in the village and personally experienced the rather creepy atmosphere of the graveyard of St. Nicholas Church in which some months after my visit a young local girl was frightened by what she saw among the tombs.

Other case books refer to 'The Red Lady' who haunts the church and the churchyard and is thought to be the phantom of a mother searching for the unmarked grave of her child, but it was no such ghost that the girl saw one evening in 1975. She was walking home from work approaching the church and, as is usual in such instances, thinking of "nothing in particular" when she saw in front of her a figure gliding among the stones. "It looked like some woman in a long white gown. I was a bit puzzled as to who it could be," she said, "but then, just as I got to the wall, the thing vanished. I ran all the way home. I've never been so frightened."

The vicar has been so concerned with the stories that he has carried out two services of exorcism in the churchyard, but freely admits that "there still seems to be something which affects the atmosphere there."

I cannot help but wonder whether this latest witness had in fact seen the Red Lady, but because of the length of time since she was last seen, she has lost her colour. There is the idea that to remain in full glorious technicolour a phantom must be recharged by the act of being witnessed, otherwise it begins to fade and finally disperses completely.

It is not far away, a few yards from the Blacksmith's Arms, that an old watercress woman is supposed to have accidentally burnt herself to death. But all that is seen nowadays is a faint pink glow sometimes on the stones of the bridge carrying the road over a stream where she died.

LANCASHIRE

Royal Umpire Museum,*OP
Moor Road,
Croston.
Junction of A581 and B5249 – Nearest Station – Croston

This museum is quite unconnected with cricket but is devoted to displaying various objects associated with folklore and life in bygone days. Mr. W. Parker, secretary of the Preston Society for Psychical Research, told me in April 1976 that the building is genuinely haunted but, despite reports in other publications, only by poltergeist activity.

"Nothing has ever been seen here," he said, "but in September last year in an adjoining barn, eight of us distinctly heard the sound of heavy breathing coming from an empty room at the back. We all thought it was a tramp but when we went in the sound seemed to recede through the back wall. We even wondered if it was an owl snoring but checked with an expert who assures us that it couldn't have been."

The barn was originally a church and still retains its memorials, crosses and distinctive windows.

Serious investigations have recently been carried out in the museum by members of the Society to establish the cause of the poltergeist activity. "We had a shower of stones thrown at us last time we went," Mr. Parker said, "what will it be next, I wonder?"

What caused errors in previous reports was the fact that when Mr. Kevill, owner of the Museum, moved a cross which signified where a priest was buried in the garden, an apparition of a young woman was seen the following day standing at a bus stop. It was assumed, incorrectly, that the two incidents were linked.

Legend has it that sometime during the Reformation a young maid employed in Gradwell Farm, as the museum was originally known, killed herself by jumping into a well at the back of the house. The reason given for this suicide was the heart-breaking sorrow felt by the girl on learning of the death of a priest who had been illegally hidden in a priests' hole in the house. When he died he was buried in unconsecrated ground, but sometime later a cross was erected to his memory. It was this cross that Mr. Kevill decided to move.

The apparition, known locally as 'The Sascoe Lady', is of an unknown woman who has been seen several times walking across the fields from Sascoe Farm and standing by the bus stop near the museum. She was seen in 1957 and assumed to be a potential passenger by a bus driver who stopped for her. Only when the conductor enquired as to the reason for stopping did his colleague realise that the young lady he had seen had vanished.

Samlesbury Hall, OPA
Preston New Road,
Near Preston *On A59 – Nearest Station – Preston*

Because this fine 14th century manor house is constantly used for social purposes, official meetings and wedding receptions, it is open for general viewing by appointment only.

Mainly half-timbered it stands in a six-acre garden and houses another unidentified 'white lady'.

The house was originally owned by the Southworths, a devout Catholic family who allowed the house to be used as a meeting place and temporary residence for members of the priesthood. Because of this and the anti-clerical feeling of the time two priests' holes were incorporated into the structure. A box was found in one of these which contained various accessories for the celebration of the Mass.

There are romantic tales of the phantom being Lady Southworth who fell in love with a Protestant. He was killed by her brother and as a result she died from a broken heart or joined a nunnery. Actually, as Winifred Hayworth says, 'the family pedigree knows nothing of her existence'.

So who haunts the old Bezza Lane, the path which leads to a dower house and formed a meeting place for members of the religion? And who is it that appears as a 'wraith-like figure' standing in the garden near the outer wall of the building at dusk?

Adding to the mystery, a few years ago workmen fitting additional drainage revealed the major part of a man's skeleton lying against the foundation wall within feet of the spot where the phantom 'woman in white' appears.

Descriptions given by numerous witnesses always feature the same woman, sometimes gliding down the pathway to stand near the wall and also seen moving silently up one of the stairways in Samlesbury Hall itself.

LEICESTERSHIRE

Brooksby Agricultural College, OPA
Brooksby,
Melton Mowbray (5 miles) *On A607 – Nearest Station – Melton Mowbray*

In my book *Our Haunted Kingdom* (Wolfe) I expressed disappointment at failing to find any more than one modern ghost in the county of Leicester. One lady was kind enough to write and provide details of eight hauntings and virtually told me to 'get cracking'. Unfortunately only one of these had been experienced in the 20th century and that was the ghostly lady of Grace Dieu Priory.

However, as a result of his own appeals in the local press and on local radio, Colin Smith of Birmingham was able to obtain details of several other cases in the area and has been kind enough to supply a selection of these to me.

One relates to another 'multi-haunting' in this college of agriculture, though admittedly the Principal has never experienced any phenomena. However there are some living witnesses to a few of the occurrences. A really peculiar incident, reminding me of the song telling of the train which steams through the dining room, is the sound of a coach and horses which gallop through the middle of the hall, stop, unload "something heavy" and then gallop on. One elderly lady has heard it three times and her husband twice in recent years.

The rational explanation offered for this weird situation is that the front of the hall used to be the site where coaches used to stop. But this section, together with a complete wing of the building, was destroyed during the 19th century and the present section was rebuilt, with the result that the road was reconstructed on a different site. The same witness to the sound of the coach has also seen a man and a woman "in long clothes" glide across the road between Brooksby and Rotherby. As far as the female phantom is concerned, this is of 'Lady Caroline'. She may be in some way connected with a woman's skeleton discovered in 1892 when Captain Stanley Williams owned the property.

Unfortunately the exact site is now the subject of doubt for some say the bones were found under a step being replaced and others claim she was discovered in a tiny room, accompanied by the skeleton of a baby. Adding to the confusion, the second tale also states that playing cards were scattered all over the floor of the cupboard in which the remains were revealed. What relevance, if any, these cards have is conjectural. However, the phantom of the good lady has been seen fairly recently in various parts of the ground floor. Perhaps, being a Lady, she is looking for a 'Royal flush'?

Grace Dieu Priory, OP A
Shepshed *Off A512 – Nearest Station – Leicester*
Thanks to Edwin Chapman of *B.B.C. Radio Leicester* I am able to include one of the lesser known, but nevertheless interesting hauntings of Leicester. Mr. Chapman tells me that Nikolaus Pevsner, in his series of works on *Buildings of England*, says that the Priory was founded for Augustinian Canonesses in 1240 and in 1539 it became the home of John Beaumont. Sir Ambrose Philipps destroyed most of the Priory in 1696, though a large quantity of the ruins was still standing in "Buck's time (1730). The most interesting single feature . . . could be a chancel. Otherwise all the still recognisable details are early and late Tudor . . . and also a chimney with three fine brick stacks."

Who was "Buck"? Mr. Chaman, through his extensive research, says that he has seen a woodcut of a rare print of 1 730 entitled 'A North West View of Grace Dieu' which is "probably the only surviving record of the founding of the Priory and its subsequent ownership." The illustration was the joint work of the brothers Samuel and Nathaniel Buck.

These gentlemen, in the dedication of the print to Ambrose Phillipps, state that the building was "a nunnery founded by Roisia, wife of Bertram de Verdun, in the 24th year of Henry III, for Cistercian nuns . . . King Henry VIII granted this house to Sir Humphrey Foster by whom it was alienated to John Beaumont, Esq."

There is no clue as to when the nunnery became a priory or who is correct as to the religious order involved, Augustinian or Cistercian. The ghostly lady involved could by that of Roisia de Verdun who "came of a knightly family" but "tired of the world" and joined the Grace Dieu Nunnery herself and died there seven years later. She was buried in the chapel in 1247, though the monument to her in Bolton Church is of a much later date.

It was surprising to me to learn that Wordsworth had referred to 'the ivied ruins of forlorn Grace Dieu' and claims that the nunnery was Augustinian. So you 'pays your money and takes your choice.'

To account for the ghost, there are two tales one suggesting that she is the victim of a car crash and the other that she is the phantom of 'The Lady Roisia' herself. As there is no record of a fatal accident near the Priory bend on the site of her appearance one could be right to assume the identity is of the nun, even though her appearance is unusual.

"She is old and bent," says Mr. Chapman, "and has a shopping bag in her left hand," but this could well be her handbag of network that a lady of that period would carry. "She is in white from head to foot, including her conical hat."

Several motorists have seen her shuffling along some fifty feet from a bus stop and one or two have stopped to offer her a lift only to find that, as soon as they get out of the car or wind down the window, the figure has vanished.

LINCOLNSHIRE

St. Botolph's Church, OP
Boston *On A16 – Nearest Station – Boston*

The dominating, 272-foot-high octagonal tower of this parish church is taller than that of Lincoln Cathedral.

Known affectionately as 'The Boston Stump' the 14th century church stands beside the River Witham and overlooks what was once a flourishing seaport. An old legend to account for the breeze which so frequently howls round the tower is that the devil is still trying to blow it down. The top of the tower remains lighted, for the benefit of seamen as in olden days, thanks to a handsome subscription from residents of Boston, Massachusetts.

A local tale to account for the well-worn slabs of stone surrounding the base of 'The Stump', is that there have been so many suicides from the tower that the surface has been chipped away. This is obviously more than doubtful, but there are known to have been at least two deaths from the roof in Victorian times.

A young mother, grief-stricken by the sudden loss of her husband, clambered to the top of the tower and, clutching her newborn babe, threw herself to the ground, hoping to end her misery forever.

During autumn evenings, a grey shadow holding a darker bundle is sometimes seen at the top of the ancient building and accompanied by a sudden strong gust of wind, the shadow glides silently downwards and vanishes on touching the ground.

Is it the ghost of the young widow, or merely a couple of owls?

Barn, PP
Deeping St. Nicholas.
A couple of years ago the *Lincolnshire Free Press* uncarthed a haunting tale about a barn not far from the level crossing in this small village which lies between Spalding and Stamford and is bordered by the North Drove and South Drove Drains. Many haunted sites are associated with water and although there is plenty around these parts I do not think it is the cause of the ghost.

The local paper discovered that the cause of the appearance of a woman in white seemed to be that a man hanged himself from a rafter in the building sometime in the 1800's. He had been refused by his lady love and could not bear to live without her.

The lady in question, appalled by what her frigidity had caused, died of a broken heart years later but she continues to return to the site of the tragic ending of her one-time lover.

There are certainly many villagers who recall the tale and some of them freely admit to having seen the phantom, even to hearing 'weird moans', though these could be caused by wind rustling through the undergrowth at the sides of the road.

"Sometimes," says the report, "the white lady appeared cradling a white cat in her arms." This must be one of the very few cases of ghostly cats which exist. Unfortunately, neither has been seen for some time, so perhaps they have finally died away.

Doddington Hall,* OP
Doddington *Off A46 and A37 – Nearest Station – Lincoln (5 miles)*
When I first saw Doddington Hall I thought it was built as an early Victorian prison. Its austere appearance can easily give the casual visitor that impression, but actually the Hall was built by Robert Smythson in 1593-1600 for Thomas Taylor.

Although the exterior has never been changed the house was completely redesigned and refurbished in 1761 and now contains a marvellous collection of furniture, tapestries and porcelain.

My guide for the day told me that the current owner, Mr. Jarvis, dismissed the legend of a screaming girl jumping off the roof as pure Victorian romantic fiction, but his wife had seen a charming old lady looking at her from the upstairs landing. She was clothed in an 'old style brown dress' and although emitting a feeling of friendliness, faded away after a couple of seconds.

I also learnt that one or two visitors claim to have seen the 'dear old soul' as well, but nobody seems to have any ideas as to her identity.

LONDON

Former Magistrates Court (closed)
Aylward Street,
Stepney, E.1.　　　　　　　　*On A13 – Nearest Station – Stepney Green (District)*
Early in 1976 Lila Joseph, a clairvoyant, was asked to help identify the ghost of a woman frequently seen in the matron's room of this unusual site for a haunting. Kevin Moss, a warrant officer in 'the service', had been mystified for some time by the constant reports and decided to clear up the matter.

After a meeting was held in the room and some subsequent questioning of Doreen Chandler, a member of the staff, it was established that the phantom was, or is, Mrs. Chandler's mother, Lillian Browne, who died in 1946 at the age of 77. Mrs. Browne had been a matron at the Court for some 30 years and was therefore a very familiar figure. One can only assume that she was an extremely conscientious worker taking a real pride and delight in her work.

Editor's Note: This magistrates' court later served as a maximum-security court handling terrorism and serious crime charges but has since been closed and converted into private residences.

Tower of London,* OP
Tower Hill, E.C.3.　　　　　　　*On A 100 – Nearest Station – Tower Hill*
No selection of ghosts could be complete without a brief mention of what is probably the most haunted building in London, for here have been seen phantoms of Lady Jane Grey, Anne Boleyn, the Countess of Salisbury, Viscountess Rochford, Catherine Howard and a host of other spectres of the past.

One of the most recent incidents was in 1975 when a Mrs. Chalmers of Bognor Regis, taking an American friend on her first visit to the ancient monument, was puzzled when her young companion asked about the lady with the long dark hair standing near a window in the Bloody Tower.

The description she gave seemed identical to that of the mysterious female seen five years earlier in the same locality and reported in the London Evening News. "The figure was in a black dressit looked like velvetand there was a gold coin hanging round her neck." That renowned expert on the ghosts of the Tower, James Wentworth Day, believes that the phantom was of Lady Jane Grey, 'the pathetic child queen who died with such childish dignity' in 1554.

But who, one wonders, was the 'young woman wearing the costume of Henry VIII's time' who passed Mrs. L. Jackson of Hornchurch when she visited the Tower in 1965. She was walking near Traitors' Gate and, turning round to see more of the lady, was astounded to see the figure "vanish, apparently through a brick wall."

Admiralty House,* OPA (parts)
Whitehall, S.W.1. *On A4/A1 – Nearest Station – Trafalgar Square*

Unless you work for the Admiralty, or are a Minister, there is not much chance of seeing the ghost who floats around a ground floor flat in this establishment of the Establishment.

Denis Healey, then Defence Secretary for the Labour Government, lived in the flat with his family in the 1960s and it was during this period that *The Guardian* stated that there had been reports of the phantom being witnessed in one of the bedrooms. She had been seen so frequently that the family were treating her as a friend. Mr. Healey himself would not admit to anything. "I have nothing to say about it," but Sir Winston Churchill, while First Lord of the Admiralty, mentioned the apparition.

As far as identifying the lady is concerned, it is pointed out that she strongly resembles a portrait in the State Room showing Margaret Reay, mistress of the Earl of Sandwich in the 18th century. This attractive woman was shot dead by that unusual old gentleman, the Rev. James Hackman, when she was leaving a performance at Covent Garden.

The Department of the Environment are non-committal, preferring to believe, or at least claim, that the trouble was due to "a fault in the water system."

Editor's Note: Andrew Green duly contacted the Ministry of Works and in April 1972 received a short and laconic reply simply informing him that "The flat in question is one of three official residences in Admiralty House, Whitehall, London SW1". The letter was signed 'M.J. Ray' which was either a coincidence of names or someone at the Ministry having a bit of a joke. Andrew Green then wrote to Denis Healey, by then no longer Minister but an Opposition MP. Healey replied on 5 May 1972 stating, "I am afraid that my wife and I are not able to give you the material you wish as the person directly involved does not wish to be approached." Accordingly, Andrew Green included an entry on the haunted flat in his book the following year but included no more information than had appeared in the original *Guardian* report. No further sightings were received and there the matter again rested until 2010 when, on my having become literary executor to the Andrew Green estate, I made some enquiries with the by then ennobled Lord Healey. He kindly replied to my enquiry, telling me in a letter that "We did all see a ghost in our bedroom in Admiralty House but it was not Martha Ray but Duff Cooper's bride Diana" (Personal communication, Lord Healey, 17 March 2010). Thus, the original rumours had some foundation in an actual sighting, even if the ghost had been erroneously identified, and it is good to be able to put the record straight with such a case (a tradition that *The Guardian* always prides itself upon honouring, of course). Denis Healey was a cultured man, with interests extending far beyond politics, clearly had taken the experience of the ghost in his stride.

Birdcage Walk,* OP On A40
St. James Park,
S.W.1 *Nearest Station – St. James's (District)*
During the 1960s, when working in Tothill Street, I used to walk to Waterloo Station to catch my train home by way of Cockpit Steps, Birdcage Walk and Westminster Bridge. I always found the walk, especially on summer evenings, very pleasant, giving me the opportunity to see the flower beds and the ducks in St. James's Park, lateworking Civil Servants hurrying home from the Admiralty and finally the occasional member of Parliament flitting over to the local pub for a 'quick one' before a Division bell.

It was during this period too that I used to idly reminisce about the long-forgotten days when the Steps adjoining a cockpit were surrounded by the houses of Lord Grey, Lord Dacres, and the Earl of Lindsay. Those were the days when 1,424 people died in the City of London of old age and in 1790 there were over 5,000 cases of consumption, 4,485 of convulsions, five of 'grief and eleven of 'Evil', whatever that was.

Thomas Pennant writing in that year tells of 119 deaths by drowning, seven executed, thirteen suicides, one licked by a mad dog but thankfully none 'frightened'.

In 1804 a Coldstream Guardsman from the nearby Wellington Barracks was 'frightened', or rather 'alarmed', by seeing the ghostly figure of a headless woman 'rise from the earth' only two feet away from him as he was approaching the Cockpit Steps. It was in 1784 that a sergeant murdered his wife, cutting her head off and burying it in the grounds of the Barracks and throwing her body into the lake in the park.

A full Court of Inquiry was held to examine the report of the Guardsman seeing the apparition, but naturally no satisfactory conclusion could be reached. There is, however, a conclusion that the woman still haunts Birdcage Walk for in 1974 a motorist nearly hit her when she ran across the road towards Cockpit Steps. In 1975 an early morning taxi driver also reported seeing the same figure and took the rest of the day off to recover.

Clapham Bingo Hall, OPA
Clapham High Street, S.W.4 *On A3 – Nearest Station – Clapham Common*
One of the most unusual hauntings recorded in recent years was that experienced in this old cinema, now used as a bingo hall, for not only has the apparition been seen, but also heard, recorded and sensed. Several researchers have carried out intensive investigations into the phenomena and various people have described the ghost who continues, it seems, to visit the 'hall of entertainment'.

In 1905, it is said, a music hall artiste who was intensely interested in opera and once had ambitions of becoming another Dame Nellie Melba, that popular coloratura soprano, realised she had neither the qualities nor the luck needed to achieve her ambition.

One night, choosing the site of her only success, she clambered on to the roof of the building and there, alone and desolate, sang to the empty skies. It is, of course, possible that the woman was somewhat intoxicated. With the final notes of the song from some well-known opera ringing round the silent buildings, she fell through a skylight to her death. A tragic ending to a tragic story.

First reports of the haunting reached the press in 1972 when doors bolted by the security guards were found to have been opened and heard to bang. Mysterious footsteps had also been heard on the roof and on the stairway leading to it. Puzzled by the incidents, one of the security guards left a tape recorder on the stage all night and on his return the following morning was astounded when, on playing the tape back, he heard a woman's voice singing snatches of an opera, and the sound of a door banging.

By 1973 the reports of the hauntings had increased in number and some members of the staff stated that they had seen a vague figure of what seemed like "a headless woman" standing on the stage.

Due partially to the publicity that the case attracted, investigations were curtailed and research visits ceased. But does that sorrowful reminder of music hall days still return to the site of her unfulfilled ambitions?

The Plough Inn, * OP
Clapham Common, S.W.4. *On A3 – Nearest Station – Clapham Common*
The ghost here, Sarah, has caused a lot of trouble, both psychic and non-psychic.

Sited in one of the worst traffic-jam areas of the Capital, this 150-year-old pub has intrigued customers and a few landlords for some time. In September 1970 the doorway to a mystery room was discovered with a sealed window, often seen from the outside to be open. It was in an adjoining room that a resident barman had woken and seen the figure of a tall woman with long black hair, wearing a white gown, standing by a window. She slowly faded away, but the experience was enough for the witness to hand in his notice.

The pub dog was frequently frightened by something upstairs that no human could see and weird, inexplicable noises were heard coming from an empty bedroom.

It was as the result of an amateur investigation that the ghost was identified as 'Sarah'. The licensee in 1970 told me that although he had neither seen nor heard anything he had felt a "prickling sensation" and learnt that several members of the staff had felt the same thing whenever near the 'haunted' bedroom. Unfortunately, the brewers felt that enough was enough and a new licensee was appointed, one who states that the place is not and never was haunted. It is a pity that the existence of the lady has to be denied.

Editor's Note: The Plough is now one of the O'Neill's pub chain. The peak of the phenomena was clearly in the autumn of 1970 with the then Plough briefly earning the reputation of being the most haunted pub in London, with attempts to investigate the ghost with equipment and the resultant publicity about seances deemed by the proprietors as being detrimental to the business. As such they removed their licensee a Mr Felwyn Williams whom Green interviewed. A message spelt out in a séance held by six staff declared that 'Sarah' would appear on 11 September 1970 but when investigators waited no materialisation occurred (*Clapham New*s 25 Sept 1970; London *Evening Standard* 26 Sept 1970). Mr Williams was dismissed soon afterwards and the owners announced it had all been imagined (see also *Haunted London* (1973) by Peter Underwood pp 163-164).

Wandsworth Prison, OPA
Heathfield Square, S.W. 18. *Off A3 – Nearest Station – Wandsworth Common/Tooting Bec*
There cannot be many women ghosts haunting prisons for men, but Wandsworth was originally opened in 1851 as a house of correction for both sexes. Some fifty years later the total population of prisons in England was 14,800 and in 1950 over 20,000.

It would not really be surprising to learn that the majority of gaols are haunted considering the traumas that must be suffered within their grim walls. Gloucester Jail has a haunted cell, and a few years ago I learnt from a freight forwarder that 'mysterious noises' had been heard in what is left of 'The Clink' beneath Cannon Street rail bridge. The site is used for storage and warehousing of goods pending despatch to all parts of the world and it was from here that a few passengers joined the Mayflower before sailing for America to set up a new colony. The phantom seen by both warders and prisoners in Wandsworth is affectionately known as 'Annie'. It is thought that the wraith is of one of the workers, probably a cook, and not one of the criminals. She appears wearing a Victorian type of grey dress and has been described as "of middle age with greying hair."

Sarah Siddons School, OP A
North Wharf Road,
Paddington, W.2.   *On A404 – Nearest Station – Paddington*
Paddington Green acquired special fame when the film '*The Blue Lamp*' was made there in the 1940s. I watched some of this film being made and would occasionally glance at the Sarah Siddons monument in the nearby churchyard when working in the area. I certainly did not realise then that the nearby school which bears her name is haunted by this renowned actress.

Although one could perhaps assume that her ghost would take the form of Lady Macbeth, one of the roles in which Mrs. Siddons achieved fame, the figure which is seen and recognised as the actress is normally dressed. She wears a smallish grey hat with a band, and a high-necked blueish gown and is normally witnessed near one of the doorways of the old building.

It may be recalled that she died in 1831 after gaining public acclaim as Britain's finest actress.

Boston Manor House, Brentford, where two of the paths in the grounds are haunted by 'ladies in white'.
London Borough of Hounslow.

Boston Manor House, OP •
Boston Manor Road,
Brentford. *Off A3 – Nearest Station – Boston Manor (Underground)*
There are possibly two ghostly ladies here, though it may be only one being seen in different places, for the descriptions by witnesses are identical. The house, occupied by the National Institute for Housecraft, was once the home of Lord Boston and his wife. She, according to some rather legendary tales, was murdered by her husband, who discovered her with Lord Fairfax and threw her into the river Brent.

Another version is that Lord Boston, overcome with remorse, actually buried the body of his wife beneath a large cypress tree where the lovers used to meet.

A skeleton of a female, perhaps that of Lady Boston, was discovered by members of the Roman Catholic Sisterhood who occupied the premises before the war and was reburied in an ivy-covered mound. The phantom of a 'lady in white' has been seen gliding down the back lawn to the lake and another (or perhaps the same) figure, walks from a back door of the house along a paved path and disappears beneath the cypress tree.

To account for the 'Lady of the lake' there is a story which tells of a woman who committed suicide as the result of a broken love affair in Victorian times.

Roundshaw Estate,*OP
Croydon. *Junction of A 23/A232 – Nearest Station – Purley (2 miles)*
Although the majority of the residents in the vast complex of the Roundshaw Estate realise that their miniature town of 1,800 houses, 4 schools, a health centre, library and shopping centre is situated on the site of the old Croydon airport, few

Roundshaw Estate, Croydon, haunted by three nuns killed in a plane crash. *Author's collection.*

seem interested. Due to the siting of the controversial development Roundshaw seems to be unconnected either with Croydon or London. It is a separate community lacking integration into the surrounding environment, standing as stark and unfriendly as a cluster of factories. Nevertheless it is a community providing comfortable homes for those with a modern outlook and independent attitudes.

In 1939 Croydon Airport, one of the first to be constructed in the country and formed of the two earlier 'dromes of Beddington and Waddon, became one of the 'triple star' fighter bases for the Battle of Britain. As one could expect, it was attacked many times and during one raid in August 1940 some 60 people were killed and 170 injured.

After the war the need for Croydon dwindled. There was already talk of a new airport at a village near Hounslow in Middlesex. But the aerodrome that saw Amy Johnson leave for her historic flight to Australia continued to be used until 1959.

It was during a snowstorm in January 1947 that a Spencer Airways Dakota bound for Salisbury and Johannesburg taxied down the runway prior to take-off and crashed into another aircraft booked for a flight to Czechoslovakia. Immediately both planes were enveloped in searing flames and choking fumes.

Of the passengers for South Africa, 12 people, including two children and three nuns, were killed the latter, it seems, were burnt to death in an attempt to help the others escape.

It was learnt that one of the nuns might have had some premonition for she told a friend shortly before arriving at the airport, "If I do not finish this journey to my station, I will finish it in Heaven."

Kevin Desmond, intrigued by this particular case, also tells me that he learnt the nuns were Sisters Helen Lester and Eugene Martin and Mother Superior Eugen Jousselot, the Mother Provincial of the Congregation des Filles de la Sagesse in Nyasaland.

In late 1975 and early 1976 several reports were received that three ghostly nuns were seen on the walkways of the estate and imagination added to the tales. One witness claims that she saw a nun standing at the end of her bed holding her head out in her hands and had told a little boy a bedtime story 'voices from space' in fact. Another woman was so distressed at frequently seeing a phantom of a nun that she moved out of her house.

Nevertheless the evidence for witnessing the spectral trio is strong. Mr. Desmond was able to establish that the descriptions of the clothing matched that of their habits. Many of the witnesses stated that the figures were in grey capes and coifs, a white starched linen material which covered the forehead, encircled the sides of the face and covered the shoulders. The description of the Mother Superior was even more accurate for she was seen as 'very old with a lined face and she was wearing a crucifix.'

Photographs had been taken of the departure of the passengers but the nuns were all shown with their backs to the camera and it is therefore impossible for the witnesses to have remembered the accurate details of the ghosts. There are other spectral incidents which have occurred on the estate involving the sighting of a motorcyclist without a face and the sound of community singing in the boiler house.

The Old Palace, OPA
Old Palace Road,
Croydon *Off A23/A232 – Nearest Station – Croydon (East or West)*
Originally the Manor House of the archbishops of Canterbury, this ancient building, standing next to the parish church, is now owned by the Community of the Sisters of the Church who allow the public to view the house on certain days.

It has a distinguished visitor's list, for at least four royal personages have at some time stayed in the Palace, including Henry III, Henry VIII and Queen Elizabeth I. Even James I of Scotland was held prisoner within its walls before he became King.

It was in 1758 that the Archbishops left after 750 years of occupation and this created such a deterioration of interest in the house that by 1780 it was abandoned. An attempt was made to save it from complete degradation but the image was hardly improved when it became a bleaching factory. This change of use was soon to end for it became a school for lost orphans, and it is believed that it was at some time during this period that the ghost which inhabits the Palace was created.

She is seen as a woman in grey, but with what appears to be a white ruff at her neck, though this could be a kerchief or a bandage perhaps? The sorrowing female is thought to be that of a mother looking for her lost child. Maids and the occasional visitor have seen her, wringing her hands with worry while desperately searching the building for the missing youngster.

LONDON

Crown and Horseshoes,* OP
Horseshoe Lane, off Chase Side,
Enfield *Off A110 – Nearest Station – Enfield Chase*
Some provincial newspapers always seem to find a suitable haunted pub at Christmas time, but John Fennelly, in his feature in the *Enfield Gazette* of December 25th 1975, really seems to have found a genuine ghost mixed, as usual in the circumstances, with a touch of poltergeist activity.

Licensee Ray Williamson and his wife Sue have seen nothing except the refusal of their dog and cat to go into the cellar, but Ray has on certain occasions felt a cold chill downstairs so cold in fact that he has hurriedly returned to the ground floor.

As far as is known the only person who has actually witnessed the cause of the trouble, which includes the ringing of the bar bell well before 'time', is Brian Bullock, a local resident. He was waiting outside one day when he saw the vague figure of a little old lady pass one of the windows. The pub was found to be empty.

There appear to be only two sudden deaths associated with the pub. Benjamin Danby, a sailor, was murdered there in 1832 and the body of licensee John Draper was found in 1816 at the bottom of a well. John Fennelly asks, 'could there be a connection?' There might be.

Although James Tuck, a former landlord, was accused and charged with the murder of Draper, the evidence was not strong enough and he was acquitted. The reports say that a Mary Holbom discovered the body, but who was she? Did she die as a result of what she knew? Is she the ghost?

Mrs. Williamson told me in February 1976 that doors continue to bang mysteriously and weird footsteps have been heard not only by herself but by her mother and husband. One night Ray was so convinced that his mother-in-law had been walking along one of the corridors that he went to find out if she was all right, only to find her asleep in bed. "Other than the footsteps and the doors, nothing much happens these days," said Mrs. Williamson, "except that the dog refuses to come round to the bar now."

Editor's Note: More activity was reported from the Crown and Horseshoe in 2013 by the landlord and landlady Byron Furness and Lynette Clarke. The *Enfield Independent* of 8 October 2013 reported that just three days after taking over in October 2012 Mr Furness was locking up after closing and realised he had left some keys downstairs. He was quoted as saying, "I came down and saw her standing at the bar, a clear outline of an old lady. I jumped and froze. She was there for four or five seconds." Other phenomena including alarms going off for no reason and the 21-year-old son of the licensee had a strong impression of a presence.

Hampton Court Palace, OP
Middlesex.   *Off A308 – Nearest Station – Hampton Court*
As Christina Hole so rightly says, "nearly every ancient royal house in Great Britain has at least one traditional phantom." The Tower of London, Holyrood, Windsor, Richmond, St. James's and Kensington all house ghosts of the past. Here at Hampton Court there are at least two ghostly ladies.

One of the most famous is that of Catherine Howard, for not only has she been seen fairly frequently in the Haunted Gallery, but also the reverberations of the original screams and shrieks that she gave on that fateful day in 1541 when she rushed down the hall to beg forgiveness from the King have been heard.

Some years ago an occupant of one of the grace and favour flats told me that she so often heard the pitiful sounds that she accepted them as a matter of course. And it was only a few years later that a Canadian visitor asked an attendant who the woman was who rushed past her "in that weird old gallery." She heard nothing, but "the woman was obviously distressed. I liked her gown, but I've never seen anything like it before except in an old painting." The painting was that of Catherine Howard and the figure she had seen had vanished.

The Lady Howard with loose flowing hair has also been seen in the gardens, usually during summer evenings, wandering about in a white gown.

Jane Seymour is supposed to have been seen gliding around the Silver Stick Gallery, but the phantom, which was seen in 1964 by Leslie Finch, the actor, was that of the 'Lady in Grey'. She was first reported in the 19th century and identified as Mrs. Sybil Penn, a nurse to Edward VI.

The incident which seems to have increased the number of her appearances was the discovery of her old spinning wheel in a previously unknown chamber in the south west wing of the Palace a couple of years ago. Her footsteps are also heard near to where the spinning wheel was found.

Editor's Note. The earliest account of a ghost at the palace appears to be a crisis apparition seen by a resident, recorded by Charles Dickens in *All The Year Round* for 22 June 1862. Nothing further had emerged by the time that John Ingram published *The Haunted Homes and Family Traditions* (1888) but later sources mention sporadic reports from the 1860s, with tales of hauntings really seeming to take off from the mid-1890s when residents of the grace and favour apartments in the building announced they were troubled by strange noises. In 1894 *Cassell's Family Magazine* carried claims of loud screams being heard in the dead of night, and a further wave of ghost reports coincided with renovation and opening up in 1905 of what became the 'Haunted Gallery', a section of the building formerly used as a lumber room. Between 1999-2002 Mr Ian Franklin a custodian at Hampton Court kept a log of incidents reported by visitors and staff. Since then the palace has embraced its ghostly reputation and was the scene of experiments conducted by Dr Richard Wiseman, centred on the premise of sensitivity to magnetic fields at certain spots as the reason why people thought they had encountered ghosts. (See 'An investigation into the alleged haunting of Hampton Court Palace: psychological variables and magnetic fields' by Wiseman, R., Watt, C, Greening, E., Stevens, P. and O'Keeffe, C. (2002) in the *Journal of Parapsychology*, 66(4) 387-408.)

In 2003 an image obtained by a security camera (and again in 2015 on a camera phone) were claimed as possible apparitions (the latter even being proposed as 'Sybil Penn') but neither stood up as anomalies to technical or rational analysis.

MERSEYSIDE

Poulton Road,* OP
Bebington. *Off A41 Birkenhead. – Nearest Station – Bebington*

In September 1974, a Mr. Cartwright was travelling from Higher Bebington along the Poulton Road when he noticed a girl on the verge whom he thought was waiting for a lift. She had long dark hair and was wearing a long coat. As he pulled up to offer his services, the youngster "slowly vanished into thin air" leaving the motorist slightly shaken. Two very similar incidents occurred four years earlier and in March 1970 a nurse from Clatterbridge Hospital had seen the figure standing at the roadside and had gone over to ask if she could help. "She looked so lonely in the empty street and it was getting rather late." But when she was only a few feet from the ghost, it disappeared. A local novice is known to have died in this area early this century whilst walking from Poulton Hall to a nunnery. Local legend has it that a broken love affair caused her to take poison.

Speke Hall,* OP
Liverpool. *On B5170 – Nearest Station – Widnes*

This is a house of controversy as far as the ghost is concerned. On referring to the Tapestry Room, Mr. P. W. G. Lawson, assistant keeper of the Hall in 1973, told me that "an inaccurate story does not reflect on the validity of the room as a haunted site. A considerable number of people have discerned a presence in the room." The Hall is a magnificent example of a 16th century half-timbered house created as a reception centre for priests arriving from overseas.

According to Winifred I. Hayward in *Country Life*, a wing was added in 1598 which contained numerous hidey holes and secret rooms, many of them linked with hidden shafts and corridors to accommodate anonymous visitors. With the exception of only a few changes and additions on the eastern side, the house looks now as it did when the Norris family owned it in 1612.

One story relating to 'the phantom lady of the Hall' is that she is one of the Beauclerks, a family who inherited the property in 1736. Upon learning that her husband had staked and lost her home at a gaming table, she threw herself and her baby from the window of what is now termed 'The Haunted Room' into the moat.

Yet, as Miss Hayward so rightly points out, although the room involved has "a small cross outside and a hiding place in the wall" the angle and the distance make the suicide most unlikely.

So another version is that Lady Beauclerk threw the child from the Tapestry Room window and then killed herself in the Great Hall. Unfortunately there is no evidence to suppose that the Beauclerks ever lived here, which leaves us with an unknown ghost. But ghost there is. Alastair MacGregor in *The Golden Lamp* states that the late Adelaide Watt was somewhat disturbed to see a female figure disappear into the wall of a bedroom. Investigations here, close to a window, revealed a secret passage leading down through an outer wall.

And, reverting to the opening paragraphs, a considerable number of people have seen the ghostly lady. Does it really matter who she is?

NORFOLK

Raynham Hall, PP
Near Fakenham.

This private home of the Marquis of Townshend is not to be confused with the National Trust property in Essex known as Rainham Hall which is open to the public by appointment.

The ghost of Raynham is very well known, for a photograph of her, or at least some phantom or other, was taken by Mr. Indre Shira, a Court photographer, and published on 26th December 1936 in *Country Life* and then in a score of other publications. All attempts to repeat the performance have unfortunately failed.

A lot of people have actually seen the 'Brown Lady', as she is known, including Captain Frederick Marryat in 1836, the Marchioness of Townshend and Mr. Hawkins. For an interesting and detailed report, readers should consult The World's Strangest Ghost Stories by R. Thurston Hopkins and *Ghosts and Witches* by J. Wentworth Day.

One of the latest incidents was in 1954 when the phantom female was seen carrying a candle and moving along a corridor upstairs, only to vanish when she reached the top of the stairway on which she had been photographed years earlier.

She has been identified as Dorothy, daughter of Robert Walpole of Houghton and second Viscount Townshend. She died of smallpox on 29th March 1726 when she was only 40 years old.

Editor's Note: Over the years the balance has swung away from the photograph of the Brown Lady of Raynham Hall being a genuinely inexplicable apparition, with the rediscovery of a file compiled by Mr C.V.C Herbert for the SPR, dated 14 January 1937. He interviewed the photographers and examined the original camera and prints. He found the camera was faulty, and he explains the photograph as a combination of an accidental double exposure and light leakage. Herbert considered that the camera was shaken vertically at the time of exposure, at the moment Indre Shira thought he had seen something on the stairs. A combination of some of the circumstances and features of the picture hint at a double exposure in the alternative. The glowing shape had none of the detailed features reported by actual witnesses to the Brown Lady, sufficient to identify her from portraits as Dorothy Walpole. In 1937 the then Marchioness of Townshend for her part wondered if the photographic image represented an appearance of the Virgin Mary (see Murdie, Alan (2006) Photographing Phantoms', *Fortean Times* No. 215, October 2006, pp. 50-53).

Oxfam Shop, OP
19 Magdalen Street,
Norwich.   *On A1151 – Nearest Station – Norwich*
With a bridge over the river Wensum and angled from the mediaeval styled Elm Hill, Magdalen Street, once the centre of the old weaving industry in the City, is currently being restored by the Civic Trust. As in most large towns Oxfam have one of their charity gifts shops here, opened by them in 1972, but unfortunately it has, or had, problems with the premises. Although there had been reports of a haunting in the old building for some time before the fund took over, the tales were ignored and probably derided.

However, within a couple of months of opening, one of the voluntary workers had been mystified to see a typewriter working by itself and had frequently heard footsteps in a former office, empty at the time. The noises were heard by other volunteers and then one afternoon the ghost of a young girl was seen by a new member of the staff, standing at the top of the stairs. This witness had heard nothing about the tales of the shop being haunted and was puzzled at seeing the figure. She was even more puzzled and a little scared when she said 'Hello', for the visitor promptly disappeared.

On discussing the incident with her colleagues, the witness learnt that three other volunteers had seen the phantom. The number of voluntary workers had fallen off from a staff of eight to a total of three by January 1973, but hopefully the group have now realised that their unpaid unearthly supervisor does no harm. She is simply interested.

Aylmerton, OP
Sheringham.   *Off A 148 – Nearest Station – West Runton*
The phantom of a tall woman dressed in white and silently weeping has been seen gliding round the ancient pit dwellings which still exist in this area. In the Victorian days she was also heard to 'scream with anguish' and the prehistoric site became known as 'The Shrieking Pits'. Rumour has it that she is still searching for her baby, murdered and buried in one of the pits by her husband in a fit of insane jealousy during the 19th century.

Editor's Note: The story is first recorded in the *Guide to the Essex, Norfolk and Suffolk Coasts* (1870) by M.E. Walcott and E.R. Suffling's charming little book *History and Legends of the Broads District* (c.1882) and more recently Neil Storey's *Norfolk A Ghost Hunter's Guide* (2007) and appears to be an example of a White Lady apparition discussed in Part Two, chapter four.

NORTHAMPTONSHIRE

Old House, PP
Hind Style,
Higham Ferrers.

A few years ago Ann Hale was cleaning upstairs and heard footsteps coming down a non-existent staircase a few feet away from where she was working. Having heard from guests and friends of the family about the ghostly old housemaid that they had seen on the path outside the kitchen door, she decided to investigate the phantom footsteps 'to the bitter end.'

It was not really surprising, "but very exciting," when she discovered behind a wall an ancient flight of stairs which once led to the original servants' quarters, now an integral part of the home. Despite the disturbance, the figure of the old woman in parlour maid's uniform is still seen, though less frequently.

Talbot Hotel, OP
Oundle.   *Junction of A42 7/A 605 – Nearest Station – Peterborough (14 miles)*

Used as a centre by boating enthusiasts, the town being bordered on three sides by the River Nene, Oundle has many attractive old houses, a 14th century church and this haunted hotel. Although it has changed considerably since its original construction as the Talbot Inn, the foundations show that a building was situated there in the 12th century.

Many of the interior furnishings, including the main staircase, have come from Fotheringhay Castle. It was at Fotheringhay that Queen Mary was imprisoned before her execution in the 16th century and some people seem to think that when the stairway was fitted in its new abode Mary came too.

Recently some guests have complained of an inexplicable drop in the temperature of a particular bedroom and of being disturbed by a 'peculiar wailing' in the early hours which could not be associated either with the central heating system or members of the staff working late. Some others staying in the hotel have remarked on the sounds of a lady walking along the corridor late at night, though the floors are carpeted. One gentleman was more than a little shocked to hear the footsteps walk past him when there was nothing to see.

A few people have enquired about the cries of distress coming from the room next to 'the cold area', describing the sounds as of a 'woman sobbing'. The room was always empty on these occasions.

There are not many people who have seen the unknown phantom but one witness told of seeing a figure near the reception counter. "She was wearing a fawn-coloured dress with what looked like a white blouse and a small cap. There was also a dainty apron on the front of the long dress and when I enquired as to the name of the guest I was told that the hotel was empty that night."

The phantom has occasionally been seen looking down into the yard from a window on the landing. Her small cap and white blouse identify her as the same figure seen by hotel guests. Her name remains a mystery.

Samuel Pepys Hotel, (closed)
Slipton.   *Off A60 – Nearest Station – Kettering (6 miles)*

Early in 1973 Harry Rogers, the landlord of this small hotel, and his wife Rose reported that they had frequently heard the sound of shuffling footsteps in an empty room over the bar. They accepted the noise as being caused by the ghost of some unknown entity who neither harmed nor frightened anyone. But when, a few weeks later, their seven-year-old nephew became a resident in the haunted room, the couple were a little disturbed to learn that the lad was being scared by the continuous visitations of "a little old lady in a blue frock." The figure of this mysterious old soul would stand beside his bed and look down on him for a few seconds and then gently fade away. Confirming that mysterious things happened in the hotel when he was licensee, Alfred Sutherland said that on one occasion some heavy ornaments "literally jumped off the mantelpiece" and a doll, torn to shreds, had been found in what is now the nephew's bedroom. Is there any connection with this phenomenon and the fact that a woman and her physically handicapped son died in the hotel many years ago? The idea should not be easily dismissed.

Editor's Note: The pub was listed closed and advertised as 'to let' as of November 2022.

NORTHUMBERLAND

Craster Tower, OPA
Craster,
Alnwick.   *Off B1399 – Nearest Station – Alnmouth (6 miles)*

Before Mr. J. H. Craster became of owner of Craster Tower, Sir John Craster had told me about the haunting of this ancient building. Both he and his wife had heard many "strange hangings and things coming from the wall dividing the front from the back libraries" and had on one occasion found the perfect outline of a naked foot in a pile of soot behind a fire-screen.

In his own work *North Country Squire* (Oriel Press), Sir John details other incidents which have occurred in Craster Tower including the witnessing of the 'grey lady'. She is usually identified by the sound of her rustling skirts and one witness said that she comes in by the first-floor front landing window, moves slowly towards the pele tower and then vanishes.

Another well-known author, James Wentworth Day in *A Ghost Hunters Game Book* (Muller), tells of the experience in 1955 when his young daughter enquired about the woman who opened the front door, came upstairs and went into the drawing room. He saw and heard nothing, but it was obvious that 'a presence was definitely there'.

The tower is 'supposed to have been built about 1290, but the modern part dates from 1730'. The identity of the 'grey lady' remains a mystery.

Langley Castle, OPA
Langley. *Off A686 – Nearest Station – Haydon Bridge (2 miles)*
A 14th century fortified towera pele towerbuilt as a defence against border raids, Langley Castle is a mere four miles from the better-known Hadrian's Wall. It has recently been purchased by a company who have carried out extensive restoration work and opened the castle as a centre for mediaeval banquets.

In common with many ancient fortresses, Langley had a strong reputation for being haunted, but by what and by whom no-one seemed to know or care.

It was only when Duncan McClellan, one of the directors, heard from a kitchen helper that the castle's two Irish wolfhounds refused to move when taken near the stairs to the top floor, that he realised there was something unusual about the place.

One afternoon Mrs. Manning, a helper from Haydon Bridge, was idly looking over the battlements when she felt a strong push from behind, though she was alone on the roof.

Several members of the staff have also been puzzled by the sound of singing when the building has been empty, and the noise of a door opening and closing where there is no aperture. The most awesome sight however is that experienced by several witnesses at dusk.

Described by one of the staff as the ghost of "a woman in a white chiffon dress" a figure has been seen walking up the drive until nearing the front door, where she suddenly vanishes. Several unsuccessful efforts have been made to establish the identity of the night walker and more especially why she continues to stride so purposefully towards the ancient building.

OXFORDSHIRE

The George Hotel, OP
High Street,
Dorchester-on-Thames. *On A423 – Nearest Station – Didcot (4 miles)*
This delightful old half-timbered inn, frequented by the ghost of a 'miserable young woman' is a mere stone's throw from the Abbey Church of St. Peter & Paul. The church itself is an interesting remnant of an Augustinian abbey founded in 1140 at the junction of the Rivers Thame and Thames.

Evidence of the ideal siting of the village, which dates from before the Bronze Age, is the fact that the foundations of a large Roman settlement have been discovered here and it has always been a favourite stopping place for travellers on their way to and from London.

The George stands on the site of an inn which was probably the ale house for the monks of the abbey, but whether the phantom is associated with those days is not known. She has been seen as recently as 1971 in 'The Vicar's Room' which leads off a gallery at the top of a stairway in the coaching yard.

The room was once used by the first Duchess of Marlborough, but there has been no suggestion that the white-gowned young phantom, who stands at the foot of the bed contemplating the occupant, is that of Sarah.

Because she peers with such sadness towards the pillows before she turns and vanishes, the probable cause is that a loved one died under tragic circumstances in the bed that existed there at the time.

Church of St. Michael and All Angels, OP
Milton Common. *On B4013 – Nearest Station – Oxford (9 miles)*

More commonly called Rycote Chapel, one of the few administered by the Department of the Environment, this is in fact a 15th century domestic place of worship with several unusual features which include a west tower and two interesting family pews erected by Lord Williams. The second storey of one of these pews contains an organ. The mansion house to which it originally belonged was destroyed by fire in the 18th century and it is thought that it was during this fire that a near relative was burnt to death.

Mr. A. Clifford Morris, custodian of the chapel, is one of the witnesses of the phantom thought to be Lady Arabella. He first saw the female, known as 'the Grey lady', at 3.55 pm on 1st December 1968.

"She appeared near to the 800-year-old yew tree," he said in his report, "and my first impression was that she was one of the ladies from Rycote House in fancy dress. She was tall and slim and was indeed of a pale grey colour with a kind of sheen, something like satin." Mr. Clifford Morris went over to the yew tree and found no one there, but on looking across the lawn on the southern side of the Chapel, saw her again, standing close to his office.

"As I watched her," he continued, "she moved across the grass and passed behind the east end of the chapel." She glided along the original route from the site of the house to the chapel and as she reached the level lawn at the bottom of a slope beneath a chestnut tree, the lady vanished

Her dress was in the early Tudor style with every detail so clearly defined that the custodian made a rough sketch of the phantom. Later he compared the drawing with portraits of Tudor ladies and realised that the design tallied.

"The dress was ground length with a bell-shaped bottom, tight at the waist, square necked and with heavy voluminous sleeves. The lady also wore a flowing veil attached to a circular head-dress fitted closely to her head." At least two dogs have been affected by the appearance of the Grey Lady.

The Chapel of Rycote House, near Oxford, where a 'lady in grey' has been seen near the 800-year-old yew. Author's collection.

Church of St Lawrence, Ludlow, Salop, where the ghost of an old woman haunts the churchyard on summer evenings. *Aero Film Ltd.*

SHROPSHIRE

Church of St. Lawrence, OP
Ludlow. *On A49 – Nearest Station – Ludlow*

This cathedral-like sandstone church is not far from the impressive castle which was built in the 11th century and said to be haunted by the sounds of heavy breathing in the Hanging Tower. It is claimed that the noises are of one of the soldiers who attempted, unsuccessfully, to gain access to the fort by climbing up a rope ladder during an attack on the Castle in the 1 6th century. This parish church was built in the 1 4th century and is the largest in the county. It features a window dedicated to St. Lawrence, patron saint of the town, and in its graveyard are the ashes of A. E. Housman, the well-known poet who died in 1936.

The churchyard also accommodates the ghost of an old woman wearing an unusual dress of heavy material described by some witnesses as a dressing gown in a "greyish blue colour." She has been seen occasionally during summer evenings walking from the nearby rectory, through the graveyard and disappearing at the doorway of the church. It has been stated also that mysterious footsteps associated with the walker have been heard in the rectory.

Dennis Ainsley from Andover was recently making his way to the 17th century Feather Hotel in The Bull Ring when he saw the figure of an 18-year-old girl with long black hair wearing a mini-skirt and, of all things, a transparent blouse, walk "straight through my parked car. I couldn't believe my eyes," he said. On reaching the hotel he told the licensee, Mr. James Falconer, of the amazing incident expecting a guffaw of laughter in response. He was very surprised at the reply. "Oh yes. That must be the same girl who walked through a sports car near here in 1962."

Crowcombe Rectory, PP
Crowcombe.
Not far from Williton, the fascinating fossil laden beach of Blue Anchor and abutting the Quantock Hills, one finds the pleasant little village of Crowcombe. In the Rectory, parts of which are Elizabethan, an occasional phantom of a 'lady in blue' has been seen. Unfortunately, like so many female phantoms, nobody knows who she is or why she haunts, but she is completely harmless and worries neither the occupants nor the occasional visitor.

She is probably associated with either the Civil War or even the battles involving the Duke of Monmouth, as are many of the ghosts of the South West.

STAFFORDSIDRE

Hoar Cross Hall, OP
Hoar Cross.   *Off A515 – Nearest Station – Burton-on-Trent (6 miles)*
Situated in 50 acres of woodland adjoining a hamlet just south of Needwood Forest, one finds this isolated 70-room house, purchased from the Meynell Trust by Mr. and Mrs. Bickerton-Jones in 1973.

Although it appears to be of a great age due to the style of architecture, the hall was actually built in 1871. Modelled primarily on the genuine Elizabethan Temple Newsam in Leeds, it contains some fine plaster ceilings, an interesting oak panelled private chapel and a large private collection of European and Eastern armour, which is displayed in the Long Gallery.

Shortly after they moved into their new home with their three young children and had started extensive renovations of the old property, with the intention of opening it to the public and holding mediaeval style banquets, the new owners saw a young girl dressed in clothes of "the Victorian era" in one of the upper rooms.

Believing the youngster was one of their own daughters 'dressing up', they took little notice. However, a few days later they saw the girl again in the same room and Mrs. Gwyneth Bickerton-Jones was puzzled as to why the same clothes had been chosen for the game. She called her daughter's name and one can imagine her astonishment when the figure of the child vanished in front of her.

As soon as they have time to carry out some research the owners hope to be able to find out who the young lady is, but until then, work is being concentrated on restoring the formal gardens, which house some beautiful ponds and a fine collection of trees and shrubs.

St. Johns Churchyard, OP
Burslem,
Stoke-on-Trent   *On A50 – Nearest Station – Stoke-on-Trent (3 miles)*
It was here at Burslem where he was born that Josiah Wedgwood learnt his trade as a master potter and later at Bell works introduced the cream-coloured ware which was so popular with Queen Charlotte.

In 1748, when Josiah was 18 years old, a local woman named Molly Lee died at the age of 63 and was buried in the graveyard of St. Johns' Church with her pet raven. It is doubtful if the potter knew her for she lived in an ancient cottage near Hamil Grange and occupied herself by selling milk to the townsfolk.

She was a peculiar old biddy, thought to be a witch, and was accused fairly frequently of watering the milk that she sold. On one occasion she caused acute embarrassment to the populace by removing her stockings in public. The number of complaints increased against the old woman anyone over 50 in those days was considered 'old' and the Rev. Thomas Spenser was persuaded to shoot the pet raven which used to sit on her shoulder and accompany her whenever she went out. He immediately fell ill which was proof to the locals that Molly was a witch. Unfortunately for the superstition, the woman died and the priest recovered.

Her body was buried lying not in the normal east to west position but north to south. On the day of her funeral the rector visited her cottage out of curiosity and saw her ghost sitting on a chair with the pet bird still on her shoulder. In a very scared state he insisted the coffin be re-opened to assure himself that Molly had been truly buried. She was.

However, on 17th July 1967 Mr. and Mrs. Boland were visiting relatives in Burslem and at about 10.30 in the morning were passing St. Johns' Churchyard. They later told Colin Smith that "an old woman raced past us at the main entrance and then just vanished into thin air. As she entered the churchyard it couldn't have been anything else but a ghost. She had white hair and what I can only describe as dishevelled clothing, a shawl and a long black dress."

Had old Molly Lee come back to see all was well?

The Bolands had told nobody else of their experience for fear of being scorned. It is unfortunate that there are still some unthinking folk who prefer to laugh or sneer at facts they cannot understand.

Blithfield Hall, OP
Near Rugeley. *On B5013 – Nearest Station – Rugeley*

The home of the Bagot family and their ancestors, the De Blithfields, since 1086, this magnificent Elizabethan house with Georgian and Regency additions contains a superb carved oak staircase. It is built round a central courtyard, whilst the stables contain some of the family coaches, and a 14th century church within the grounds heightens the general atmosphere of the erstwhile days of manorial privileges and high society.

With such a long history it is hardly surprising to learn from my Birmingham colleague, Colin Smith, that there are in fact five ghosts which inhabit various parts of the estate. Two of these are male, two female and one, because the haunting is merely a noise, of unknown gender.

This mystery sound is that of rustling skirts which could be either that of a woman's gown or a priest's robes, the latter idea deriving from the records which show that a man of the cloth sought sanctuary in the Hall in the early 1700s. One room is termed 'the priests' room' and the noises are heard most frequently at 11.20 pm along the lower gallery by occupants of the bedrooms leading into it.

Another unknown apparition was first seen in 1973 by a cleaner, and later her daughter, in a drawing room at about 3 o'clock one afternoon. The description given is that of a man dressed in dark clothing who stared at the floor whilst rubbing at an unusual ring on a finger of his left hand. Initially treated as a joke the tale gained strength, for the existence of the anonymous spectre was obviously known to older members of the staff but they are reluctant to provide any details.

A much older ghost is that of a victim of an accident some two hundred years ago. One of the elderly gardeners was trying vainly to save a small child who had fallen into the well in the Archery ground. Unfortunately his attempts failed and he slipped and fell to his own death with a pitiful scream, his body hitting the chains as he fell. Earlier this century some of the gardening workers reported seeing the vague shape of an old man clambering on to the well head and suddenly vanishing.

Nowadays only the sound of a "creepy wail is heard issuing from a certain spot on the ground, for the well, its surround and the chains were removed many decades ago.

Seen three times by a Mrs. Woodcock is the phantom of a woman wearing a "long frock with what looks like a grey macintosh over it and a flat straw bonnet" which, to me, sounds like a fashion of the 1920's. At first Mrs. Woodcock thought the figure was that of a guest staying at the house, though she puzzled at the mode of dress.

She was witnessed walking behind a large clump of azaleas on the east side of the house but failed to appear on the other side. On the last occasion the witness ran across the lawn to speak to the woman but, as she says, "it's a bit odd when someone disappears into thin air in front of you."

None of the shades of Blithfield appears to cause any fright; they are just accepted for what they are, visible or aural reminders of past events.

The main phantom, known as 'The Grey Lady of Blithfield', seems to have no set haunt and no predetermined time for her appearance. She has been seen in the early morning, afternoon and evening and in almost any part of the house. She was last seen in the upper gallery in September 1970.

She is always seen as a middle-aged woman wearing a long grey dress with a white collar and a lace cap. At her waist hangs a chatelaine with a bunch of keys on a short leather thong. Witnesses are first attracted, not by the figure itself, but by her shoes, for they are embellished with a pair of sparkling silver buckles.

The most recent appearance was recorded by a gardener and his wife whilst they were having their morning coffee in the upper gallery, only a few days after 'the lady' was seen in a bedroom in the east wing.

Even in this marvellous home with its five ghosts, the female phantoms are dominant.

SUFFOLK

Bury Abbey, OP
Bury St. Edmunds.   *On A134/A14 – Nearest Station – Bury St. Edmunds*
This site of a Saxon township known as Beodricksworth and chosen as a suitable locality for a monastery in 636 AD, Bury St. Edmunds is now the county town of West Suffolk.

The monastery was granted Abbey status by King Knut, better known as Canute, and the entire precinct of this holy structure survives, though the buildings are considerably changed. The most complete are the two gatehouses, one of Norman construction, the other dating from the 14th

century, but the only portion of the huge abbey church which remains is the west front. The tomb of St. Edmund was a pilgrimage site second only to Canterbury, for it contained such peculiar relics as 'the parings of St. Edmund's nails, the coals that St. Lawrence was toasted with and St. Thomas's boots'.

I cannot help but wonder what happens to such souvenirs, for one never finds these fascinating tourist attractions in modem churches, except perhaps in those in Roman Catholic countries.

The ghost of St. Edmund himself is, according to legend, supposed to have materialised and killed a Danish king when he attacked East Anglia in 870.

The 'real' ghosts of the Abbey are those of a grey lady, thought to be Maude Carew, and a regal female, believed to be Queen Margaret from Provence, though I find this difficult to accept. Certainly one, sometimes two, phantoms of women are seen in the Abbey precincts and occasionally in the Cathedral Churchyard.

There is a ghostly monk as well, wearing a brown habit and seen in the cellars of Cupola House which was once linked with the Abbey.

Maude Carew was a close friend of Queen Margaret, wife of Henry VI, and also enjoyed the admiration of Brother Bernard. The Duke of Gloucester, believing that the monk was a heretic, ordered him to be burnt at the stake, but the Queen, on learning of the plan, persuaded Maude, a nun, to poison the Duke.

Unfortunately for the murderess, she failed to realise the potency of the fatal liquid and was herself affected. A few hours before her death: the monk found her outside the Duke's room and cursed her for her action.

Editor's Note: Whilst Duke Humphrey did indeed die in the town in February 1447, the cause was apoplexy and the tale in which Maude Carew herself also succumbed to the deadly poison and then returns as "the Grey Lady" to haunt each February 24th turns out to be a fiction, derived from a novella *The Secret Disclosed: A Story of St Edmund's Abbey* (1862) written by an 18-year-old local woman Margaretta Greene, the daughter of a local printer. Nonetheless, on February 24th 1862 the tale was enough to cause a crowd of 400 people to assemble in the churchyard of St Mary's Church in the hope of seeing her. When the ghost failed to appear the crowd rioted pelting the Greene family house with stones and breaking windows. The mob also pelted Margaretta's nephew John Greene with sticks and stones after he rashly decided to roam the churchyard wrapped in a sheet, either to provoke the disappointed mob further or to try and placate them.

Links with the Cupola House began when the story was given new impetus after being recounted in the 20th century, with these claims of other ghost sightings used in good faith as a source for *Phantom Ladies* (1977). Stories of a ghostly figure in grey appearing in a house built from parts of the Abbey Ruins in 1946, and experiences of what was deemed to be a female ghost called 'Maud', in a house in Fornham Road, close to the ruin of St Saviour's Hospital where Duke Humphrey died, help sustain the story. She is continued sporadically at no less than six locations around Bury St Edmunds, all being dubbed "the Grey Lady" as if it had become a convenient local brand or label to apply to otherwise anonymous manifestations.

Ghostly phenomena were reported from the 1970s at Cupola House, which operated as a pub until 2006, and are documented into the 21st century. In October 1993 landlord Roger Stone told the *East Anglian Daily Times* that an unexplained figure of a woman had been witnessed in the bar, and a strange shape seen in the cellars. Strange noises of footsteps on the stairs, furniture being moved, a strange light were reported. In February 2000 an apparition of a woman in an "old-fashioned white dress" identified as Victorian or Edwardian was seen standing at the foot of the stairs in the Cupola House by a barman who left the pub soon afterwards. On October 10th 2000 the then licensee Claire Holmes had a tactile impression of walking into a female presence on the central wooden staircase. In June 2001 members of the Ghost Club held an all-night vigil at the Cupola with one Joanne Kelly, also experiencing what she felt was a chilling female presence on the staircase, although at that stage she had not heard of Mrs Holmes's experience.

One of the last licensees, Marian Thomas also complained of interference with the mechanism of lager barrels in the cellar and had the impression of someone sitting on the barrel. Minor poltergeist phenomena were also reported in 2006-2007 after the conversion of the building into a pizza restaurant. In June 2012 the building was gutted by fire, eventually being restored 4 years later. No further reports have been received. Whether this calamity has exorcised the ghosts or driven them elsewhere remains to be seen, or if there will be reports of "the Grey Lady" transferring her attentions to a new location. Sources: *Bury Free Press* 1-15 March 1862; *Daily Mail* 1 March 1946. *Bury Free Press* 22 June 2012; *Journal of Paraphysics* (1973) Vol 6 *Classified Directory*; *East Anglian Daily Times* 27 October 1993; *Haunted Bury St Edmunds* (2007) by Alan Murdie; BBC Suffolk website 22 October 2008.

Thorington Hall, OPA
Stoke by Nayland.   *On B1068 – Nearest Station – Colchester*
Built about 1600 as an oak-framed gabled house, this 'Hall' was enlarged in 1700 within retaining walls and completely restored in 1937. It is now primarily used as studios, but the artists are occasionally disturbed by the phantom of a young girl wearing a "brownish frock" gliding along a corridor on the upper floor. Sometimes inexplicable footsteps are also heard.

Who she is nobody knows, although there are the usual tales of a long-forgotten suicide brought about by some unfortunate love affair.

SURREY

St. Mary the Virgin,*OP
Bletchingley.   *On A25 – Nearest Station – Redhill*
S. P. B. Mais, in his work *The Home Counties* (Batsford) refers to the monument in this church of Sir Robert Clayton, an 18th century Lord Mayor of London, and quotes Dryden as describing him 'as good a saint as usury ever made'. At the suggestion of a friend, I visited the church in 1975 and noticed an inexplicable and rather sudden drop in temperature when about eight feet from the Clayton memorial. Puzzled, I reported back and learnt that a few weeks earlier he had seen, on the very same spot as I had felt the cold, an apparition of a woman in what he believed to be a 17th century gown "perhaps of the William and Mary period," he suggested.

A local resident confirmed that there were rumours of the church having been haunted by a phantom lady', but who she is nobody knows.

Multi-storey Car Park, OP
Sydenham Road,
Guildford.   *On A25 – Nearest Station – Guildford*
Considered to be the most important town in Surrey, Guildford offers a variety of interests and entertainment difficult to match. Surrey University is overlooked by the dominant Guildford Cathedral, which took some 30 years to complete, vies with the Yvonne Arnaud Theatre on its own little island only yards from the former home of Lewis Carroll. Known to most tourists visiting the ancient town is the overhanging clock of the Guildhall in the High Street, the 17th century Abbots' Hospital and, tucked away near the multi-storey car park and approached through an old gateway, the towering keep of a Norman castle.

In 1670 the Society of Friends, commonly termed 'Quakers', having already attended their first meeting house in London, decided to form another group in Guildford and purchased a building on the south side of North Street together with a plot of land for burials immediately opposite. One of the first local families to join the 'new religion' lived in a house practically next door to where the Holy Trinity Church now stands and although their name is not known it has been established that they had a daughter called Lorna. In some of early history books of the area one finds reports of the ghost of a woman wearing a grey gown and a small black cap being seen in the locality.

Over the years the belief developed that she was the phantom of Lorna who had been thrown out of her home by her fanatical father because of her love for a local lad who refused to join the sect. The girl was killed when she fell into a small quarry near her home. When I lived in a nearby village this area was a car park. Reports of the ghostly 'lady in grey' continued to be made throughout the Victorian era, but gradually diminished until the whole story was re-awakened by a report in the local paper in 1969. Finishing touches were hurriedly being made to the barriers on the second floor of the newly constructed multistorey car park in time for the Christmas rush of traffic. Building the new park caused considerable controversy locally, for it had meant the demolition of a great deal of old and interesting property, but as usual the demands of the motorist had to be given priority.

Two of the workmen painting the wooden fencing on the edges of the second level suddenly noticed the figure of a woman standing on the edge of the floor. One of the men called to her and started to walk over to find out what the trespasser wanted. The woman turned to face him and he stopped, slightly surprised by her beauty.

"She was a really beautiful girl," he said, "with a thin face and sort of grey-blue eyes and golden hair, but she looked terribly sad and utterly miserable. I thought at first she might be a potential suicide, but I also remember thinking at the time that the colour of her dress matched her eyes." Just as the workman was about to enquire whether he could help the figure "slowly faded away, like a mist." Locals immediately recalled that Lorna's former home had been one of those demolished to make way for the new development and where she had been seen would have been the site of her bedroom. It must have been in that room that she made her soul tearing decision to put love before her father's wishes and where only a few hours later her torn and bleeding body had been laid.

Editor's Note: Philip Hutchinson, author of *Haunted Guildford* (2006) and the creator of the Guildford Ghost Walk, considers that the name 'Lorna' may have been randomly chosen with no written reference before 1860. He also confirms there are several versions of the story in circulation and the precise locality where she lived and died has become garbled (there being two multi-storey car parks, the first in Sydenham Road with her death at Rack's Close at the edge of the castle site, and the second in York Road which is actually built into a quarry). However, he recalls attendees on the Guildford Ghost Walk 'who have seen a young lady in a grey dress walk through the walls of an old passage' on the Sydenham Road site, 'or have seen her standing at the end of said passage'. Therefore it is conceivable that the story has grown up and applied to an actual manifestation as means of accounting for it.

Hayes Lane,* OP
Kenley
Surrey *Off A22 – Nearest Station – Kenley*

Kenley, the home of a major Battle of Britain aerodrome, is also renowned for 'The Grey Lady', a phantom nun frequently seen in the Hayes Lane and Welcomes Road area.

Mrs. Phyllis Fretwell, now of Steyning in Sussex, was kind enough to provide much of the information regarding the haunting, in fact detailed over 15 separate instances of what is officially termed as 'spontaneous phenomena'. Unfortunately it has been impossible to identify the figure, though she was known locally as 'Sister Mary'.

Shortly after the end of the war a tenant in some flint fronted cottages in Hayes Lane was woken shortly after falling asleep by the sound of her baby screaming. Running, she was appalled to see a misty shape in the form of a woman bending over the cot, but as she ran to her child the figure faded away.

A few months later an Indian nanny told her employers that she "didn't like walking along Welcomes Road in the evenings because of the lady in dirty white who is not of this world." Associated with the haunting was the perfume of narcissus which used to waft around a room in a house in Welcomes Road, and the sound of footsteps heard to walk straight through the building.

One evening Mrs. Howland, a former owner of Welcomes Farm, glanced towards Barn Cottages in Hayes Lane and saw the figure of a 'lady in a grey gown' standing in the front garden. Mistaking it for Mrs. Fretwell she waved and called out. Only when the apparition faded away did she realise that she was merely another witness to the nun.

Another impressive sighting was in 1968 when a gentleman driving home one afternoon was puzzled at seeing what looked like a nun "walking in my driveway." As she seemed deaf to the sound of his car or his horn, he stopped and got out to ask the lady to move aside. But when only a few feet from him the figure vanished, "it melted into the hedge."

At least four other local residents have seen the figure at varying times, sometimes at 8 o'clock in the morning, and she is believed to be the ghost of a nun who had an illicit relationship with a monk. Occasionally the phantom has been seen carrying a small bundle in her arms believed to be her baby, the result of her love affair. Children playing in the woods opposite the cottages claim that a small grotto in an old wall is where the nun prays. Other more imaginative youngsters say it is the site of the grave of the child. All I could find at the spot was an old kitchen sink half buried in the thickening undergrowth. Admittedly, it could hide a shallow tomb.

It is a fact that a chapel existed in the area, foundations of it having been discovered by the local archaeological society in 1966 and they also found 20 skeletons in the adjoining area. The aim of the dig had been to establish the site of the village of Watendone, which was deserted in the time of the Black Death.

The cause of the haunting by the 'Grey Lady' remains conjectural, but the genuineness of it does not.

St. Mary's Church, OP
Chart Lane,
Reigate. *Off A25 – Nearest Station – Reigate*

One evening early in 1975 Mrs. Christine Bell was walking home with a friend past this beautiful church when they suddenly heard what sounded like a choir singing inside the building. Not unusual perhaps, but the church was in darkness and locked for the night. A few days later Mrs. Bell was again near the building and saw a lady of "medium height" walking slowly along the path to the church and when only a few feet from it, the figure faded away. The apparition was wearing a long white gown, "rather like a wedding dress."

In March 1975, Simon Barnes of the Surrey *County Post* in featuring Jack Hallam, another collector of ghost cases, mentioned that another "reliable and normal witness" had seen the lady in white, but at a much later time in the evening.

Wray Farm, PP
Reigate.

A few years ago someone researching at Wray Farm in Cumbria found mention of this Surrey counterpart in which the ghost of an old man had been seen upstairs in a bedroom. Unfortunately there has been some difficulty in establishing the real history of this delightful property, but what is known is that it is haunted.

Records show that the building is officially listed by the Department of the Environment as 17th century and there is no mention of any murder or suicide in the house during the last 100 years. The farm was probably part of the estate of the Castlewhich, incidentally, was used purely as a fort and when the grounds were divided, the Augustinian Priory took over the administration in about the 14th/ 15th century. The Priory itself still exists but is now a school.

In the 1880s it was occupied by a Mr. Simpson who caused severe displeasure to Queen Victoria by purchasing an Academy picture that she wanted to buy. A family named Gillman lived there in the 19th century and returned to it in 1920.

Recent owners, the Richards, bought the farmhouse, understanding that it was 13th century and situated on the estate once owned by the Archbishop of Canterbury.

At approximately 4pm one afternoon in May 1973, Mrs. Richards was making up the fire in the huge oak-beamed sitting room and on hearing the door open, turned round to see a little girl walk in. Thinking it was Esther, her young daughter, "she had the same colouring, dark hair and blue eyes but wearing a beautiful Victorian dress with pin tucks and lace edging, I admonished her for wearing the strange dress and asked where she had got it from." At that moment the figure vanished.

Edward Pratt, a clairvoyant friend of mine who had the great pleasure of visiting the house with me in October 1974, told us that he could 'see' the outlines of an old building on the left-hand side of the lawn and when we went to examine the site complained of a peculiar feeling in his stomach and of suffering from a very dry constricted throat. "Why are my legs trembling?" he asked, "Did someone hang himself here?"

Wray Farm, Reigate, Surrey, which appears to house several ghosts, including a group of children and a kindly old lady. *Author's collection.*

Mrs. Richards told us that she had recently learnt that earlier this century a youngish man, dominated by his mother with whom he was having an illicit relationship, starved himself to death in a large shed that was originally situated on the spot.

We returned to the sitting room where Eddie was able to see the little girl witnessed by the owner, and also the figure of a man standing in what had been a doorway. "The man is wearing highly polished riding boots," he told us, "and I think his name is James Thurber or Herber." When we moved into the sitting room a group of four children could be 'seen' by the clairvoyant and consisted of "Jimmy, a young boy wearing a cap with a tassel, Katherine the oldest, and two other happy little girls. They have just come tumbling into the room and they are singing. Can't you hear them? 'Boys and girls come out to play, the moon doth shine as bright as day'."

Mrs. Richards had told me earlier that she had seen the figure of a charming old woman "wearing a sort of shawl on her head and a divided crinoline, sitting in the corner by the inglenook fireplace. Eddie now promptly described the same figure and thought that she was from the "end of the 18th or beginning of the 19th century."

It is this dear old soul who was frequently seen by the previous owner, the mother of a local M.P., and continues to be seen by Mrs. Richards, young Timothy her son, who often smiles and waves at the ghost, and the family dog. Visitors have often mentioned the feeling of a presence in the dining room and all agree that she is "so sweet, like a favourite granny".

To me it doesn't matter who she is, for to house such a charming, friendly shade of the past just adds further to the more obvious attractions of the homely atmosphere and general enchantment of Wray Farm.

SUSSEX

Deans Place Hotel, OP
Alfriston. *On B2108 between A27/A259 – Nearest Station – Selmeston*
Built in about 1700, this large 45-bedroomed hotel lies just on the southern outskirts of this attractive village and within a stone's throw of the old Clergy House and the church. There used to be a local tale that a ghostly dog would make its appearance in the lane leading to the Hotel every seven years, but like so many legends there is no one alive today who can remember ever having heard of a witness to this haunting.

On the other hand, the story of a lady in a long blue dress seen walking into a bathroom has been confirmed and witnessed by several guests. A Mrs. Saddler of Hastings told me that her five-year-old daughter asked who the lady was when they stayed in the hotel about ten years ago. She was puzzled and enquired about the apparition only to be told by a member of the staff that she was thought to be that of a woman who was "cut up and put in a settle."

Unfortunately I was unable to find out any other details and, on speaking to Mr. T. H. Brewster, one of the owners of the hotel, I was told that they have recently carried out further modernisation and extension plans and that 'the lady in blue' may now find herself 'out in the cold'.

Preston Manor, OP
Preston Park,
Brighton. *Off A23 – Nearest Station – Preston Park*
I was introduced to this charming but rather cold Georgian house and museum by Frank Hennig of B.B.C. Radio Brighton during an interview. The building, owned by the Borough of Brighton and administered by the Royal Pavilion Art Gallery and Museums, contains many interesting bequests of fine furniture and, it seems, one or possibly two ghosts.

Marion Waller, Keeper of Preston Manor and Rottingdean Grange, was kind enough to provide some information about the history of the former home of Lady Thomas-Stanford who died there with her second husband in 1932.

In some notes compiled, probably, by Henry Robertsthe first Curator of the Manorone learns that Mrs. Magniac, half-sister of the previous owner, went to see him in 1934 to discuss the ghost. She said that in a letter to the *Catholic Magazine Lady* Thomas-Stanford's son had stated that a Mrs. Studd was the only person to witness the apparition, but this was inaccurate.

Mrs. Magniac, who lived in the house until her marriage in 1894, claimed that 'the Lady in White' had been seen by many people, including herself. She went upstairs after a tennis party to change her shoes and on reaching the first landing saw a woman in a white dress standing beside her.

'She did not know her and did not recognise her as one of the players; she spoke but received no reply; she spoke again and still received no reply, so put out her hand to take the lady's hand but the figure vanished'. She was a little nervous after this experience but on telling Lady Thomas-Stanford's mother of the incident learnt that several other people, including Captain W. W. Sandeman, had also seen the phantom.

It was learnt that the body of a murdered woman was buried on the terrace outside the dining room and a few years later, when drains were being replaced, a skeleton was unearthed. The bones were enclosed in a very small space, head to feet and, according to a local doctor, were at least 300 years old. They were re-buried in a nearby churchyard.

Although there are no actual recorded reports that the phantom has been seen in recent years, a visitor in 1975 reported that he had seen a dog running through the house. On being shown the painting of Lady Thomas-Stanford's 'Kylin', which hangs in the hall, the gentleman stated that the dog he had seen certainly resembled the animal portrayed.

During the interview with Frank Hennig he asked me if I felt anything in the bedroom in which we were being filmed. I had to admit that, to me, it had rather an uncomfortable feeling which seemed to emanate from a corner cupboard. Marion Waller says in a letter to me, " . . . the room in which you were televised, the north west bedroom, is often felt to have an unpleasant atmosphere by our visitors."

Two or three people have also told me that they have seen" a sort of white shape" on the landing, but if this is the 'remains' of the murdered woman then there must obviously have been an earlier building on the site. In fact the house was originally built in 1250 and rebuilt and extended in 1738.

Nan Tucks Lane, OP
Buxted. *Off B2102 – Nearest Station – Buxted*
This lane and Hadlow Down Road are two sites of a haunting by the wraith of someone the church turned away. The belief is that in the 17th century, when Buxted was a smaller rural community than it is today and more interested in ironwork that chickens, there lived a teenager called Nan Tuck. Like some of the youngsters of today she was terribly shy, appeared morose and could even have been considered 'simple'.

As a result of this individual nonconformity, she had to be an out-cast or a 'probable witch'. An incident in the village started people talking. Perhaps the harvest had been poor or there had been an inexplicable accident at the forge. Whatever it was made the superstitious villagers look askance at Nan and murmurings grew to threats. Finally, aiming at giving her the traditional 'witch treatment' of ducking or worse, a militant group made their way to the girl's home.

Realising that for some unknown reason the village had turned completely against her, Nan ran to the vicar pleading for sanctuary and help. However, the representative of the church, no doubt scared by the raging mob, turned her away and into the arms of the furious villagers. They grabbed her and began the frightening trial, but Nan was able to escape by running down the narrow twisting road which now bears her name.

The partially satisfied crowd eventually dispersed and returned to their homes, perhaps intent on getting even with the lass in the morning. The following day, however, their rage was thwarted by the discovery of the girl's body swinging from the branch of an oak tree in the wood. The conscience of the group took over and she was cut down and buried in the hope that her death and the incident which caused it would be forgotten.

Unfortunately it cannot be, for a dark grey figure has been seen flitting along Nan Tuck's Lane and occasionally gliding through the hedges of Hadlow Down Road at dusk on September evenings.

It was one evening in 1971, at a time when I had no knowledge of this story, that I was driving along the Lane and was puzzled by a shadow which persistently kept just in front of my headlights moving in the hedgerow. Risking blocking the twisting road, I stopped to check my lights. There was no cause for the peculiar impression so I resumed my journey, but for at least half a mile this human sized and shaped darkness kept flitting along. Then suddenly, it was not there any longer.

Some two months later I heard about poor little Nan Tuck.

Alice Bright Lane, OP
Crowborough. *On A26 – Nearest Station – Crowborough & Jarvis Brook*
During the First World War a young girl hurrying home one evening in the pouring rain slipped and fell into a stream near to the Rose and Crown. Her cries for help were never heard and in the morning her drowned body was discovered by some local farm workers.

As in the case of one of the Robertsbridge hauntings, her little ghost is sometimes seen during floods and bad weather hurrying along Alice Bright Lane, but unfortunately it is not established as to whether she was the original Alice Bright.

Shovells,* OPA
All Saints Street,
Hastings. *Off A259 – Nearest Station – Hastings*
How many famous personalities, on reaching stardom, forget their origins and more especially their mothers? Sir Cloudesley Shovell was born in 1650 and at an early age was apprenticed to a shoemaker. His father was a poor man and unable to finance his son, so the lad decided to make his own way in life and ran away to sea, becoming a cabin boy to Sir John Narborough.

He had a frank and lovable disposition and so rose quickly in rank and favour and in 1690 played an active and gallant part in the battle of Beachy Head. His claim to fame, however, was the major assistance he gave as an Admiral of the Blue Fleet to Sir George Rooke in the storming and eventual capture of Gibraltar in 1704. His ship was lost off the Scilly Isles shortly afterwards.

Evidence of his love for his mother was that she was consigned in the 1700s to one of the seven paupers' cottages in All Saints Street, then available to ladies suffering from severe financial difficulties.

Shovells, All Saints Street, Hastings, still 'inhabited' by a former owner who lived there for forty happy years. *Author's collection.*

In 1962 a Mrs. Prideaux died, having spent many years in one of the surviving cottages and carried out, in the forty years of residence, a complete modernisation of facilities.

It was this somewhat dominant and forthright character who ensured the provision of mains water and drainage and electricity to her home without harming the character of the ancient structure built, it is believed, in 1435. In fact she expressed her own individuality by adding doors here, cupboards there, but all constructed in ancient wood. Some cupboards still bear old painted texts of church plaques from which they were made.

Some two years after the death of Mrs. Prideaux the cottage, now named 'Shovells', was purchased by Mrs. Jane Taylor Lowe who has further enhanced it by a careful choice of attractive old and comfortable furnishings which blend so well into the charming surroundings. Her overnight lodgers, in what is now a small guest house, have all expressed the general feeling of homeliness, even the gentleman who a few years ago witnessed the ghost of a lady in black standing at the foot of his bed.

He was apprehensive, but not frightened at the sudden appearance of the phantom. Nevertheless he requested to be allowed to move to another room for the following night.

The haunting was confirmed in 1970 by two friends of the owner who had been sitting in the hall one evening and asked Mrs. Taylor Lowe the identity of the old lady sitting on a chair a few feet away. The couple had not noticed her arrival during their conversation nor her departure but were able to describe the visitor's clothing and some of the jewellery she wore. It matched that of the figure seen upstairs and that of Mrs. Prideaux whose portrait now hangs, albeit temporarily for it is only on loan, a few feet from where she was last seen some eight years after her death.

Hastings Castle, OP
Hastings.   *On A259 – Nearest Station – Hastings*

As one of the first castles to be built by William the Conqueror, it might be surprising if the fortress was not haunted, although little of the original construction now remains. It fell into decay in the 13th century and was further damaged by plunder and the encroachment of the sea. However, at the time of the Norman settlement the castle was one of their principal bastions with a moat over 100 feet wide. There seems to be some attraction for a certain type of suicide to use high buildings for their last journey. Westminster Cathedral in London was at one time a much-favoured sitetop of the drops in factas was Beachy Head. But jumping into the void has lost its popularity since the introduction of tranquillisers, for these prove to be a much easier method of really getting away from it all.

Women with babies seem to be high on the list of suicides and here, at Hastings, there is a typical case.

A vague figure of a woman in a brown dress holding a small bundle "resembling a child" has been seen walking up and down the east wall of the castle ruins. After a few seconds the figure reaches a point near the cliff edge and, with a sudden movement forward towards the sea, "simply fades away."

Local residents claim that the baby is her illegitimate child, fathered by a fisherman of the town, and that she committed suicide over 150 years ago.

One recent witness to the haunting was a Mr. Gibson who was exercising his dog one evening in 1974 and saw the rather frightening incident "quite clearly."

Pevensey Castle,* OP
Pevensey.   *On A259 – Nearest Station – Pevensey Bay*

Many people seem to forget that, although William the Conqueror had a battle at Battle which was later called the Battle of Hastings, he did in fact land at Pevensey but the troops at the Roman castle there failed to stop him. Before the 12th century the Normans had started to build an inner bailey and a keep within the impregnable walls. It was considered impregnable by King Stephen in 1147 and in the 13th century walls, towers and a gatehouse further strengthened the fortress.

The claim is that Lady Jane Pelham glides around at night, but when I asked the attendant in 1974 about the tale he laughed in derision. "Who is around to see?" he asked, but continued, in a serious tone, "we often have youngsters scrambling over the walls and one evening at about 4.30 in August last year I saw four of them run off in an awful hurry. I managed to catch one and realised that he was not so frightened of me as of something he and the other lads had seen.

When two of his friends came up to see what I was going to do they confirmed that they had all seen the figure of a woman actually on the wall, but because she was so 'filmy' and just 'vanished' when they looked at her again they ran." He also told me several people had felt something in the dungeon just on the right-hand side of the gateway as one goes in. "I must admit," he said, "I don't go down there if I can help it and no dog will enter it. I've tried to persuade my own."

Leaving a friend who was reluctant to accompany me at the top of the narrow stairway, I walked down into the darkened cell. The atmosphere was most uncomfortable, perhaps claustrophobic, perhaps something else, and I returned rather hurriedly.

There is another story about the haunting of the Mint House, a wholesale antique supplier opposite the castle, in which it is claimed that a small room on the right-hand side of the ground floor is haunted by a young woman murdered in the 16th century.

It is only a couple of miles away at the Crumbles that in 1924 Patrick Mahon brutally murdered Emily Kaye, his mistress, and then threw portions of her body on to the railway line between Waterloo and Richmond. If it is horror you are after, just think of the murderer's feelings when he was trying to burn Emily's head during a raging storm. The expansion of the muscles caused by the intense heat resulted in the eyes suddenly opening.

Pevensey Castle, Pevensey, Sussex, where a ghostly woman has been seen on the walls. *Author's collection.*

Ghosts, if you can call them that, of both Irene Munro, slaughtered in 1920, and Emily Kaye are supposed to have been seen in the locality, but the descriptions are of 'vague misty shapes' which is exactly what they could be misty shapes.

Public Library,* OP
Battle Road,
Robertsbridge. *On A21 – Nearest Station – Robertsbridge*

One of the initial problems of gauging whether a haunting is genuine or not is, as far as I am concerned, to assess the type of witness and the circumstances involved. In certain cases I think it unwise to dismiss a case merely because there is only one known person who saw the apparition. There may well be others who are reluctant to divulge that they too saw a ghost or have moved away from the district.

What impressed me about the incident, which confirms that this old building still houses a former owner, was that my informant had only been to the village once and had no knowledge of the history of the building involved.

The building was constructed in the mid-17th century and is now used as a branch library, the Youth Employment Bureau, the meeting place of the old people's club and, three days a week, by the local youth club. A new deputy youth leader had been appointed and was travelling from his home at Battle to attend his first function.

It was fairly early one June evening in 1972 and as he approached the house, he noticed that an upstairs light was on. "It should have been empty at that time of day," he told me, "and I was puzzled but assumed somebody had left it on accidentally. As I drove past to the car park I glanced up at the window and saw an old woman peering out. Having parked the car I came back to find the place in darkness and the door locked. I opened up and went all over the building but found nothing out of place and nobody about so I forgot the incident."

However, when talking to some colleagues later that evening, he mentioned seeing "the old dear at the window" and was more than surprised to learn that he had described the former owner of the house who had died many years previously. A senior Youth Club official from another area told me independently that when she visited the youth club she had several times heard the sound of footsteps going up the stairway, though the house was empty. "I never liked being there alone," she said, "I feel that someone is watching me, and I have heard of one or two other people who have mentioned the footsteps up the stairs."

This type of phenomenon can often be explained by the sound carrying through a partition wall from another building, but this house is detached. There is a wide alley on one side and a field on the other.

The Grange Antiques,* OP
High Street,
Robertsbridge.   *On A21 – Nearest Station – Robertsbridge*

When Mrs. M. Wilmot-Brown first moved into this 15th century cottage she decided to open the premises as a small guest house. One of her first guests was a senior lecturer who, on regular monthly assignments, would stay for a couple of nights. Shortly after his first visit he asked who the ghosts were, for he had been woken "two or three times" by the sound of children dancing around on the floor. The owner, having heard nothing, was unable to provide an answer.

Shortly before his last visit the gentleman said that the sounds appeared to be getting louder and were certainly those of children.

Another guest also commented on the noises during a visit in 1967.

Within the last few years Mrs. Wilmot-Brown has turned the premises into an antique shop and stresses that she has still heard nothing unusual herself, but freely accepts that some people are more receptive to phantoms than others.

Only a few weeks after moving in she was told that the previous owner had seen the ghost of a woman in one of the double bedrooms, "but it was many years ago."

A neighbour who helped out occasionally also confirmed that he too had frequently heard "not footsteps so much, but the sound of children's voices and a child crying."

Although the building is one of a row of ancient cottages and the loft covers a couple of adjoining properties there are no children in the terrace, so the answer cannot be of 'travelling sound'. Even when there were a couple of youngsters at the far end of the block, they certainly did not dance around at 3 o'clock in the morning.

Pashley Manor, Ticehurst, Sussex, where a little old lady has been frequently seen on the stairway and in the hall. *Author's collection.*

Pashley Manor,* PP
Ticehurst.

Sitting in gently rolling countryside surrounding the River Lymden but hidden from the main road to Wadhurst by a mass of trees, is what must be one of the most attractive ancient buildings in the area. The front of the building was, up to a few years ago, hidden by various Victorian embellishments which thankfully have now been removed to reveal a 16th century countenance. The rear portion of the building is a large Georgian addition of 1730, whilst the cellars reveal a probable 13th century foundation.

The manor, standing in many acres of a beautiful estate, takes its name from the Passelewe family, though according to Judith Glover in her *Place Names of Sussex* (Batsford 1975), it is derived from 'Paecci's clearing which in 1230 became Pesselegh'.

The first owner was Robert, Archdeacon of Lewes, who in 1232 became Treasurer of the Exchequer and it was his influence which enabled Sir Edmund de Passele to acquire a vast area of Kent and Sussex, evidence of which is contained in a Charter granted to Sir Edmund in 1317 and still held by a Mrs. Margaret Cole, a direct descendant of the family who owned Pashley in the 16th century.

There are numerous intriguing features about the house and its environs, one of which is the strong belief that the first house was a hunting lodge built on an island in the largest of the three ponds which still exist in the extensive grounds. For centuries the cluster of ponds has been termed 'the moat', but any sign of an earlier building is hidden by the trees and shrubs which abound on the plot.

For a fuller history of the manor readers would perhaps be interested to read my *Ghosts of the South East* (David and Charles 1976), but suffice to say that in 1539

Sir James Bulleyn, uncle of the famous Ann, sold the property to Thomas May of Combwell for 360 when the estate consisted of 600 acres of land and a water mill.

In 1918, when Doctor Hollist was the owner, there was considerable talk in the household of a ghost which had been seen frequently and Madge, one of the last of the servants who still lives in the village, told me in 1974 that when she was an under-parlour maid in her teens she too saw 'the lady in grey.'

She was clearing up following a shooting party and was collecting the muddied boots for cleaning. "I glanced up towards the open door," she said, "and saw, gliding along the front landing, the figure of a woman with her arms swinging as if walking with some considerable purpose on a special errand.

She had white hair, piled on her head rather like a bun, and wore a high-necked shirt blouse shaped and gathered into a very small waist, but as she had just turned, having come up the stairs, I was unable to see her face. I was in one of the ladies' bedrooms at the time and certainly wasn't scared by the phantom even though I couldn't see any legs. The figure faded into nothingness at the waist."

Madge followed the apparition into what was then known as The Violet Room but found it empty. Poltergeist activity had also been reported by those 'below stairs' and the cook had, with great relish, told of a pair of phantom hands she saw one winter evening grasping out through the balustrade at the top of the stairways.

During the last war some young soldiers who were billeted there reported being scared by 'the phantom lady of the manor' but no details are known.

The new owners, Captain and Mrs. Forsyth, decided to try to restore the manor to its former splendour and it was during their period of 15 years occupation that the 'Phantom Lady' became more active. Lindsay Forsyth, when nine years of age, frequently saw the old lady "in a grey dress walking through a partition wall from one bedroom to another" and was so used to her appearance that she complained to her father, when he bricked up an old fireplace in a bedroom, that "the little old lady won't be able to visit me anymore."

A sensitive friend and neighbour of the Forsyths surprised them one day by asking who the little old lady was whom she saw standing in front of "the funny old building on the island." She accepted the figure as that of the ghost but was puzzled by the appearance of the non-existent building which just faded away. Was this some sort of proof that foundations of the original manor will one day be found on the island?

The next owners were Doctor and Mrs. Cole who were told of a ghost of an old woman who had been seen walking down the main stairs and through the wall opposite on the ground floor, and had also been seen on the terrace, gliding towards one of the pools.

Mrs. Cole told me that although she never actually saw the phantom she was often aware of "a friendly presence" in the hallway and, like the entire family, was "absolutely thrilled" to find, when some old plaster had been removed from a wall in the hallway, the carved framework of a Tudor doorway. It was this doorway that the old lady had been walking through.

Another rather mysterious figure was seen, however, by Mrs. Cole during her occupation and this was of a small silhouette in the doorway of a bedroom adjoining that of the room in which her young son was lying in a high fever.

Two other areas of the house have also been affected by previous long forgotten occupants. One is a child who would cry out from somewhere near the moat, and the other is an unseen walker heard climbing an outside stairway to a flat once occupied by a gardener and his wife.

The current owner, David Le May, who is no relation to the original May family, seemed disappointed that so far none of his family had ever seen any signs of the old lady. "But," he said with a smile, "there's always the chance that she will come back again some time."

SUNDERLAND

Washington Old Hall, OP
Washington. *Off A182 – Nearest Station – Newcastle-on-Tyne*

Owned by the National Trust, this house remains a link with America, as the name 'Washington' implies. The house was built in the early 17th century but it incorporates sections of a much earlier mediaeval building, for it was the seat of the Washington family from 1183 to 1613. Other branches lived in Sulgrave Manor in Northamptonshire which was completed about 1560 by a direct ancestor of George. It is here, at Sulgrave, that a coat of arms carved over a doorway, and consisting of three stars and two stripes, is claimed to be the origin of the American flag.

However during the last few years a few of the many visitors to the Washington Old Hall have enquired about the figure of 'a lady in a long grey dress' which is seen gently wandering along an upstairs corridor. Several of the witnesses claim that there is a likeness to one of the family portraits hung in the Hall. I'm not doubting it, never having seen either the paintings or the ghost, but wishful thinking is a pleasant pastime.

WARWICKSHIRE

Hilborough Manor, PP
Evesham Road,
Bidford on Avon.

Now owned by John Barton, a director of the Royal Shakespeare Theatre, this 15th century timber-framed house with an Elizabethan stone wing and 18th century additions was, until about 20 years ago being used as a farmhouse, but then left empty to fall into a pitiful state of disrepair.

In 1968 it was purchased by Mr. Barton and completely restored. Only a few yards away is the Roman road known as Ryknild Street, leading to the Roman town of Alcester. From information kindly provided by Penelope Gold of the Royal Shakespeare Company, one learns that the manor was the hub of a once thriving village community which, due to the plague and enclosures, died in the 16th century. Legend has it that one of the ghosts is that of the last survivor of the village, a shepherd, who could well have stormed into Hilborough to rage at the Lord of the Manor who was responsible for destroying the life and people of the village.

The other phantom, for which there is more evidence, is that of Anne Whateley, a girl who is thought to have nearly married William Shakespeare.

There is claimed to be a 'mysterious marriage licence issued to William on the day prior to his obtaining approval to marry Anne Hathaway'. "Various explanations for this anomaly have been offered," says Penelope, the most generally accepted being that the record is "the result of a clerical error." It seems that Anne's father was so keen on litigation that the clerk might have been confused and issued the licence inadvertently completed for Whateley's daughter rather than Anne Hathaway. The fault was discovered in time and the next day a correct licence was issued.

The alternative is that Shakespeare blatantly jilted Anne Whateley and because of her broken heart she continues to haunt the Manor.

Sadly, though she has never been seen, she certainly makes her presence felt. Several people in recent years have sensed someone in a particular bedroom and one, a sceptic, had an extremely disturbed night. She was convinced that 'at least one person was with her in the room but became too frightened even to look'. Another young lady thought that she had had her hair pulled by an unseen hand.

Somewhat confusing the story of the phantom lady is the strong smell of cigar smoke which is experienced frequently in the kitchen during the early hours. A former housekeeper was so puzzled by the smell that on one occasion she enquired of all the male house guests as to whether they had visited the kitchen earlier in the day. None had, but one or two admitted to hearing some unusual sounds coming from the haunted bedroom when it was empty.

Harrow Hill, OP
Long Compton.   *Off A34 – Nearest Station – Moreton-in-the-Marsh (5 miles)*
Is it the ghost of Anne Tennant which was seen in November 1973 by two furniture delivery men at about 9 o'clock in the morning at the bottom of Harrow Hill?

Described as "a most hideous looking old woman, at least 70 years old, with grey matted hair and wearing a black shawl, the figure suddenly appeared from nowhere, glided past the van and vanished as quickly and mysteriously as she had arrived". James Haywood, a local farm worker, was accused of murdering an 80-year-old woman because she had "bewitched" him, "and," he said, "there are 16 other witches in the area who deserve the same fate." Mrs. Tennant made and sold mops for a living and was probably of Romany stock. The case was heard by Baron Bramwell at Warwick Assizes in January 1880 and Haywood was found to be insane.

There are other reports regarding the haunting of Harrow Hill by a phantom coach and horses, but nobody has heard or seen these for some time. Perhaps it is because few people are around in the area during the winter months, or at the right time after a rainstorm when the coach is claimed to be visible. It should be remembered that only a couple of miles to the north the famous Rollright Stones remind travellers of the prehistoric days of pagan worship and it was here in 1949 that a local man claimed he saw a group of witches practising a 'black mass'.

At Westwood Common, a few miles away, Nanny Morgan, another reputed witch, was murdered in 1875 by William Davies who killed her with an eel spear. It is not far to Lower Quinton where in 1845 the 74-yearold Charles Walton was murdered by means of a hayfork (or pricca) which resembles the practice of killing witches with a pike or skewer. The murder was never solved.

Editor's Note: The murder of Charles Walton remains unsolved but suggestions by the famed Scotland Yard detective Robert Fabian in *The Anatomy of Crime* (1970) and Donald McCormick in *Murder By Witchcraft* (1968) that this was attributable to witch beliefs in the community have been discredited. Local police suspected that a personal grudge on the part of a local farmer and an unpaid debt provided the motivation, not a ritualistic 'Wicker Man' style killing by a secret rural cult. No case ever was ever prosecuted or proven.

Ettington Park Country Club,* OP
Stratford upon Avon.   *On A34 – Nearest Station – Stratford upon Avon*
Purchased in 1975 by Mrs. Chapman, this magnificent example of Victorian Gothic architecture has an amazing history dating back to the Domesday Book in which it was mentioned as Eatendone. Some twelve months after buying the former hotel the new owner/manager told me that she hopes the present Club, featuring 'ancient and modem' folk music and dancing, will be a fully residential hotel by 1977.

She was interested to learn that the excellent film *'The Haunting'*, based on Shirley Jackson's novel, was made there in 1963 and that it was the original ancestral home of the Shirley family, claimed to be Britain's oldest.

Standing in some 40 acres of magnificent Shakespearean countryside, the building consists of 40 bedrooms, a private chapel and an old coach house. I was not able, in our short discussion, to ascertain whether Mrs. Chapman had discovered the concealed door in the dining room which leads into the chapel or the so-called 'secret door' leading from the library to the ballroom.

The house is the third to stand on the site. The original was Saxon and the second Tudor, which was rebuilt in the 18th and 19th centuries to produce the present structure. In 1952 a reporter writing in the *Evening Telegraph* stated that Mrs. Gwendoline Evans, the manageress at the time, frequently heard footsteps walking along an empty corridor in the early hours of the morning. Her father had also heard the mysterious sounds and was puzzled that although the 'walker' went to the end of the hall, it never returned.

Two members of a Devon football team slept in Rooms 21 and 22 and both claimed that they had seen "something funny." One woke to find someone leaning over him and the other felt that a veil or some other light material had been stroked over his face. For both men to have unusual dreams at the same time would be considered odd I think, but knowing footballers, they might have been suffering from a 'night on the town' anyway.

The more popular claims are of a figure of a lady in a long white dress having been seen through the decorative wrought iron panels in the cloister-like terrace beside the arched entrance. Mrs. Harrison of Torquay was one of the witnesses to the apparition, known affectionately as 'Lady Emma', one evening in the 1960s.

Another more recent incident was that experienced by Terry Hindon, temporarily acting as caretaker for Mrs. Chapman in February 1975. One evening he saw "a very old lady" gliding along in the hallway and vanish when she reached a wall, "as if she were going through it."

Other phenomena reported during the last few years have been the inexplicable opening of locked doors in the turret rooms.

As to the identity of the lady, it must remain a mystery. It is thought that she is in some way associated with a crime committed by one of the Shirleys some 200 years ago and it is this crime which is remembered as 'a bloody hand' on one of the family crests. However this was usually just a sign that the family had supplied troops to Ulster and had no other significance.

WEST MIDLANDS

Victoria Road, OP
Aston,
Birmingham. *Between A34 and A38 – Nearest Station – Aston*

As a change from ghostly ladies in white or grey comes the phantom of a woman in green, or maybe yellow, depending on who saw it. Shall we say it was a sort of yellowish green?

Mrs. Bagley and Mrs. Heath were walking along Victoria Road on 28th September 1971 at about 8.15 in the morning, "near where the old police station used to be," when they saw a "lady in a green frilly gown suddenly appear in the middle of the road and remain motionless for about a minute." As the bus neared the figure it vanished.

Sometime later Mrs. McFarlane, a former usherette in the Aston Cross Cinema, had just passed the 'tat yard', a scrap metal merchant, at approximately 9.30 pm when, according to Colin Smith, she was shocked to see the figure of a woman in a yellowish dress suddenly appear at the kerbside, cross the road and then disappear.

"There was supposed to be a ghost at the cinema," she told Colin, "I always treated it as a joke, but the figure I saw was a real ghost I can assure you." Convinced it was the same apparition, I wonder if the difference in colour was due to the streetlights being on at the time of the second witnessing. Fluorescent lighting has a peculiar effect on some colours.

Warstone Lane Cemetery, OP
Brookfields,
Birmingham. *Between A41 and A547 – Nearest Station – New Street (2 miles)*

Irrelevant but of possible interest is the fact that Ben Crouch, a body snatcher who specialised in 'resurrecting' young boys from all parts of the Midlands, is thought to have visited this large old cemetery, which is situated close to a famous jewellery quarter, and originally named Deadman's Lane. This Ben Crouch, one of the infamous 'Diggum Uppers' of Birmingham, is believed to have been the pattern for Jerry Cruncher in *A Tale of Two Cities* by Dickens and used to occupy his boyhood days by playing with the skeleton of a child given to him by his father 'to get him used to the trade'.

A few months after the last war ended, a Mr. Dixon returned home looking pale and drawn and told his wife, "I've never believed in ghosts before, but I've just seen a woman walking through a parked taxi in Key Hill," one of the roads abutting the cemetery. Mr. Dixon's widow told Colin Smith of Birmingham that her husband said the phantom was "youngish with fair hair in ringlets and wearing an old-fashioned white dress."

This is the first known report of the 'White Lady of Warstone'. It was some twenty years later in 1966 that at about 9.30 in the morning two scrap metal dealers were shocked to see "a figure in Victorian ladies' clothing come through the tunnel wall close to the graveyard."

Two years later in October at some time between 7-8 o'clock in the evening, the time she was first seen, the white lady made another appearance to Mrs. Emily McFarland and her sister, Mrs. Pamela Todd, when on their way to a bingo session. The ghost "in a crinoline type dress" was seen to walk through the railings surrounding the graveyard.

A few yards from the graveyard stands the well-known Birmingham Mint and several security men have told Mr. Smith that a "lady in a long flowing dress" has been seen in the part of the establishment closest to the cemetery. One of the unusual aspects of this haunting is that not only are the lady's footsteps heard but she seems to leave "a strong smell of pear drops behind her."

Next to the Mint is a factory in which, on at least one occasion, the phantom has been seen in the ladies lavatory, having walked through a closed door. There are many others who have admitted to witnessing the mysterious woman.

The clue to her identity may be the smell of pear drops. In Victorian days hydrocyanic acid, more popularly known as prussic acid, which is present in bitter almonds, was given in small doses as a gastric and respiratory sedative and applied to the skin as a local salve for itching. But as every murder story enthusiast will know it was often used for poisoning and would always leave behind "the smell of pear drops."

Is the lady a victim of an unknown murder?

Maxstoke Castle, Coleshill, Birmingham, where the wife of an eighteenth-century owner still haunts the scene of her violent death. *Aero Film Ltd.*

Maxstoke Castle, OPA
Coleshill,
Birmingham.

On A47 – Nearest Station – Coleshill

Situated on the eastern outskirts of the sprawling conurbation of Greater Birmingham is this 600-year-old castle built by Sir William de Clinton in 1346. Among its various claims to fame is the fact that Richard III slept in the Lady Tower in the castle on the night before the Battle of Bosworth and the same room was occupied the following night by Henry VII. There are not many homes which housed a Plantagenet king one night and a Tudor monarch the next.

The owner of the castle, Captain C. B. Fetherston-Dilke,R.N, told my colleague Colin Smith that between 1669 and 1728 it was owned by Ward Dilke who married Mary, daughter of Sir Edward Littleton.

Sometime between 1708 and the time of his death in 1728 Ward Dilke had an appalling quarrel with his wife on the staircase outside their bedroom in the Lady Tower, because she threw a bag of coins out of a nearby window. This enraged her husband and in the ensuing row Mary fell down the staircase breaking her neck. Did she fall or was she pushed is an unanswerable question, but the coins were recovered. They were obviously significant.

It is, understandably, the phantom of Mary that is occasionally seen near the landing. The owner was showing a party of visitors round the castle in 1972 and no mention had been made of the haunting. On entering the bedroom opposite the stairway one gentleman was so overcome by the' atmosphere that he had to return to the ground floor.

A legendary tale of the bedroom door mysteriously flying open is believed by Captain Fetherston-Dilke to have been started during the Civil War in an attempt to deter searchers of the castle.

Public Telephone Box, OP
Station Road,
Erdington,
Birmingham.   *On A38 – Nearest Station – Erdington*

"In September 1975," said Keith Boland, a trainee priest, "I had. been visiting some friends in Erdington and was on my way home. It was about 9.30 pm. I was walking down Station Road and decided to phone my parents to inform them that I would be home about half an hour later than expected.

"As I reached the telephone box, I noticed that someone was already using it and another couple were waiting outside, so I decided to wait. After a few moments the couple, who would be in their thirties, began to walk away and as they did so say, 'She will be there all night. We have been here for twenty minutes already.'

I waited for another five minutes or so and finally decided to ask the woman to let me have the telephone directory as I had some important calls to make, thinking this would hurry her up a bit.

I opened the door and said, 'Excuse me please', and was shocked to see the woman melt away. I say 'melt' for want of a better word. I would have seriously considered seeing an optician or a psychiatrist very quickly were it not for the fact that the other people saw her too.

The woman certainly did not look frightening in any way. In fact she looked perfectly normal to me. She was wearing a dark blue costume and a reddish coloured polo neck jumper. She would be about 25 to 30 years old I should think."

This statement was made to Colin Smith by Mr. Boland on 4th April 1976 shortly before taking him to the actual site. Colin tells me that he often uses that telephone but Mr. Boland, although not frightened, admitted to making his calls from another box that night.

I wonder if the mysterious caller was a phantom of the living, perhaps some young lady a few miles away, intent on making a vital telephone call.

Witton Lakes Park, OP
Upper Witton,
Erdington,
Birmingham.   *Off A4040 – Nearest Station – Witton*

Shortly after midnight in August 1974 Mr. Michael Phipps and Mr. Richard Cadman were exercising their four greyhounds in the park when, on nearing the boathouse by the lake, all the dogs began to whine and yelp. Mr. Phipps told Colin Smith that he then saw a 'swirling white shape floating on the grass verge some 50 yards away'. One of the dogs, 'Knockmead Squire', ran towards it, stopped suddenly, turned and raced back past us at a speed he never achieved on the trials at Norton Canes track.

"As the shape drew nearer I realised it was a ghost of a rather young woman. I wanted to run, but my legs went numb and she actually passed within a couple of inches of me. I'll never forget this as long as I live."

Mr. Cadman felt that "she wasn't old fashioned, just like an everyday woman, only very white." One of the tests for hallucinations is to close one's eyes and then open them to see if the ghost is still there. For Mr. Cadman it was. "I wanted to touch her as she passed us, but at the last minute I closed my eyes. When I opened them again she was floating towards a tree and as she reached it she vanished." The dogs are still exercised in the park but nowhere near the boathouse.

Mr Smith, in carrying out some enquiries regarding the haunting, learnt from several pupils at Perry Common School which adjoins the lakes that they knew all about the white lady. One young girl told him that her aunt had seen the figure about ten years ago "drifting by the water's edge."

Despite numerous visits to the lakes in the hope of seeing the lady, Colin has witnessed nothing unusual except a 'streaker' running round the pathway after taking an early morning dip and that was no woman.

Long Acre, OP
Nechells,
Birmingham.   *Off A38 – Nearest Station – Aston*

In the 1960s there were several reports of poltergeist activity in numerous houses in this Victorian area of the city, but among the cases investigated by Colin Smith was one in which a ghostly lady was involved.

Mr. and Mrs. Brassington saw the spectral female in their bedroom at least four times in 1969, but the appearance was "not a frightening one." She was dressed in a long flimsy blue dress and had also been seen walking along the street by a special constable in September 1962.

This witnessing by an authoritative representative of the law was noted in the official Charge Book. Mr. Smith asked the constable why he thought the figure was that of a ghost. "When you see someone walk through a brick wall, I reckon they are not normal humans," was the spirited reply.

Although the houses have now been demolished there is still a 'peculiar atmosphere' in the area which, suggests Colin, could be caused by the fact that in July 1878 the skeletons of eleven children were discovered in a back garden of one of the buildings. The owner of the house claimed that the bodies were of stillborn babies, but it is the first time I have heard of skeletons of children of that age surviving.

St. Nicholas Church, OP
Curdworth,
Birmingham.   *On A409 7 – Nearest Station – Water Orton (2 miles)*

Dating back to Norman times, though with a 14th century tower, this little parish church, set on the original old road to Birmingham, which is a mere 8 miles away, has a churchyard containing remains of many of the Civil War soldiers and, it is claimed, 'a hoard of buried treasure'. One day some unfeeling metal detecting enthusiast will no doubt try his hand at finding the gold, but he should be careful, for a headless ghost guards the spot.

St. Nicholas Church, Curdworth, near Birmingham, which has one of the very few haunted graveyards in the country. *E. P. Jones.*

More seriously though, there is a female companion phantom which has been seen occasionally floating around the churchyard. There are very few genuine haunted graveyards in the country, mainly because not many die in such places.

Described as a 'tall figure of a woman in a long green gown', it has been assumed that she was some relative of one of the Royalist officers now lying buried in a mass grave. Perhaps she killed herself at the loss of her lover, or because of the shame of the mixing of 'loyalist' and 'rebel' bodies in one tomb.

Grimshaw Hall, PP
Knowle.

Colin Smith of Birmingham, founder and vice president of the Midland Association of Ghost Hunters, tells me that this is a mid-16th century half-timbered house with "quaint little oriel windows." Although the owners, the Southalls, are unable to authenticate the ghost, they do admit that in 1967 a young lady who had been peering over the fence admiring the building was so frightened by the sudden appearance of an apparition that she was taken to a local doctor to obtain treatment for shock.

The legend of the haunting is that the ghost is of a young woman named Frances who was murdered by her lover jealous of seeing her being taken to a local ball by another man. The girl was killed in one of the bedrooms, now known as the 'Haunted Chamber', and her wraith has been seen wearing a white dress and wringing her hands in sorrow.

In August 1971 Robert Greenway was sketching the Hall and told Colin that he kept feeling that his neck was being stroked by "an icy hand" and was unable to concentrate on his work. He was convinced that someone unseen was watching him all the time.

Warley Abbey Grounds,* OP
Warley Park,
Abbey Road
Smethwick. *On A457 – Nearest Station – Smethwick West*

I was told in 1975 that a group of young researchers were so intrigued by my comments concerning Warley Abbey that they obtained special permission to camp out in these public grounds in the hope of seeing the ghost. The fact that she has only been seen at twilight and it was bound to be a waste of time was ignored, and so were the group as far as the phantom was concerned. Never mind, it must have been quite thrilling, albeit cold.

The Abbey building was torn down in 1968 after having served as a restaurant and a golf clubhouse. The grounds were laid out for the benefit of the public by the Warley County Borough.

There is not much known about the Abbey except that it is thought to have been built in the 18th century by a prominent local landowner who gave it the name 'Abbey', having taken stones from a derelict farm owned by Halesowen Abbey.

To add a touch of mystery, a subterranean tunnel was discovered some years ago, but nothing to identify the 'Grey Lady of Warley'. Some think she is the ghost of a murdered heiress. Mrs. Harrison, now of Torquay, told me in 1972 that the phantom, seen as a tall woman wearing a grey gown, was known to have appeared in the late 1950s. She still glides about on the site of the old building and vanishes halfway along a path.

Black Patch Park, OP
Foundation Lane
Smethwick. *Off A41 – Nearest Station – Smethwick (2 miles)*

Only a few hundred yards from the Birmingham Canal lies the small and unusually named public park which was used as a Romany encampment site at the turn of the century. The community was, as are most gypsy groups, very closely knit and there are many reports of old members of the 'tribe' being disposed of at their death in the traditional way, by burning the bodies in their caravans. At the turn of the century the ruler of the local group was known as 'Queen Henty', a matriarch of strong and dominant character ruling her 'family' like a firm but understanding
dictator. Was it her ghost who was seen in 1970?

Colin Smith tells me that a Mrs. Eleanor Heeley of Warley reported that one June morning six years ago she was walking through the park with her four-year-old son when suddenly a figure appeared in front of the pram.

It was that of "a very old woman wearing a long black dress and a red cape. She had beautiful long black hair for her age, and as I moved the pram to walk past her she just vanished. I wanted to run, but I couldn't. "There have been one or two vague stories of a 'ghostly old woman' having been seen in the park but as far as is known, this is the first time such a detailed description has been achieved.

An enthusiastic searcher for relevant or perhaps related facts, Colin points out that the exact site of the witnessing was a path leading to a small bridge and tells of an incident which may have caused the eventual departure of the gypsies in 1905.

Very early in the 1900s, a Yugoslavian circus family wanted to share the camping site with the Romanies and started to move on to the ground. The gypsies, feeling that they were the only rightful 'tenants' persuaded the 'gorgios' to depart, using perhaps more than a few forceful arguments. The foreigners were only temporarily thwarted for they returned a few hours later with 17 bears in an effort to 'persuade' the tribe to accept them. However, they were unsuccessful and finally left.

Penn's Lane, PP
Walmley,
Sutton Coldfield.

Walmley is best known for its two popular golf courses and is one of the suburbs of Sutton Coldfield, which is itself a dormitory town of Birmingham and boasts of a 2,400-acre park.

In 1817 the body of Mary Ashford was found near a post bridge in Penn's Lane. There is a strong suggestion that she had been murdered and the corpse tossed over a stile adjoining the bridge, but no-one was ever executed for the crime.

A few years ago, Mrs. A. K. Brown, now of Erdington, lived in a house in Penn's Lane with her mother, her husband and two sisters. One night Eva, a younger sister, had gone to a dance with a girlfriend but had failed to return home by the family's bed-time.

Suddenly there was a knock at the door which was at the side of the house by the garage. Mrs. Brown's mother, being cautious, rather than assuming immediately that the caller was Eva, went to the bathroom where, "if you stood on the toilet seat you could see down into the area of the front door."

There, waiting, stood a blonde-haired girl. Thinking that her daughter had returned the mother opened the front door but found no-one there. The woman was frightened and, with the hair on the back of her neck standing up, ran back to bed. A few minutes later the incident was repeated but this time, determined to find the answer, the mother put on her coat and equipped with a big army torch went all around the front gardens of the houses next door. No-one could be found so, after a few minutes of fruitless searching, she went back to bed.

Eva returned home later that morning, having spent the night with her friend in Birmingham.

The mysterious girl was described later as about 5 ft. 4in. tall and might well have been the ghost of Mary Ashford, or possibly a phantom of the living Eva. However, this was not the only mysterious incident in the house.

Shortly after this a phantom woman in a taffeta dress passed Mrs. Brown's mother and a friend on the landing and this visitation occurred several times. One morning the friend was so scared that they ran from the house to finish dressing in the Lane.

Even the family dog, Spot, was affected for he was found one night shivering with fright in the garage. His teeth were bared and his hackles raised.

Mrs. Brown herself thought she saw the phantom of a man standing in the doorway of her bedroom, but on screaming and waking her husband, the figure vanished. The house is situated practically opposite the bridge where the body of Mary Ashford was found in 1817.

Editor's Note: In the early hours of 27 May 1974, 20-year-old Barbara Forrest was raped and strangled at the same location close to where Mary Ashford had been murdered on 27 May 1817. The coincidences regarding the date and location and certain other aspects of both of the two cases are remarkable. The fact of a second murder in the same area raises the possibility that the apparition reported may have a more recent origin. (*The Independent* 26 December 1999; *Birmingham Evening Mail* 28 January 2010).

Manor House Restaurant, OP
Hall Green Road,
West Bromwich. *Off A4031 – Nearest Station – Birmingham New Station (8 miles)*
A few years ago the *Wolverhampton Express & Star* reported that this former mediaeval manor, restored in 1961, was haunted and the manager, John Dryden, had never believed in ghosts until he moved there. It was the incident which occurred in the old timbered building which changed his mind. "Late one night I heard footsteps upstairs," Mr. Dryden said. "I thought someone had been locked in accidentally and went to investigate, but there was no-one there."

Members of the staff later reported seeing a little old woman and a man with a black beard peering out of the windows. An electrician said that he had heard singing, even though the building was empty at the time. Various other peculiar noises and phenomena have occurred, but they only add to the mystery, for there is no clear evidence as to the identity of the phantoms and therefore no apparent reason for the incidents.

There is, however, a clue. One young girl stated that she thinks the old lady was her grandmother who died in a bedroom after falling on a fire many years ago.

Editor's Note The Manor House closed as a pub and restaurant in 2009 and the building is now back in the guardianship of Sandwell Council, and maintained by Sandwell Museum Service, being used for a variety of community projects and activities. In 2004 the site was visited by the team from the TV programme *'Most Haunted'* but little weight can be given to the claimed results, given the focus of the programme was entertainment and not an attempt to study the site scientifically.

Enquiries in March 2022 led to Dr Paul Lee of King's Lynn who at the time was compiling a website gazetteer, learning from Catherine O'Neil, who had worked at the museum for three years, that the atmosphere in the building becomes "strange" in September and Unusual noises have been heard at that time, including 'dragging noises' 'footsteps on the flagstone floors when no-one was there' and a sound 'like a human whistle'.

Two members of staff heard someone running, banging on the walls as they did so. Catherine also told of a time when keys went missing but were returned when staff asked for them.

WILTSHIRE

Littlecote House,*OP
Near Hungerford *Off A4 – Nearest Station – Hungerford (3 miles)*

A very enjoyable three years of my life were spent in the Household Cavalry working with such personalities as Major John Wills, a member of the renowned tobacco family who own this historic Tudor manor built between 1490 and 1530. Interested in genuine hauntings even when in the Army, I learnt much of the history of the ghost which resides in this early Renaissance house.

The story concerning the cause of one of the phantoms has frequently been told, but briefly it is that in Elizabethan times a Will Darrell called upon the services of a midwife named 'Mother Barnes' of Great Shefford to deal with the pregnancy of an unknown woman. When delivered, the baby was ordered to be placed on a blazing fire in the landing and Will, ignoring the pleadings of the nurse to be allowed to keep it, snatched it from her and threw the child on to the flames, keeping the body there with his booted foot.

Mrs. Barnes was returned home at nightfall and given a bag of gold, but she was later able to identify the building and Darrell was brought to trial for murder. Somehow he was acquitted. Some believe that Judge Popham was a relative and others that a hefty bribe was taken, but the outcome was that Darrell was released. He was killed soon after when his horse, startled by the apparition of a child, threw him and broke his neck.

The ghost of the mother of the baby, thought to be Darrell's sister, was seen by Sir Edward Wills in 1927. Other female phantoms have also been witnessed. In 1968 one of these walked along a narrow corridor on the north side of the building and out into the garden where it vanished. In 1969, when the Long Gallery was empty, sounds of 'feminine footsteps' were heard by some of the guides who were clearing up before returning home for the night.

A photo of the murder room was taken in 1970 by a National Trust lecturer and when it was printed an unusual semi-transparent shape could be seen through the curtains surrounding the four-poster bed.

One of the most recent incidents was that experienced by a member of the Wills family in 1972. When on the landing, he glanced towards the upper stairway leading to the third floor, which is closed to the public, and saw the figure of a woman in a dark blue gown walking slowly up the stairs. "The ghost just walked straight through the rope across the stairs," he said.

Maddington, OP
Shrewton. *Junction of A360/A344 – Nearest Station – Salisbury (10 miles)*
Now practically a suburb of Shrewton but once a village surrounded like so many in this part of Wiltshire by tumuli and pre-historic earthworks, Maddington also contains the ghost of a young woman.

Only a half mile from the village to the north east at the usual crossroads one finds a site marked on the map as 'The Gibbet'. It is not far from here that in 1970 Mr. Alexander of Shrewton was working in a barn with his daughter and, glancing up, saw the apparition of a young female wearing a "long white costume" standing only a few feet away. He glanced at his daughter and realised that she too could see the figure. When he looked back the spectre had vanished, but the sounds of footsteps as the phantom walked away were clearly heard by both witnesses and they also heard the rustling of clothing.

The ghost had also been reported a few years before by the Rev. Barnard, a former vicar, who claimed that the ghostly woman had visited the church several times but only "late in the evenings."

Two other witnesses were ladies living nearby who said that they saw the mysterious young woman glide past the kitchen on two occasions when they were making a pot of tea.

As far as I know no-one has made any real attempt to find out who the ghostly visitor is, but the locals think she is a novice from the former seminary in Maddington Manor. It seems that the manor was used as an initial centre for a nunnery associated with the Abbey at Amesbury nearly six miles to the east.

The Manor House, PP
Stanton St. Bernard.
A hangover from pre-historic days was the custom of burying the dead with their personal jewellery. Even in the Victorian era this procedure was still accepted as normal.

It is perhaps for this reason that grave robbing has not yet completely died out and proof of this activity is certainly evident at the old Highgate Cemetery in London, which probably accounts for many of the tales, even in the 1970s, of 'vampires' and 'ghosts'. I was told when filming there in 1975 that two such ghoulish morons, having successfully opened up three or four tombs a month, were netting about £1,800 per year from the proceeds of selling rings, trinkets and even watches and chains stolen from the dead. A strange coincidence involving two similar incidents which occurred in the 19th century are due either to the transference of a folk tale from York to Wiltshire, or sextons in those days not being all that they should be.

St. Saviour's Parish Churchyard in York houses many tombs and one of these was known by the sexton to contain the body of a lady who had been recently buried wearing her rings. One night, so the story goes, he re-opened the vault and the coffin and began to remove the valuable jewellery from the corpse. In order to obtain one of the more attractive rings he had to cut the finger off the body and in doing so "awakened the woman who had been in a coma." To the horror of the layman, but to the delight of her friends and relatives, the lady was restored to her home.

Whether her ghost haunted the man who restored her to life is not known but a practically identical story relates to this Manor House in Wiltshire. The woman in this case was a farmer's wife and the sexton managed to actually remove the finger before the 'corpse' recovered. Miss Kathleen Wiltshire in her book dealing with the many ghosts and legends of the county, says that on the anniversary of the first funeral the victim returns from the churchyard and stands in the dining room doorway, "her finger dripping blood."

There certainly seems to be a genuine haunting here, for the names of two informants have been given, one of whom stated emphatically that several maids had seen the ghost, with alarming consequences. One ran home screaming, another immediately demanded 'her cards' and a third dropped a tray of china. A former occupier admitted that neither he nor his family were comfortable in the room and even today stories circulate that 'the lady of the Manor' has been seen again.

Longleat House,* OP
Warminster.   *On A362 – Nearest Station – Warminster*

Promoted as 'one of the Magnificent Seven Stately Houses' and home of the Marquess of Bath, Longleat sports a huge safari park and many other tourist attractions, including a restored Victorian kitchen. But of the ghosts little is said. Perhaps visitors are so over-awed by the size of the building, the lavish decor, furnishings, paintings, and the huge 11,000-acre estate that they fail to realise that a lady in a green dress they saw in a particular corridor was not one of the guests but the phantom of Louisa Carteret.

Whilst serving in the Army I had the pleasure of meeting Major John Thynne, one of the relatives of the current owner. During an interesting chat one evening I learnt that the Elizabethan family seat is built on the foundation of a priory which was destroyed during the Dissolution and that the haunting is really the result of a family affair. One of the forefathers of the Marquess, the second Viscount Weymouth, married Lady Louisa during the reign of Queen Anne, but it was not long before the wife took a lover. Legend has it that the Viscount discovered the couple together, fought a duel with the other man, killed him and buried the body in the cellar. The site of the 'battle of honour' became known as the 'Green Lady's Walk', mainly because of the portrait of Lady Louisa which hangs there and the belief that she continues to visit the corridor where her agony of mind must have reached a peak of distress. When the current Marquess was still in his teens his father realised that central heating should be installed, and in the ensuing work the remains of a youngish man were discovered beneath some flagstones. The rotting clothing was confirmed as being of Queen Anne period. A particular linen cupboard is also haunted by a most unpleasant housekeeper, but the cause of this remains a mystery.

YORKSHIRE – North

Ripley Castle, OP

Near Harrogate. *Junction of A61 with B6165 – Nearest Station – Harrogate(5 miles)*

This has been the home of the Ingilby family since 1350. Oliver Cromwell stayed here and bullet marks on the walls of the 15th century gatehouse are a reminder of his troops' later attacks on the semi-fortified mansion. Another famous guest was James I, but if it is the Tudor period you are interested in then there is much to discover in this fascinating old building. A collection of armour and weapons of the Civil Wars is also on display, along with a floor made from the deck of a British warship.

One of the really interesting items for many ghost hunters is the priests' hole which has only recently been discovered. There is also a ghostly nun whose portrait hangs on the wall to mystify and puzzle guests and visitors. Some of the more imaginative will claim that if you stare into her eyes long enough you may go into a trance, fall asleep, or get so bored you walk away. Actually it is this female who has been seen a few times at night gliding along one of the upper corridors and there is more than one guest who has claimed she has knocked at their bedroom door to waken them. Perhaps one day there might be some information as to her identity and why she still ripples around Ripley.

Ripley Castle, near Harrogate, Yorkshire, haunted by a nun, whose portrait is on view to visitors.
R. Ackrill Ltd, Harrogate.

Editor's Note: A remarkable story appeared in the *Darlington & Stockton Times* for 17 July 2017 that a pair of antique silver candlesticks which vanished at Christmas 2014 had mysteriously re-appeared in 2017 in the castle's strong room on a shelf in a bright red Christmas carrier bag. This was a year after the owner Sir Thomas had claimed and been paid out on the insurance. Sir Thomas suspected that the candlesticks' 'movements' were down to Henry and Mary Ingilby, who died of leukaemia in the castle in the late 19th-century when they were aged only seven and five. With their re-appearance he duly refunded the insurance money prompting the claims manager of Ecclesiastical Insurance to state: 'This is certainly the first time a customer has reimbursed us for items they suspect was returned by a ghost'.

Tosside, OP
Near Settle.　　　　　　　　　　*On B64 78 – Nearest Station – Long Preston (5 miles)*

The steep road through this village beside Gisburn Forest runs down to Ribblesdale and eventually, by way of the A65, into Settle, a major market town used as a base by the enthusiastic pot-holers exploring Gaping Gill, Car Pot and other renowned underground chambers. A few yards from Tosside a tributary to the Ribble flows under the road and it is here that a couple of nasty accidents have occurred due, it is said, to the phantom of a young woman drowned in the stream some years ago. Some of the hikers who frequent the area have reported seeing what looks like a young servant girl suddenly dart across the road and vanish. Locals say that one winter, about a hundred years ago, a farmer told a milkmaid to fetch some water from the stream, perhaps not realising the risk involved. However, the lass scrambled over the frozen ground and stepped on some snow-covered ice which broke under her weight, causing her to fall to her death.

Sherriff Hutton,*　　　　　　　　　　*Off A64 – Nearest Station – York (8 miles)*

Long distance lorry drivers are occasionally referred to as 'Knights of the road' and those I have met are certainly deserving of the title. Some are imaginative, some are not, but there are dozens of both types who admit to seeing 'Nance' on the A64 and are delighted when they do.

I first heard of this helpful young lady from Jack Carter, a long-distance lorry driver. He told me that a lot of drivers who travel in fog at night to York from Malton have seen the figure of a youngish woman just on the edge of their headlights. She travels with them on the road practically all the way to the city.

"What is funny," he said, "is that if there is trouble ahead, a crash or something, she slows down. Otherwise you can travel up to about 30 miles an hour with her. I don't know who she is, but we call her Nance. I think she came from Sherriff Hutton." Referring to *The Ghost Hunter's Roadbook* by John Harries (Muller 1968), I found that she is indeed 'Nance', the phantom of an 18th century farmer's daughter who was engaged to a driver of a mail coach travelling from York to Berwick. Unable to refuse the attentions of a smooth-talking highwayman, she ran away with him only to find, when it was too late, that he was married. Sometime later the heart-broken fiancé, travelling to York one evening, found poor little Nance standing on the side of the main road carrying a small child. Still very much in love with the girl, the coachman took her with him to the York Tavern; but despite his care and tenderness both Nance and her baby died.

Some two years later the man was taking some goods to York but had to slow down because of the thick fog. Suddenly Nance was beside him. Taking the reins from him she drove the coach at speed into the Black Swan in York and then faded away. Quite obviously Nance still helps drivers delayed by bad weather conditions.

Boulby Cliff, OP
Staithes. *Off Al 74 – Nearest Station – Saltbum (8 miles)*
Practically on the border line between North Yorkshire and Durham lies this small coastal town, or is it a village? Actually it rather resembles a Cornish hamlet with its narrow twisting road leading down to the harbour and grey stone beach. Small alleys and steep paths separate the ancient cottages. It is an attractive little place and popular with the occasional tourist looking for something different. One of the noteworthy aspects of Staithes is Boulby Cliff, the highest perpendicular cliff in England at some 700 feet.

It was during a pleasant Spring evening in April 1807 that Hannah Grundy, a teenage girl from the village, was strolling along the beach beneath the cliff when something attracted her attention among the pebbles on the shore. She bent down to take a closer look, ignoring the sudden gust of wind. Suddenly without warning a knife-edged rock from the cliff above her, loosened by recent storms, fell like an axe and beheaded the young woman. The incident was witnessed by one of the fishermen tending his nets a few yards away. Today, about one hundred and seventy years later, one hears of the sighting, albeit infrequently, of the vague wispy figure of a young girl walking near the sea's edge beneath the imposing cliff, usually at Springtime. The local fishermen nod their heads. They know who it is.

York Theatre Royal, OP
St. Leonard's Place,
York. *On A 19 – Nearest Station – York*
There must be hundreds of nuns who were walled up alive according to legend, but in fact many were merely entering their own cells in a burst of voluntary fanatical fervour. These cells were common to nunneries, abbeys and prioriesin fact wherever a religious order called for intense solitary prayer, supplication or study. For some reason females seemed to take a greater delight than males in suffering this form of privation, termed as immurement, a very strict form of life imprisonment. The cell would be left with a small opening for food to be passed in, empty plates and other containers to be passed out. The colour of robes, grey or white, often provides an indication as to the status of the wearer, a lay sister or accredited nun, or the order to which they belonged. The 'grey lady' of the Theatre Royal, which opened in 1740, is actually associated not with the stage but the ruins of St. Leonards Hospital which at one time was situated in a four-acre plot provided by King Stephen. The crypt of the original hospital now forms a social centre and club room for the theatre. St. Leonards Hospital was one of the first religious foundations devoted to the care of the sick and one assumes it was also used, as most such establishments were, to house the nuns, whether they were nurses or religious devotees.

Tradition has it that one of these women was 'walled up alive' in a tiny room behind a dressing room near the dress circle. This room has fairly recently been enlarged for the benefit of the actors and actresses. John V. Mitchell, author of *Ghosts of an*

Theatre Royal, York, built on the ruins of a convent. A 'grey lady' occasionally moves across the dress circle from left to right. *Alec Russell, York.*

Ancient City (Cerialis Press), states that "many occupants of this room mentioned the strange feeling they had of being watched," whilst others experienced an inexplicable chilling sensation. Some asked to be allowed to change their rooms and some of the braver members of the cast would sit up all night in the hope of seeing the apparition. "Strange happenings still occur," says Mr. Mitchell and a former actress, Mrs. Marjorie Rowland, tells how, whilst standing at the back of the dress circle, she saw the figure of the nun, dressed in grey with a white coif, leaning over the edge of the stage box. This description seems to suggest that the ghost is that of a novice who, not having qualified for full sisterhood of the order, is unlikely to have voluntarily taken up immurement. She may therefore have been one of those few who were punished for some misdemeanour by suffering enforced entombment. There is another ghost here, but this is of an actor killed in a duel some time ago. He was seen quite recently wearing period costume and standing in the upper circle. The most prominent object was a large and awesome ring with a green stone that the phantom was wearing on 'well cared-for hands'.

In 1965 the *Daily Sketch* published a letter from Harry Bennett of Hampstead in which he said that, when appearing at the theatre with his company, permission was obtained to 'try to lay the ghost.'

"Several of us occupied the dressing room," he says, "and soon we heard footsteps. The atmosphere became eerie and cold. Then to our horror the figure of a tall woman appeared, hooded and gowned. She entered the dressing room through the closed door . . . unfortunately one of the company screamed. The lights were turned on and the apparition vanished". The most recent sighting occurred during rehearsals of 'Dear Octopus' in the Autumn of 1975. As the cast began to sing 'Kerry Dance Again', they were puzzled to see an inexplicable light slowly develop in the circle of the theatre. As they watched, it gradually increased in intensity and eventually took the form of the head and shoulders of a woman. The incident lasted only a few seconds but the rehearsal came to a complete standstill as the whole cast watched in amazement while the apparition gradually disappeared. What must be a unique situation was the fact that when the cast of ten, having recovered their composure, re-started the rehearsal, the ghostly head and shoulders re-appeared, but with less intensity. The woman has not been seen since.

Castlegate House, PP
York.
Once this ancient building housed Mount School, but Castlegate still accommodates the phantom of a 'grey lady' who has been seen gliding about the main staircase. She is thought to be a Quaker, but other than this nothing is known about the phantom female. According to John Mitchell in his Ghosts of an Ancient City there is also another female ghost in number six Castlegate, but even less is known about her.

YORKSHIRE – West

Haworth Parsonage, OP On A6033
Haworth. *Nearest Station – Keighley (3 miles)*
Is it haunted by Emily Bronte? There seems to be some controversy as to whether the ghost of the quietest of the three sisters does walk along the path leading from her home, or whether the initial story in 1972 was a fabrication, aimed at attracting tourists to a nearby eating house.

The path from the Parsonage to Far Withins certainly must have been used by Emily Jane a great deal when writing her books in the 1830s, and it would hardly be surprising if she really did haunt her old home. There is the same sort of objection to the idea by fanatical supporters of the Brontes as there is to any suggestion that Rudyard Kipling visits Batemans, his former home in Sussex. Nevertheless, during 1975 there have been two reports of the phantom of someone, a 'lady in a longish dark frock', walking towards the building used as a pattern for the Heathcliff residence.

East Riddlesden Hall, OP
Keighley. *Off A 650 – Nearest Station – Keighley*
This is another haunted National Trust property. Originally built in 1640 as a clothier's manor house, though with castellated battlements, it now houses some fine examples of armour and paintings. Standing in the small, rather formal, grounds is a rare example of a mediaeval tithe barn. Also seen in the garden sometimes is a figure of an unidentified lady in a greyish blue dress which trails on the ground. There is supposed to be another ghost of a wool buyer who used to appear in a tiny room over the porch, but no-one has seen him for a long time.

NORTHERN IRELAND
LONDONDERRY
Springhill, OP
Moneymore. *On B18/A29 – Nearest Station – Dungannon (12 miles)*
There is a bit of a mystery as to when this magnificent house was built, but from certain records it seems that it dates from about 1700. There is an even bigger problem in naming the ghost, but she has frequently been heard walking along the landing halfway up the stairs, both by visitors and the warden. This gentleman assured me that he had heard the firm footsteps when the house was completely empty and in broad daylight. Some years ago visitors had seen the vague outline of what is thought to be Jean Hamilton gliding around the stairway and 'wringing her hands in a pitiful fashion. The legend that she is Henrietta Hamilton, whose three children died of smallpox during the Seven Years War, is not borne out by the official history, for there is no lady of that name mentioned in the book. A Jean Hamilton, a widow, married a William Conyngham in 1775, but as far as is known she only had one daughter and that by her previous marriage. A slight coincidence is that Lady Conyngham, a relative of William, owns Balnagown Castle in Scotland which also houses a female ghost. She is described as 'a lady in a grey gown with copper gold hair and green eyes and is 'very gentle and friendly'. She must be striking with such colouring. Long may she haunt.

SCOTLAND
CENTRAL REGION
Stirling Castle, OP
Stirling. *Off/A9 – Nearest Station – Stirling*
Owned by the Secretary of State for Scotland, but open to the public during the summer, this royal and imposing castle stands on a sheer 250ft. crag of basalt overlooking the Forth Valley. Although it looks practically as old as the rocks on which it stands, it was built in the 15th century, replacing earlier forts which commanded the routes across the surrounding plain. It was James V who converted the building into one of the most magnificent in Scotland and it remained a royal palace until 1603 when James VI took the English throne. The female ghost associated with this ancient home is that of a woman in a pink gown, thought to be silk, who walks from the castle to the nearby church at Lady's Rock. It was at this spot that the women of the court used to watch and encourage their menfolk as they jousted and no doubt tossed the caber. There are at least two ideas as to who she is and why she still 'hangs around'. In 1304 when Edward I besieged the castle, one of the occupants is thought to have been smuggled out and it is this young female, the only one of over one hundred and forty occupants to escape, who has to return to look for her husband. But silk was not introduced into Europe until the 16th century. So perhaps the beautiful lady is Queen Mary who was so happy there. One day the lady's true identity may be discovered, but meanwhile she still glides about the castle occasionally.

GRAMPIAN REGION

Crathes Castle, OP
Near Banchory. *Off A 93 – Nearest Station – Aberdeen (14 miles)*

An imposing survivor of Tudor days and claimed to be one of the finest examples of 16th century baronial architecture, Crathes Castle is where the ghostly 'green lady' is well known but hardly ever seen. The building of the castle started in 1553 but it was forty years before it was sufficiently complete for the owners, Katherine and Alexander Burnet, to move in. Their initials are carved on one of the decorative bedheads.

Leading off the Nine Nobles Room visitors find the Green Lady's Room in which the phantom of a young woman wearing a green gown and carrying a baby in her arms has been seen. The story is that the girl became pregnant by one of the servants whilst under the protection of the laird.

The servant was apparently punished by being banished from the castle forever.

Although it is difficult to date the mysterious death of the mother and child, a baby's skeleton was found in a small recess under a hearthstone during the 19th century when modifications were being effected. Added to this, the 4th Baronet in the 18th century is known to have been horrified by the thought of ghosts. Could it be that he was connected with the deaths? It is also possible that the green gown worn by the ghost gives a clue to the identity of the female concerned. Although few people have seen the phantom in the 20th century there is, according to one recent visitor, "a definite feeling of an unhappy person in the room" and another claimed that he had heard the sound of footsteps near the fireplace.

Muchalls Castle, OP
Stonehaven. *Off A92 – Nearest Station – Stonehaven*

Mr. Maurice A. Simpson, owner of the castle, told me that he was slightly disappointed at not having witnessed any phenomena here himself, though during a weekend a few years ago he and a friend were petrified by the feeling of "a frigid icy atmosphere in the withdrawing room. The chill struck right to our bones," he said, "and it was nothing to do with the heating system."

The castle, or rather fortified mansion, was built by Burnetts of Leys in 1619 and contains many notable plaster ceilings and 17th century fireplaces. It is not far from the impressive, awe-inspiring ruins of Dunnottar Castle, the last in Scotland to resist the attacks of the Roundheads. During Lord Robertson's tenancy in 1906 a weekend guest at Muchalls saw a girl in a "yellowish frock titivating in front of a mirror" when he passed one of the bedrooms. He commented on not being last down to dinner and was astonished to learn that he was. There was nobody else in the castle that day.

Although he described the girl he saw as wearing a frock of a yellowish colour it is in fact a girl in green who haunts the castle. Perhaps the young lady's dress is beginning to fade, for another visitor in the early 1970s told me he saw a girl upstairs in what is now a dining room standing facing a wall, touching and patting her hair into place.

"Her dress was terribly old fashioned," he said, "and was nearly a ripe corn colour, not yellow nor green."

An incident which occurred in the grand old days is believed to be the cause of the phantom girl. There is claimed to be an underground passage from the castle to the 'gin' store near the sea. This store was often used for a bit of smuggling. One of the daughters of the house had a boyfriend occupied in this illegal activity and, having sighted his ship coming into the nearby bay, went down the tunnel to meet him.

The lad would be rowing straight into the entrance to the 'store', for the passage opens out as a tidal cave. Unfortunately, somehow the girl was drowned. Whether she fell in or was trapped the story fails to say, but it is this wench who is seen putting the finishing touches to her appearance in preparation for her last meeting with her lover.

Muchalls Castle, Stonehaven, Grampian Region, where a young girl in a yellow dress has been seen.
British Tourist Association.

LOTHIAN

Royal Hotel (now closed) PP
Royal Circus,
Edinburgh.   *Off A 900/A 90 – Nearest Station – Edinburgh*

It cannot be often that such a renowned personality as Dr. John Beloff of the Psychology Department of the University of Edinburgh, past President of the Society for Psychical Research and leading light in the world of parapsychology, finds himself investigating a haunted hotel. Yet in November 1973 the *Scottish Daily Express* reported that this well-known person had spent many hours with a tape recorder and a thermometer examining the evidence and sifting through the reports in an effort to establish whether the building really does house a phantom lady. Three porters had claimed that they had seen a ghost flitting through the corridors of the hotel and described it as a woman dressed in a long white dress with flowing black hair. So scared had they become that the young men not only refused to work except in pairs but had complained to their union. What they expected of the T.U.C. and whether any reply was received or not remains a mystery. Workers could hardly claim 'danger money' for working with something as intangible as a ghost, let alone a female phantom. They might, I supposed, claim 'victimisation', but even this is doubtful. And there it remains for, in common with many serious investigations of this kind, Dr. Beloff was unable to offer a definite verdict. He could not say whether genuine phenomena were occurring or not.

Editor's Note: A popular hotel through into the 1990s, the Royal Circus Hotel was originally two Georgian townhouses subdivided with cornices, false ceilings and a huge lift running through its centre up until conversion to a private dwelling in 2001. This construction may have created strange sounds in the building at times. The Royal Circus hotel was further investigated by American ghost hunter Hans Holzer (1920-2009) in 1974-75 and subsequently outlined in his *Great British Ghost Hunt* (1976). Holzer suggested in a farther garbled account that the ghost was connected to a fire in which one person died in 1973. Most interestingly during the 1920s and 1930s there were sightings of a ghostly figure of a small woman appearing at another property on Royal Circus just a few doors away. Known as the 'grey lady' she was first reported during the time the house was occupied by a Presbyterian Minister the Very Revd Lachlan Maclean. He was succeeded in in 1923 by a Mr Thomson and his family who over the next 16 years saw the figure of the woman in the house and experienced strange object movements. A ghost hunt was held at the property in 1938 organised by Mr J.W. Herries, chief reporter for the *Edinburgh Evening News* a leading Scottish journalist and secretary of the Edinburgh based Committee for the Investigation of Strange Happenings. During this a medium Some details are contained in the archive of the writer Alasdair Alpin MacGregor (1899-1970) deposited at the National Library for Scotland.

STRATHCLYDE
Inverawe House,* PP
Taynuilt.

Overlooked only by the peak of Ben Cruachan, this Scottish manor house has been associated with the clan of the Campbells for some 400 years and the ghost of the golden-haired girl in a green dress for over 100 years. Known as 'Green Jean' she is normally witnessed in the Ticonderoga Room, named after the French fort in America, where Duncan Campbell was killed in 1758.

Some of the estate workers still think that the phantom is of the legendary Maid of Collard but experts state emphatically that there is no reliable evidence to support this idea.

It is only 30 years ago that the captain of Dunstaffnage told of his meeting with Jean. He was putting away his fishing rod and, on glancing upwards, saw "a girl in a green dress walking along the gallery that overlooked the hall." She had beautiful fair hair and looked about 16 years of age. She moved into the Ticonderoga Room and vanished. In 1912 loud screams had been heard coming from the empty room. Another witness was Robert Ross who saw his flock of sheep stop to let the phantom through their ranks. Mrs. Ross has also experienced phenomena associated with the ghostly girl.

In 1967 'Jean' made herself felt to a guest in the affected bedroom and Mrs. Campbell Preston told me that, although neither she nor her son-in-law have seen the girl, her 14-year-old grandson "senses her presence." The belief is that 'Jean' only shows herself to bona fide Campbells, but I haven't checked on the identity of the latest reported witnesses. These were some workers on a nearby hydro-electrical development who claim that they saw the figure of the girl on the Inverawe Road, who vanished as she neared the house.

TAYSIDE
Glamis Castle,* OP
Glamis.

This castle of mysterious secrets, of legendary horror and remarkable history must be one of the best known in Scotland and the most haunted. Scene of the murder of Duncan in Macbeth, Glamis is basically much older than the 17th century re-modelling which offers a 'French chateau facade' to visitors. Some of the walls are 15 feet thick and there must be several secret rooms yet to be discovered. Antony Hippisley Coxe says that some workmen who have revealed sealed doorways during modifications and repairs have, it is claimed, been given cash rewards on condition that they emigrate. The author of *Haunted Britain* also tells that the latest theory regarding the 'secret horror' relates to some form of documentary record which involves Queen Mary of Scots. The fascinating and intriguing mystery continues. The 'White Lady' who haunts the Clock Tower and glides around the main avenue could be that of Janet, wife of the sixth Lord Glamis. In 1537 she was put to the stake at Edinburgh for witchcraft.

Nearly 25 years ago, in 1951, I had the great delight of visiting the castle to meet one of the residents and was made slightly apprehensive by the strange and complete silence within the huge building. It was weird and chilling, due no doubt to imagination, though I was convinced that my two companions and I were not alone.

Our hostess, Mrs. Hunter, told us of crashes that they heard in the oldest part of the building and the sounds of men stamping and shouting coming from an empty locked room close to the top of the western tower. But I was pleased to learn that something had also been seen by Mrs. Hunter. "It was the figure of the Grey Lady in the chapel," she told us, "I was in there a fortnight ago intending to arrange some flowers and there she was, kneeling at one of the pews."

It is a pity that nobody knows who the figure is or why she haunts the chapel. She has been seen by many people including James Wentworth Day who writes, "I walked into the chapel one day to examine a picture and turned round to see the 'Grey Lady' on her knees. I just tiptoed away."

Another phantom experienced by the Hunters was that seen peering from a window in the old tower. The face of a woman who looked very ill was described by some friends when walking in the grounds. A second later they all heard horrible shrieks and the face vanished. "We only wish we knew who it was," was the comment as we were handed some delicious pancakes.

Meggernie Castle, PP
Glen Lyon.
In a remote area of what used to be known as Perthshire, surrounded by mountains with names unpronounceable to the Sassenachs such as Cam Chreag and Meall Luaidhe, lies this 15th century fortress with what might be one of the most horrific female phantoms yet. Whether she is still active is not known, but not so very long ago she certainly made a very disturbing appearance to a Dr. MacKay of Aberfeldy.

It is thought that the first report of the haunting dates from 1862 when two friends were staying in the castle in adjoining rooms. They found a sealed doorway connecting the rooms, from which in the small hours issued the upper half of a woman. The apparition was seen by both men, though in different rooms at practically the same time. On discussing the matter over the breakfast table they learnt that a few days earlier a kitchen maid had seen the lower half of a woman flitting through the corridors. It had also been seen in a nearby churchyard.

A week later one of the guests saw the face of the ghost looking in at a window in one of the ground floor corridors and described her as 'sad and beautiful.' It slowly faded as he watched it, but it was clear enough for him to recognise the face as that of the weird creature who had entered the bedroom seven days earlier.

Nearly forty years later Dr MacKay had a very similar experience. He saw a female head and shoulders wafting around one of the bedroom walls near the ceiling. He was not in the haunted room but in the room immediately above it. The legend is that one of the Menzies who owned the castle became so jealous of his beautiful wife that he murdered her. In trying to hide the corpse he cut it into two parts. The two portions were both hidden in an old chest of drawers which stood in a doorway between two bedrooms. Later he managed to remove the lower half of the body and buried it in a nearby graveyard but, on returning to collect the remaining section, was himself killed by an unknown assailant.

Alasdair Alpin MacGregor gives much more fascinating detail of the haunting in his *Phantom Footsteps* (Robert Hale) and it is understood that the churchyard is still visited by 'half a lady.'

WALES

ANGLESEY

Penrhos Nature Reserve, OP
Near Holyhead. *On A5 – Nearest Station – Holyhead*
The only part of Wales that is non-mountainous, for the only peak is a mere 700 feet above sea level, Anglesey is the site where the Romans suffered one of their highest casualty lists at the hands of the Druids. Alfred Mills, chairman of the Isle of Anglesey Society for Psychic Research, tells me that the figure of a 'grey lady' walks near Point 13 of the scenic nature trail through this attractive reserve, but who she is no-one knows. Another site of her appearance is near the old 'betting stand.' She could well be associated with the cruciform Church of St. Cybi, a striking building with a 13th century chancel.

The Reserve is some two miles east of Holyhead and provides a wonderful opportunity for enjoying a delightful country walk through the forest before reaching the town on Holy Island.

Here, in a building in Station Street, a ghost of an old lady dressed in long period clothes has been seen and recognised as a previous tenant. Not far from the caravan site at Trearddur Bay, two miles to the south of Holyhead, the figure of another woman has been seen close to a cricket pitch and identified as that of a lady drowned many years ago.

Llanerchymedd, OP
Llangefni-Benllech Road. *On B5109 – Nearest Station – Holyhead*
On the south side of this country road, close to the California Inn, a young girl was killed when horse riding some years ago, according to Alfred Mills of Holyhead. Several residents and the occasional visitor to the island have seen the vague figure of a young woman sitting on a stone stile which stands at the spot where she was thrown from her mount.

DYFED

Manorbier Castle,* OP
Pembroke. *On B4585 (off A41 39) – Nearest Station – Tenby (4 miles)*
Sir Francis Dashwood in his leaflet about this attractive fort uses the words of Gerald de Barry, Archdeacon of Brecon, to describe the area as "the pleasantest spot in Wales." I find it difficult to disagree, having spent many delightful hours here. The Welsh call the castle 'Maenor Pyrr' (Pyrrus's abode). The same Pyrr, a Celtic Abbot, was known to have lived on the offshore island of Caldey in the 6th century.

The oldest parts of the castle are the round tower and ruined square tower together with the Baronial Hall, all of 12th century construction. The first record of Manorbier is the death in 1130 of Odo de Barri, a Norman who held the lordship under Gerald de Windsor.

The de Barri's held the manor until the 14th century when it became a gift to various Royal favourites, one of these being the mother of Henry VII. It eventually passed to the Philips family and finally to Lady Dunsany. But who is the lady in a long dark gown who glides down the entrance drive to the gatehouse?

I learnt of her when staying in a nearby hotel and was told that she is seen about twice a year, usually in September and mainly by tourists or visitors. I am slightly suspicious of tourist attractions but was assured that the mystery woman is hardly ever spoken about. The Welsh are very reticent about ghostly matters and certainly she is not a figment of somebody's imagination.

A member of the hotel staff admitted that she had seen the drychiolaeth apparition which vanishes a few feet from the gateway and knew of "two or three others who have witnessed the lady in black."

The reason for visitors seeing more of her than locals, I was told, is that, as is the case with all such attractive places, the people who live in the locality hardly ever visit it. One of the most recent witnessings was when a party of five school teachers visited the castle and three of them saw the phantom. The two others are still puzzling over their inability to see the woman who passed within a few feet of their colleagues.

POWYS

Red Bridge, OP
Newtown Road. *OnA492 – Nearest Station – Caersws*

On a Thursday night in November 1972 Mr. Bill Hopkins, then headmaster of the Churchstoke Primary School, was returning to his home at Hyssington, having been lecturing at a WEA meeting in Llangurig, when he noticed a hitchhiker at the side of the road. He had just reached Llanidloes and pulled in to ask the young man where he wanted to go.

He replied "Newtown" (about 14 miles to the north). Just as he was about to get into the car the potential passenger asked the time and was told "9.50." Mr. Hopkins was a little surprised at the response for the lad said, "Thank you. In that case I won't come." Slightly aggrieved, but puzzled, the teacher drove on.

In his letter to Mr. Colin Smith of Birmingham, to whom must go my thanks for his help in this case, Mr. Hopkins continued by saying that it was a clear and fine night with a full moon.

About a mile and a half outside Llanidloes the road crosses the railway and runs alongside the river Severn at a point known as Red Bridge. Quoting directly from the letter :

"I was travelling at about 45-50 mph when suddenly out of the hedge stepped a woman. She was outlined by the headlights. I braked, the car swerved and skidded. I can recall saying out loud, 'my God, I'm going to kill this woman.'

I braced myself for the crunch. There was none. I was aware of a mist-like substance passing either side of the car and reforming into a woman."

The impression was that Mr. Hopkins had driven right through the figure. When he first saw her she was looking at him through the front windscreen and then gazing at the back of the car through the rear window.

What mystified the teacher even more was that he could still see the figure behind his car even though there were no headlamps to "show her up." He was not aware of her costume nor the period of her clothing, only that the woman had "large soulful eyes." On arriving at Llandinam he called in at a pub to steady his nerves and, on telling his experience to a group in the bar, was surprised to learn from another customer that he had experienced an identical incident some months earlier and at the same spot on the road.

Mr. Hopkins concludes his reports by saying that he has no doubt that what he saw was a ghost. Mr. Smith wrote to the Lion Hotel in Llandinam to try to obtain further information, but they denied any knowledge of the haunting and referred to a local press report which featured the story of Mr. Hopkins.

The report in the County Times and Express (of Mid-Wales) dated June 2nd 1973, seven months after the incident, quoted two other people, Mr. and Mrs. Gwilym Swain of Llandinam, who had a similar experience six years previously.

"A woman just stepped out from the ditch," said Mr. Swain, "straight into the path of my car. There was no impact and she disappeared."

Editor's note: A few months after *Phantom Ladies* was published, a number of people wrote describing similar experiences in the same locality. A Mrs Gladys Bennett of Craven Arms described how 'When on the Llandidnoes side of the railway bridge a ghost-like figure suddenly appeared to come straight at me.' She had been walking home with a friend to her home at Dolwen but her companion saw nothing.(In *Ghosts of Today* (1980) by Andrew Green).

Further Reading/References

A Ghost Hunter's Game Book J. Wentworth Day. Muller 1958
Folklore, Myths & Legends of Britain (1973) Readers Digest
Ghost Hunter's Road Book John Harries. Muller 1968
Ghost Tour Jack Hallam. Wolfe 1967
Ghosts & Legends of the Wiltshire Countryside Kathleen Wiltshire. Compton Russell 1973
Ghosts and Witches J. Wentworth Day. Batsford 1954
Ghosts of an Ancient City John V. Mitchell. Cerialis Press 1974
Ghosts of Dorset, Devon & Somerset Rodney Legg, Mary Collier & Tom Perrott. Dorset Publishing 1974
Ghosts of London Jack Hallam. Wolfe. 1975
Ghosts of the South East Andrew Green. David & Charles 1976
Ghosts of the South West James Turner. David & Charles 1975
Haunted Britain Antony Hippisley Coxe. Pan 1973
Haunted Inns of Britain Jack Hallam. Wolfe 1972
Murderer's London Ivan Butler. Robert Hale 1973
North Country Squire Sir John Craster. Oriel Press 1958
Our Haunted Kingdom Andrew Green. Fontana 1975
Phantom Footsteps Alasdair Alpin MacGregor. Robert Hale 1959
Plague House Papers Robert Neumann. Hutchinson 1969
Science & the Spook George Owen & Victor Sims. Dobson 1971
Sometimes into England James Turner. Cassell 1970
Stately Ghosts of England Diana Norman & Tom Corbett. Muller 1963
The Home Counties S. P. B. Mais. Batsford 1942
The Realm of Ghosts Eric Maple. Pan 1964
The World's Strangest Ghost Stories R. Thurston Hopkins. Cedar Books 1955
White Lady of the Priest Hole Article by Winifred I. Haward in Country Life 1974

PART TWO

Aspects of Phantom Ladies

By Alan Murdie

CHAPTER ONE

PHANTOM LADIES FROM THE PERSPECTIVE OF PSYCHICAL RESEARCH

In compiling *Phantom Ladies* Andrew Green provides a survey and snapshot of haunted sites across the length of the British Isles during the mid-1970s. There is no doubt that both the 'Phantom Ladies' of the title and other ghostly manifestations were being widely reported to the extent that the number of entries could have been greatly increased with further research, and given that the percentage of cases that come, rather like crime, to the attention of researchers and the press is only a small fraction of the total number of paranormal experiences.

It may be thought that much of the evidence would not meet the strictest standards of psychical research but it may often be forgotten that the conduct of research and investigation was often far-more laborious in pre-internet days requiring physical searches of press reports and archives backed up by interviews conducted in person or communications via telephone and post. It may also be noted that the quality of many witness reports and cases being reported in local media was much higher than today.

A decline in the quality of witness evidence and a decline in full-formed human apparitions (both male and female) was noted in the following decade by Dr Peter Hallson writing in the *Journal* of the Society for Psychical Research in 1986. Hallson compared cases of apparitions collected in the Victorian era with many modern reports observing "the present-day series and supporting testimony is very much poorer in quality. Reports from Victorian days were clear and well-defined. To-day they are often vague and sometimes silly such as stories of black shadows, indescribable odours and attacks by evil spirits."[1] However, there has not been a fading away of ghost experiences as might be thought, for over the decades since *Phantom Ladies* was published, people have continued to see, experience and perhaps more importantly to report female apparitions, both at the locations in this book and at many other places.

Before considering the scope for further investigation and re-investigation of these cases, it is worth examining in more detail the types of phenomena which are being consistently reported. Although the quality of reports might not often be high, the large number of separated reports show marked similarities between them, suggestive of their being underlying patterns to such phenomena, various 'signals in the noise' which emerge.

The existence of such patterns in widely separated cases is indicative of an underlying reality to the phenomenon, it being improbable that separated witnesses with no known connection between them would yield strikingly similar accounts and descriptions. Termed similar fact evidence in a judicial context, this principle is used as a means of proof in courts of law concerning events occurring outside laboratory and clinical conditions in the wider world. From the patterns that emerge in accounts it may be possible to draw some tentative conclusions about the nature of the experience and the phenomenon itself.

Visual Apparitions

Female apparitions where a recognisably female (or perceived as such) apparition is seen at a certain location predominate in reported cases throughout *Phantom Ladies* as examples show: e.g. "When I saw her, she was in Katherine Parr's nursery, but did not give me the slightest feeling of fear. I thought she was a real person until she vanished as I approached her."(Janet, Sudeley Castle, Gloucestershire); "I saw the figure of a woman in white standing in a corner of the bedroom and as I looked she slowly vanished, just faded into the wall," (Mrs. Springthe Royal Oak, Havant, Hampshire).

Contemporary surveys conducted in the years before *Phantom Ladies* was published confirm this predominance of visual sightings as an overall trend. The *Journal of Paraphysics* published by the now-defunct Downton Paraphysical Laboratory in Wiltshire undertook a number of studies of cases reported in UK newspapers in the decade before *Phantom Ladies* appeared. These were published in summary form in a series of 'Classified Directories' with a rudimentary statistical analysis. Their national survey of reports in UK newspapers conducted between 1967-1971 and then between 1972-74 discovered an average of 47% of cases involved a human figure, with those identified as female being slightly more common than those deemed male. These findings were in line with a smaller national study and analysis of trends in hauntings conducted over six months between January to June 2007 by the Spontaneous Cases Committee of the Society for Psychical Research. Analysing 106 reports it was discovered 43% of reported hauntings involved a human apparition, with the figure being considered male in 19% of hauntings and female in 23% confirming this pattern.[2]

The figure may be fully formed and indistinguishable from a living woman. In other cases the form is transparent or partially formed, sometimes only a part of the body such as the legs or face alone. More difficult to ascribe gender are sightings involving apparitions in which a human form cannot be discerned, such as shapes, lights, luminous patches, shadows or other visual anomalies – though occasionally someone may describe a shape as a 'male-looking' or 'female-looking'. Additionally, some sites generate reports of non-human apparitions, including animals and inanimate objects, as with the 'tall woman, a young child and a black dog' claimed at Swan Pool.

The precise mechanism operating with all classes of visual apparitions remains a problem for psychical researchers despite many decades of contemplation, partly because the precise working of ordinary perception remains subject to many uncertainties. The two alternatives presented for the data are that either apparitions are objective and part of the visual spectrum reflecting real light photons which impinge on the observer's retina, or else the whole scene is produced at a higher level inside the brain and is an illusion and mimicry of normal optical effects. Since the 1890s the majority of psychical researchers have considered that such experiences are hallucinatory but occur with persons who are not dreaming, ill, mentally unwell or under the influence of drugs, when they see a figure or object which could not be that of a real person or object.

Some of these hallucinations may be termed 'veridical' in that they exhibit correspondences, not easy to explain, with external events (i.e. coinciding with a death at the time or previously at the same location). These appear to transmit information not obtainable through normal sensory channels at that moment or show consistencies between multiple and widely separated percipients when the same ghost manifests on different occasions, sometimes weeks, months or even years apart. There is much suggestive evidence that certain species of domestic animals such as dogs, cats and horses display sensitivity to apparitions and haunting phenomena.

Auditory phenomena

In a considerable number of cases the Phantom Lady is heard as opposed to being seen, although the two experiences rarely come together (few apparitions are heard speaking in modern cases). In some cases the gender of the apparition is purely assumed on the basis of a tradition or story since it is not possible to ascribe sex to most purely auditory phenomena as Green acknowledged, a factor complicating analysis of reports from premises where it is considered there is more than one ghost active. This difficulty was encountered at Blithfield Hall near Rugeley, Staffordshire, reputedly haunted by a pair of males and a pair of female ghosts together with a further phenomenon that "is merely a noise, of unknown gender". The mysterious sound was that of rustling skirts "which could be either that of a woman's gown or a priest's robes." This also applies in cases where footsteps are heard e.g. at the former Manor House restaurant "Late one night I heard footsteps upstairs," Mr. Dryden said. "I thought someone had been locked in accidentally and went to investigate, but there was no-one there.' In some cases we are probably faced with a guess by the witness that the footsteps were those of a woman rather than a man, or these may be accompanied the sounds of a swishing skirt which is treated as determinative for the witness, from suggestive sounds from perceptions of footwear or an altogether more indefinable sense of presence. More reliable are likely to be cases where a voice is heard which is recognisable or identified as that of a woman.

Tactile

In a number of cases witnesses report the sensation of physical interaction and being touched by a presence. e.g. "One night Mrs. Todd was woken at "about 3 o'clock by what felt like someone touching my forehead very lightly" (Lorton Hall, Cumbria) or Robert Greenway who was sketching the Hall and told Colin Smith that he kept feeling that his neck was being stroked by "an icy hand" at Grimshaw Hall. Tactile hallucinations are for the most part even more trivial than auditory ones, and there is, naturally, not much variety in them. Often they are quite vague and fleeting and not associated with any definite idea of an external object; but possibly the lighter the touch, the more prone the witness may be to interpreting it as a female contact. Sometimes, however, the impression is more definite and less easy to forget as with a heavy blow, a shaking of the body and, in a few cases, where the feeling is more subtle such as the sensation of a kiss.

Nothing in *Phantom Ladies* quite approaches the sensation of a full body embrace of a naked woman experienced by the Revd. Merryweather at the manor house near the now demolished haunted church at Langenhoe in Essex, scene of numerous phenomena from the 1930s onwards until its demolition in 1962.[3]

Some tactile cases involve sleep paralysis and a hypnoid state of catalepsy which in other cultural contexts is often ascribed to a hostile female presence, dubbed 'the Old Hag' ascribed to a malevolent female presence encountered in a heightened state of suggestibility.[4]

Olfactory.

Smells can be ghostly, for example the witness at who perceived the perfume of 'lily of the valley' at the same time as a sighting (Bramshill Police College, Hampshire). Historically and today, women make greater use of scents and perfumes than males, so an inexplicable fragrance is likely to be considered female. Andrew Green made the point that smells were differently perceived by different witnesses, so a degree of subjectivity and personal interpretation may creep in.[5]

Sense of a presence

In a number of cases a sense of a presence of an invisible woman is engaged. 'Mrs. Cole told me that although she never actually saw the phantom she was often aware of "a friendly presence" in the hallway (Pashley Manor Ticehurst, Sussex).

Another example included was a site where, 'Visitors have often mentioned the feeling of a presence in the dining room and all agree that she is "so sweet, like a favourite granny" (at Wray Farm, Reigate, Surrey). In other cases, there may be an intangible sense or feeling accompanying an experience involving another sense impression. In this regard, I can say this regarding my own experience of seeing an apparition in 2011 which I recognised as a woman known to me. I knew exactly who it was although I could make out little more than a shape and profile in the darkness. This depressive feeling stayed with me well into the morning, hours after seeing the apparition which disappeared within 30 seconds.[6]

Temperature variation

At a number of haunted sites witnesses report the sense of variation of temperature e.g. S.P.B. Mais, "I visited the church in 1975 and noticed an inexplicable and rather sudden drop in temperature when about eight feet from the Clayton memorial" (St Mary the Virgin Church, Bletchingley Surrey) or the account from Craster Tower, Northumberland 'the atmosphere becoming eerie and cold'.

Electrical interference, equipment malfunction and object movements

A range of physical phenomena are recorded, especially lights being switched on; e.g. at Chadderton, Greater Manchester, where 'Switches and lights would be turned on or off and tools would be moved'; lights of a fruit machine coming on without explanation at the former Pussycat Club in Plymouth. Some are poltergeist in nature e.g. "heavy ornaments literally jumped off the mantelpiece" and a doll, torn to shreds at the former Samuel Pepys Pub near Kettering, Northamptonshire. One of the more unusual noted is the appearance of 'the perfect outline of a naked foot in a pile of soot behind a fire-screen' at Craster Tower.

Photographic anomalies

A small number of anomalous images recorded on cameras are mentioned at a number of sites. For example, at Berry Pomeroy Castle in Devon it was reported that the unexplained profile of a woman was obtained. However the number is small and with the exception of claims of the Brown Lady of Raynham Hall the photographers did not see anything unusual at the time. As *Phantom Ladies* was compiled before the arrival of digital photography, images would have been recorded on physical film and occasionally on analogue TV and would suggest an effect involving the electromagnetic spectrum.

What is noticeable with alleged ghost photographs both before and since the arrival of digital photography is that the images produced as suspected ghosts do not represent some of the previously detailed descriptions of apparitions recorded by eye witnesses. In the decades since there has been a vast expansion of CCTV coverage in public places and many private sites but little in the way of convincing pictures have emerged.

This raises the strong possibility that many alleged ghost photographs are artefacts produced by the camera itself. Similarly, images obtained on camera phones can be attributed to artefacts produced by the camera (for example, images taken at Hampton Court in 2015). This Rorschach ink-blot quality means much depends on personal interpretation. The possibility remains that some of these images may be the effects associated with the ghost experience for the user of the camera or a form of equipment breakdown also encountered with sound recording.[7]

Altogether this range of persistent anomalies at multiple locations is sufficient to suggest something is going on, it is not yet possible to form any complete and comprehensive theory as to what lies behind phenomena. Nonetheless, within these diverse accounts are further patterns which Green noticed were discernible, spread over different sites across many years.

Ghosts of the living

It may come as a surprise that Green considered that up to 40% of ghosts in his estimation were potentially those of still living people rather than representing psychic traces of the dead. Green took the view that most examples of what are classed as hauntings could be explained by telepathy or psychokinesis produced by the living, rising to up to 60% of reports if poltergeist phenomena were included.

This raises the possibility that at least some female ghosts are appearances of women still alive and wrongly assumed to be dead, for instance the figure of a young woman seen inside a Public Telephone Box in Station Road, Erdington, Birmingham.

A contemporary case involving a phantom woman who was very much alive at the time was collected by Andrew Green too late for inclusion in *Phantom Ladies* at the now demolished Ancient Britain pub in Mile End in December 1975. The ghost who was seen twice was identified as Mrs Florrie Clark a former but still living landlady of the pub. One witness was the landlord Jim Marling who had seen the ghost standing in the cellar with her arms folded. The previous tenant had also seen Mrs Clark sitting at the bar. In fact, she had not set foot in the pub for seven years but said she was always dreaming about the place. On learning of the situation, the *Dagenham and East Barking Post* took Mrs Clark to the pub to meet Jim Marling and they were photographed having a drink together. A telling comment from Mrs Clark was published, "I was landlady for more than 14 years and was very happy. I often wish I was back." It is easy to see how this may have been mistaken as a ghost of a dead person in different circumstances.[8]

Telepathy and the state of mind of the witness

Examples of ghosts of the living encouraged Green into taking the view that telepathy between the living could account for a number of cases of apparitions. He stated: "Before pursuing the investigation of a case I would suggest that a major requirement is an understanding of telepathy. Although telepathy is still a matter of controversy and to some people remains unproven there is, I feel, sufficient tangible evidence and personal experience to accept that thought transference does occur."[9]

This echoed the views of early psychical researchers who studied hundreds of cases of recognised apparitions typically seen by friends or relatives of the person who appeared as a ghost. Subsequently it was discovered that these apparitions coincided closely in time with the person perceived dying or suffering some kind of trauma. Numerous examples were collected by the early Society for Psychical Research and published in a two volume work *Phantasms of the Living* (1886) by Frederic Myers, Edmund Gurney and Frank Podmore. The authors theorised that these apparitions arose from telepathy between the dying person and their friend or relative. Such appearances were labelled 'crisis apparitions' in 1946 by Dr Donald West and the term stuck. *Phantom Ladies* did not tackle specimens of this category because they were one-off sightings and experiences. The numbers of crisis apparitions have declined since 1945, perhaps because of changing patterns of death or because of more immediate systems of communication such as mobile phones, and so on although they still occasionally continue today.

Because of their once-only nature, crisis cases were not included in *Phantom Ladies* but Green believed that during times of stress, such as physical pain or emotional upset, the brain is able to projects a telepathic image beyond itself and that this might, in the alternative, form the basis of a haunting at a location.

Relaxed state of mind

Green noticed that few, if any, people ever saw their female ghost when in a state of high alertness on investigations or when individuals were thinking of ghosts or when deliberately searching them out. Generally, visual experiences were much more common when people were absorbed in daily living activities and routine tasks (e.g., at work, seated in a restaurant, or touring a site but not thinking about ghosts at the time). On asking witnesses what they recalled thinking about at the time he found they mostly answered that they were generally in a reduced state of alertness and arousal and not concentrating upon anything. Generally, he found the witness was as '…usual in such instances, thinking of "nothing in particular" as with the witness who saw a figure gliding among the gravestones at St. Nicholas Church, Pluckley. This was consistent with experiments in telepathy which suggest that when a person is in a more receptive state and relaxed the best results occur at least as regards the 'receiver' of the images.[10]

The connection of sightings with semi-waking states

The tendency of apparitions to appear when the percipient was in a highly relaxed state (e.g., daydreaming, awaking or going to sleep, sleeping, or meditation) was particularly pronounced. This pattern has been noted in the literature. Such states have been clinically labelled hypnagogic (half asleep) and hypnopompic (half awake) states with the same connection made by Andrew MacKenzie in *Hauntings and Apparitions* (1982) who found that about one-third of apparitional experiences occurred just before or after sleep, or when the percipient was in a state of relaxation.[11] A number of cases in *Phantom Ladies* show such experiences occurring when the percipient is alone, often when resting in bed. Experiences vary from dream-like or unrealistic impressions to vivid and realistic figures mistaken for actual persons. Exemplifying the link was the mother who was tenant in a flint cottage in Hayes Lane in Kenley, Surrey who '…was woken shortly after falling asleep by the sound of her baby screaming…. she was appalled to see a misty shape in the form of a woman bending over the cot'.

Another was the experience of the White Lady seen at the Royal Oak pub in 1969 by Mrs Spring who recalled that she "….heard someone moving around and assumed it was my young daughter who had been known to sleepwalk. So I got out of bed to lead her back and saw the ghost".

Other examples included the Flight Lieutenant at Chicksands Priory, Bedfordshire, who woke up at 3.45 am, switched on the light and saw "a woman with a ruddy face and untidy hair, wearing a dark dress with a white lace collar" and the incidents at the Ettington Park Country Club In Warwickshire where "Two members of a Devon football team slept in Rooms 21 and 22 and both claimed that they had seen 'something funny'. One woke to find someone leaning over him"…. All these confirm the fact that the point between sleeping and wakefulness is a conducive one for seeing a ghost. Similar results have been reported for other types of entity and spontaneous experiences.[12]

Tendency of ghosts to fade with time

Green considered that some ghosts had a 'half-life' in the sense of the image fading away in time, with few ghosts being reported that were more than 400 years old. In some instances this can be seen to occur in stages and may be even more noticeable over the years with female ghosts. In his *Ghost Hunting A Practical Guide* (1973, 2016) Green describes how during the 18th century, the ghost of a woman in red shoes, a red gown and a black head-dress was observed in a little-visited corridor of a mansion.

Many years passed before the apparition was seen again, and by then, perhaps because the original full description of the ghost was not then known, it appeared as a female in a pink dress, pink shoes and grey head-dress. She was not witnessed again until the mid-19th century, when the figure had dwindled down to "a lady in a white gown and with grey hair. Just before the Second World War all that was reported was "the sound of a woman walking along the corridor and the swish of her dress". In 1971, shortly before the demolition of the property involved, workmen "felt a presence in one of the old corridors".[13] This suggests the possibility that phenomena may evolve and change with time. A similar process may have been at work with Castle Rushen on the Isle of Man. Castle Rushen's Grey Lady seems to be fading away or transforming into a shadow now known as the 'Black Lady' or 'just a mist' when I made enquiries at the site in September 2012.

Green speculated that the ghost is recharged from time to time by being seen, leaving a possibility that if this is not done, then the phantom will gradually fade away. The continuation of a haunting over a very long period (say 250 years) might be explicable by regeneration which he believed could be linked with a drop in temperature. It would appear that for a mentally created image or phantom to be witnessed over a period may require re-energising by heat extracted from the atmosphere. This was suggested by 'a common feature in paranormal occurrences is a very rapid drop in temperature'this sudden chill is always experienced before the appearance of 'Agnes' at Woolston Hall Country Club, in Essex or from the individual is necessary, or that emotional energy – such as the shock or fear at seeing a ghost – could in some way energise it. In other cases, a person may feel a loss of physical energy from their bodily system.

Theories of Ghosts

Broadly speaking, psychical research theories concerning ghosts and hauntings have fallen into two classes – those viewing ghosts as enduring mental images generated by once living people detectable by sensitive individuals and those considering ghosts as being spirits or a survival of a portion of a once-living human personality. These theories themselves having been further refined by proposers but without definite proof for either of them.[14]

A case can be made for both viewpoints. Parapsychologists and psychical researchers generally tend to favour ghosts and apparitions being impersonal images. Green's view was that ghosts were entirely without consciousness like the images in a film or photograph. His view had some similarities with a theory advanced by Frederic Myers (1847 – 1901) one of the founders of psychical research. In his *Human Personality and Survival After Death* (1903) Myers considered ghosts might be 'a manifestation of persistent personal energy, or….an indication that some kind of force is being exercised in some way connected with a person previously known on earth" adding "this force, or influence, which after a man's death creates a phantasmal impression of him, may indicate no continuing action on his part, but may be some residue of the force or energy he generated while yet alive".[15] Thus, it constituted a trace or imprint of consciousness but with no self-awareness. On the evidence, there is generally little sign of personality that emerges in hauntings with simply appearing or figure repeating without showing any awareness or interaction with of observers. In other words the apparition may just be a residue of a personality, an emotional complex that needs airing existing in some form which we cannot yet conceive.

Traces of once-living personalities?

Green postulated an electromagnetic basis to these lingering mental images. His theory envisaged that energy was released at the moment of death by the person whose apparition was later seen. Alternatively, it could be generated by a living person in a state of high emotion or stress and who could leave an emotional imprint on his/her surroundings whilst still alive. His hypothesis proposed mental images were electromagnetic in nature and were persistent, in that they could continue after the death of the person who originally created them. This energy went on to 'haunt' the premises and could then be picked up mentally and perceived by sensitive people and animals.[16]

The psychical researcher George N.M. Tyrrell (1879-1952) outlined a mental images theory of apparitions in a lecture delivered to a meeting of the Society for Psychical Research held, appropriately enough, on the evening of Hallowe'en 1938 and later set down in a book *Apparitions* (1942, 1952). His ideas derived from an extensive analysis of cases collected by the Society for Psychical Research over more than fifty years and visits to haunted houses. Tyrrell maintained ghosts to be mental projections produced by telepathy and constructed within the mind of the witness or percipient. His view was that an apparition represented a perceptual expression of a mental imagewhich he termed an 'idea-pattern'operating on, or through, the subconscious mind of the witness. Periods when the mind was relaxed or when on the verges of sleep were most conducive to this process.

Tyrrell viewed this as a two-stage process. The earliest stage is some ways the most mysterious – the apparition arises at some level in the unconscious, Tyrrell suggested that paranormal cognition occurs at the first stage by telepathic contact occurring on an unconscious level. Sometimes the idea that generates an apparition originates with a living person, in others with a person as they die (so-called crisis apparitions) and in some cases possibly involves an idea lingering after the physical death of its originator. It is not a cut-and-dried 'message', but a relatively general idea or 'theme'. This theme is then 'signalled' up into consciousness which the mind duly develops in the second stage where the information is then processed into consciousness, through dreams and certain waking experiences that resemble ordinary cognition and perception, that of 'seeing' a ghost.[17]

In this second stage, the signal undergoes creative dramatization in the mind, sometimes highly symbolic (e.g. a person who has drowned being seen dripping with water). This image is worked up and coloured by the unconscious and is then projected on to the 'screen' of the subject's surroundings and 'seen' as a ghost.

Labelling these two stages Tyrrell humorously dubbed them 'the producer' and 'the stage-carpenter'. In his model, the 'stage carpenter' element is responsible for the detailed imaginative dramatization, as within dreams – an accomplished dramatist, costumier, make-up artist, director, editor, location manager, stunt and fight-arranger and animal trainer as the case may be, providing, at its best, life-like and full-blown figures complete with features, apparitional clothes and accompaniments (e.g. horses, carriages, cars or walking sticks) to match. In the process, this answers the old chestnut 'Where do the ghostly clothes that ghosts wear come from?". The answer is that their clothing and costumes are as hallucinatory as the rest of the apparition itself.[18]

Ultimately, Tyrrell concluded: "The work of constructing the [apparitional] drama is done in certain regions of the personality which lie below the conscious level" and arguing that it involves "something between the two extremes of consciousness and mechanism . . . which is to a certain extent like an idea, and ... to a certain extent like a pattern" with the apparition "... the sensory expression of the idea-pattern".[19]

To extend Tyrrell's metaphor further we might say that the conscious mind is then in the position of being the theatregoer or spectator who watches the apparitional drama created by the unconscious.

Needless to say this is only the sketchiest of hypotheses and how the mechanics of this might work is not possible to determine. From a rigid scientific perspective, Tyrrell's theory was very much a case of 'new ghosts for old', replacing traditional entities or spirits with nebulous terms couched in scientific phraseology and carrying the idea of telepathy over into an unseen world and a dimension after death.

One obvious (hitherto unanswered) question is just where such idea patterns would be stored in the environment and the period between sightings. Tyrrell himself also questioned whether accounts of a Grey Lady were or could be taken literally as an expression of a human personality as it often seemed that it was a ready and 'all too convenient' explanation just given to otherwise unexplainable phenomena to fill an explanatory void with otherwise anonymous manifestations.

Spirits of the Dead?

In contrast, many amateur ghost hunters – who tend to be far more active in site investigationoften uncritically embrace the idea of unquiet spirits being present at localities. These envisage the surviving presence of a personality in discarnate form.

Their ideas may overlap and appear indistinguishable from the beliefs of spiritualists who consider that communication with the dead is readily possible through mediums and senses. Many believers in the spirit hypothesis readily imbue ghosts with a consciousness and awareness and consider a form of communication can be established with them. But on occasions the experiences seem targeted to individuals and signs of a personality do manifest as with the movement of objects.

Until 2018 Cambridge King's Parade opposite King's College incorporated Britain's only haunted vegetarian restaurant, *The Rainbow Café* which was located in a spacious former cellar below a row of 17th century buildings. Previously, it formed part of a building owned by Mrs Sadie Barnett for about fifty years before her death in August 1991. Sadie enjoyed a fearsome reputation as a landlady who kept student lodgers under a strict regime on her premises. (There was no truth in the rumour that she murdered her first husband and buried the body in the wall of the cellar where the Rainbow would be set up). Several members of staff, including a chef, quit because of the appearances.

At about 10pm, early in August 2003, close to the anniversary of the death of Sadie Barnett, Mrs Sharon Meijland, the proprietor was locking up the building when she felt what she described as being like a physical push as though she was being forced from the building. One chef quit over sightings of an apparition and in August 2008 Joshua, Mrs Meijland's son, glimpsed a figure which he thought was a customer near the stairs but when he looked again a few seconds later no-one was present. More often footsteps descend the outside stairs, typically at about 10pm when the premises were quiet. Staff would go to look for a late customer, but all too often there was no-one to be seen. These phenomena carried on periodically up until the Rainbow Cafe closed in November 2018.[20]

Even where manifestations are interpreted as signs of communication what emerges is often fragmented and nonsensical in content, suggestive more of a living person in the grip of dementia and showing no proper awareness. Swiss psychologist Carl Jung (1875–1961) described a personal encounter originally published in Germany by Fanny Moser in her book *Spuk* (1950). In 1920, Jung was spending a weekend at a reputedly English country house a friend had rented. During the night there were a range of manifestations suggesting a haunting, including raps on the walls, noxious odours, and the mysterious dripping of liquid. Whenever these incidents began Jung suffered a sensation of incapacity and a cold sweat. Incidents culminated in the appearance of a ghostly old woman 'with half a face' next to him in bed. Leaping from his bed he spent a fitful rest of the night in a chair. Jung's respect for the existence of ghosts as a possibility increased thereafter but no messages emerged from the manifestations.[21] Other more elaborate theories involve the possibility of some glimpse of the past, including experiences of so-called timeslips.

Whilst these theories are stated, an argument against all visual apparitions being pure telepathy is that the form may be witnessed on different occasions, suggesting that the apparitional form has some independent existence. As Dr Alan Gauld pointed out in his book *Mediumship and Survival: A Century of Investigation* (1983), the ESP which must be occurring in a multi-witnessed case far exceeds anything normally recorded in laboratories and points to the apparition having some degree of spatial reality, which is external to mind of the observer.[22]

Thus, in one sense, ghosts might be understood as spatially fixed psychic effects that persist after death. But on what level of reality for the experience?

The possibility is that the unconscious mind is also generating psychokinetic energy of some kind to trigger the effects and sensations. There is extensive evidence to indicate that consciousness may affect matter in various ways, with much poltergeist activity being ascribed by parapsychologists to the mind of a living person under stress. The results demonstrate that poltergeists are not purely random compilations of manifestations but a phenomenon showing identifiable characteristics with those centring on a living person and those that lacked such a focus. Gauld found 76% of poltergeist cases lasting six months or less with disturbances centring on particular individuals. These suggested human agency with more females than males as the postulated foci. However, 24% of longer-term cases (1 year or more) seemed unconnected with an individual and appeared to be more place centred. Occupiers might change (haunted pubs exemplify this). Such longer-term poltergeists displayed noticeable differences with the shorter cases, resembling traditional hauntings, suggesting a purely mental origin or link with a living human and the longer-term suggesting influence from external haunting entity or presence engaging in rudimentary communication.

Gauld's analysis showed that patterns are discernible within amorphous collection of facts and cases. Gauld's cluster analysis, a statistical examination of some 500 recorded cases to search for common characteristics, went someway to confirming Professor William Barrett's observation of 1911 that, 'The disturbances may be centred on persons of either sex, and appear to be attached to a particular place as well as to a particular person; some animate as well as inanimate *point d'appui* seems to be essential'.[23]

Although Green excluded short-term poltergeist cases from *Phantom Ladies* there are a number of instances which suggest poltergeists may occurr as part of long-term hauntings. Mixed discarnate presence and adolescent psychokinesis was considered in Enfield in North London between 1977-79. Guy Playfair had previously encountered poltergeist activity in Brazil between 1973-75 and was familiar with spiritist explanations but did not consider them sufficient for all aspects of the phenomena.[24]

Sceptical approaches

That problem of accepting conjectures without evidence to support them is not a fault exclusive to ghost hunters, but one also detectable in the willingness of some sceptics to accept any plausible sounding theory in attempts to 'explain away' hauntings.

For instance, a publication by one researcher Vic Tandy proposed the hypothesis that suggested some hauntings in enclosed premises were attributable to infra-sound below the normal range of human hearing which affect the brain and eyeball. His theory was based on a single instance where the source of infra-sound was traced to a defective fan within what was becoming known as a 'haunted' workplace. The actual frequency and amplitude of the infrasound were never directly measured but estimated based on the authors' personal experiences, mathematical calculations and the observation of the effects. From this it was suggested that infrasound at a specific frequency range (around 19 Hertz) was causing disturbances, a sense of unease and causing eyeball vibration resulting in visual disruption effects which were in turn misperceived as apparitions by the person affected.

Tandy later conducted a series of infrasound measurements in a 14th-century cellar beneath a tourist information centre in Coventry, using environmental monitoring equipment that seemed to confirm a frequency of 19 Hz was present within the location, apparently supporting his earlier observation. Tandy's infrasound hypothesis was quickly picked up by the media and the paranormal community, and for a period it became fashionable to propose infrasound as the explanation for anomalous experiences. In fact, later analysis shows that no such relationship was demonstrated or that these findings were replicable. The hypothesis could not explain for apparitions seen in the open air, cases where the same apparition was reported by separate people or that infra-sound could cause detailed hallucinations. Whilst it is a factor that might be considered any such claims are unsubstantiated and must be treated with caution.[25]

Whichever particular theory is favoured by a researcher is likely to influence and dictate how an investigation is conducted. It is therefore important that researchers remain open minded and do not readily reach conclusions that simply fit their own preconceptions and preferred theory of choice and appreciate that a currently fashionable theory is liable to be replaced. In this regard it is salient to note the opinion of psychical researcher Maurice Grosse (1918-2006) who commented in 2001:

> *'In the past we have had underground streams, ley lines, absorbent building materials, planetary influences, faulty observation, delusions, over-active imaginations, alien visitors, low and high frequency sound, earth tremors, temperature changes, to name but a few of the reasons to account for PK, haunting and all the other phenomena associated with our subject. I look forward to the next popular and fashionable revelation.'*[26]

However, Grosse did not give up on ghost investigation and was active in the Spontaneous Cases Committee of the Society for Psychical Research until a few months before his death.

Notes & References

[1] Hallson, Peter (1985) *Journal* of the Society for Psychical Research. Vol 53 No. 803. pp.331-332.

[2] Cassirer, M, Driver, Herbert Benson, *Classified Spontaneous Directory* in *Journal of Paraphysics* vols 1,2,3,4, 1967-71; Cassirer, M *Classified Spontaneous Directory Journal of Paraphysics* vols 5,6, and 7 1972-74; Murdie Alan & Colvin, Barrie *Analysis of Ghosts and Poltergeist Reports in the UK and Irish Press between January and June 2007*. Spontaneous Cases Committee of the Society for Psychical Report.

[3] Underwood, Peter, (1971) *Gazetteer of British Ghosts* pp 123-131; Underwood, Peter, *A Host of Hauntings* (1973) Leslie Frewin Publishers. pp. 180-218.

[4] Hufford, David (1982) *The Terror That Comes Back By Night*. University of Pennsylvania Press.

[5] Green, Andrew (1973, 2016) *Ghost Hunting A Practical Guide* chap 5 Arima Publishing.

[6] Murdie, Alan (2015) *Fortean Times* 'Ghostwatch'; Murdie, Alan (2013) *Journal* of the SPR;

[7] Murdie, Alan (2005) Correspondence in *Journal* of the SPR vol 69 No. 880 July pp169-171.

[8] *Dagenham and East Barking Post* 10 December 1975.

[9] Green, Andrew *Ghost Hunting A Practical Guide* (1973, 2016)Arima Publishing.

[10] Green, Andrew (1973,2016) n.9; Ellison, Arthur Presidential Address (1982); *Alejandro Parra and Jorge Villanueva Mirror-Gazing Facility and Psi: Examining Personality Measures 1 Mirror-Gazing Facility and Psi: Examining Personality Measures* (2011) *Journal* of the Society for Psychical Research; Parker, Adrian (1975) *States of Mind: ESP and Altered States of Consciousness*. Malaby Press. London.

[11] MacKenzie, Andrew (1982) *Hauntings and Apparitions*. Paladin. pp1-47

[12] Houran, James (2000) *Toward a Psychology of 'Entity Encounter Experiences' Journal of the Society for Psychical Research Vol 64 No 860 141-152;* Haraldsson, Erlendur (1988) Survey of claimed encounters with the Dead. *Omega: Journal of Death and Dying 19,* 103-113.

[13] Green, Andrew, n.9 p.33

[14] Hart, H. (1956). Six theories about apparitions. *Proceedings of the SPR, 50, 153-239;* Ralphs, John D. (2014) 'Blue Sky Thinking: Psychical Research – An Assessment' in *Paranormal Review* No.70, 28-33 published by Society for Psychical Research.

[15] Myers, Frederic (1903) *Human Personality and its Survival of Bodily Death*. Vol II Longmans & Co. Chapter 8 para 703 p 4.

[16] Green, Andrew (1973,2016) Ghost Hunting: A Practical Guide. Arima. Chapter 3.

[17] Tyrrell, G.N.M. (1942, 1952) *Apparitions*. Duckworth pp.83-115

[18] Tyrrell, G.N.M n.17, ibid; Hallson, Peter (2013) 'The Traits of Apparitions' *Paranormal Review* No. 66 24-25.

[19] Tyrrell, n.17, ibid

[20] Halliday, Robert and Murdie, Alan (2010) *Cambridge Ghosts*. Arima Books pp.54-55; personal communications from Sharon Mjeiland 8 August 2003.

[21] Jung, Carl Gustav *Psychology and the Occult* (London: Routledge, 1982, pp. 174-183; Moser, Fanny (1950)*Spuk Irrglaube oder Wahrglaube?* Baden Germany chapter 5

[22] Gauld, Alan (1983) *Mediumship and Survival: A Century of Investigation*. Heinemann.UK pp 224-249.

[23] Barrett, William (2011) 'Poltergeists Old and New' *Proceedings* of the SPR Vol 25 pp 377-412 at p. 410

[24] Playfair, Guy Lyon (2018) Personal communication

[25] Tandy, Vic (2000) 'Something in the Cellar' *Journal of the SPR* Vol 64 July 2000 pp 129-140; Parsons, Steve T. 'Infra-sound and the Paranormal' in *Journal of the SPR* Vol. 76.3, No. 908 150-179.

[26] Grosse, Maurice (2003) Correspondence in *Journal* of the Society for Psychical Research vol 67 63-64.

CHAPTER TWO

HUMAN ISSUES AND IMPACTS

One sunny Saturday lunchtime in September 1944 Andrew Green, then aged 17, climbed to the top of a tower of a now demolished house at 16 Montpelier Road, Ealing. Dating from the 1880s, the house had stood empty for 10 years on account of being haunted. He was accompanied by his father, a local air raid official, who had been ordered to inspect the property and who brought Andrew along as he was interested in science. Leaving his father downstairs, Green went off exploring the empty building and eventually set about climbing the stairs and then a ladder fixed up the ornate tower at the back of the house. Lifting a trapdoor in the topmost ceiling he gained access to the flat tower roof and looked out over the parapet of the across to central London in the distance, a striking vista then unimpeded by post-war development. Suddenly, a message began to form in his mind. He recalled, "As I stood admiring the view I slowly developed an urge to look over the parapet." Peering down to the crazy paving in the overgrown garden some 60-70 feet below, he felt no fear but instead an overwhelming urge to step off the tower.[1]

The compulsion was so strong that he swung one leg over the parapet as an internal voice in his mind seemed to compel him with a message, "Walk over the parapet, it's only 12 inches on to the lawn. You won't hurt yourself."

Fortunately for Green – and the future of modern ghost hunting – just as he was preparing to take a fatal jump his father came up to the tower and pulled him back muttering that they 'didn't want any suicides in the family'. Green at that point had been in a semi-trance state, honestly believing he would not harm himself if he launched himself into space. Leaving the house soon after he took a photograph of the front of the building. When developed there seemed to be the unexplained figure of a young woman looking out from an upstairs window. Green made enquiries with the local police and learned that the house was reputedly haunted by a young girl who had jumped from the tower in 1884.

There were other claims of more than dozen suicides from the tower in the next 50 years, the last a murder and suicide committed by a nanny who threw a baby from the top and then jumped to her death in 1934, whereupon the house was abandoned. Redeveloped in 1948 and converted into flats, successive occupiers experienced footsteps, banging sounds and strange smells into the 1960s. The building was eventually demolished in 1971 and replaced with modern flats. Nonetheless the story persisted locally of a ghostly girl or woman haunting the site and who had once lured people to jump to their deaths from the tower when it was still standing. Subsequent research has cast doubt on the history of multiple deaths, but Green considered the house genuinely haunted by a female presence over the years and for him his near lethal experience set him off on his 60-year career of ghost hunting.

The year after Green's near brush with death, in 1945 the writer and artist Paul Huson was a small boy evacuated from London to Lincolnshire and billeted with his parents at Thorpe Hall, a 16th century mansion near Louth for what was treated as a short holiday. The owner of the hall was away and it was the housekeeper's day off. After lunch young Huson was sent for an afternoon rest by his parents who were sunning themselves, and taking his leave he went into the bedroom.

"I was fairly used to my parents bringing friends of theirs into my room to visit me, so when I saw the woman in a green dress standing beside my bed I greeted her matter-of-factly and asked if it was time for me to get up. Unfortunately, I don't remember if I received any reply."

Only later that they learned of the legend of the Green Lady, the daughter of a Spanish grandee whose ghost is supposed to walk to walk the corridors of Thorpe Hall, her faithful English lover's old home. Her phantom had been seen repeatedly since the time of the Spanish Armada – a woman in a green dress seen moving sadly in the house and its grounds. Paul Huson's account is little known, being just a personal anecdote he brought into the penultimate chapter of a popular book on testing and developing ESP published in the 1970s. His experience was ascribed to over imagination; if so, it at least potentially revealed a sign of his capacity for creativity and visualisation which he later displayed as an artist and writer. Possibly it contributed to his own path as a writer on paranormal and esoteric matters.[2]

In the autumn of 2021, a female figure was seen on the first floor of *The Eclipse Inn*, on the marketplace in Winchester, coinciding with a being couple shown round for a ghost tour, owing to the long-standing story that the building and surrounding area was haunted by a Grey Lady, reputedly 'Lady Alice'.

Mr Fearne, 28, who had arrived earlier in the summer of 2021, duly provided a tour of the building and told them of its history, pointing out the most active areas "up on the corridor and near the ladies toilet". This corridor was one of the places which 'Lady Alice' reputedly walked.

However, as often happens, the real activity was taking place unnoticed by the would-be investigators. Another couple had arrived downstairs and sat on the opposite side of the bar room and were not involved with the conversation. Mr Fearne recalled, "This lady walked in, her husband bought drinks, she went to the toilet then sat down and said she had a conversation with a lady upstairs."

Astonished at over-hearing this this, Mr Fearne asked "Are you telling me that you have just seen a lady upstairs?" She said 'yes'. Speaking at once with the ghost-hunting couple, they both confirmed that no other woman had been upstairs with them. This announcement shook everyone as the mystery lady must have been a ghost, all the more remarkable for being missed by a couple interested in ghosts and seen by one not thinking about the subject. For his part, Mr Fearne had witnessed strange object movements and twice heard inexplicable sounds in the pub late at night.

This experience, together with the inn's central location on the market square in Winchester, has proved irresistible for ghost tourists and Mr Fearne has maintained a tradition of encouraging ghost hunters to visit.

Tradition holds the Grey Lady to be Dame Alice Lisle (1617 -1685) executed outside the pub on the marketplace in September 1685 for her part in sheltering two supporters of the Monmouth Rebellion against Charles II. The night before she hanged she was kept prisoner at a room in the Eclipse. Ever since her ghost reputedly walks the corridor outside the room where the Lady spent her last night on Earth in human form.

According to Christina Hole in *'Haunted England: A Survey of English Ghost Lore'* (1940) 'Tradition says the sound of her silk dress and tapping of her heels were long afterwards heard in the corridors of Moyles Court, and that sometimes she was seen passing down Ellingham Lane in a driverless coach drawn by headless horses.' The main focus of her return is the pub itself. One mysterious sighting of a woman in the upstairs part was made by a female customer accessing the toilets. Fresh enquiries by Sarah Gerard from the Ghost Club in September 2022 indicated that, as is common in the pub trade, Mr Fearne had since moved on to pastures new but that the phenomena were continuing with staff talking of an atmosphere and the unexplained movement of glasses.[3]

The appearance or experience of a ghost naturally focuses attention on the apparition as something strange and unusual. But in order to have an apparition it is necessary to have an observer. All too often insufficient attention is given to the observer and the impact the experience may have upon them. In their eagerness to investigate, many would be researchers of recent years have often overlooked the importance of speaking and listening to first hand witnesses of ghostly phenomena. It should be remembered that without witness reports at the outset there would be no cases of hauntings to investigate. For it remains the case that ghosts do not come to order and our primary source of data on ghosts remain such experiences from people who have actually encountered them.

In terms of understanding the nature of the Phantom Lady phenomena, the collection such first-hand testimony and assessing the credibility of the witness and seeking out any corroborating accounts are of key importance. Whether for percipients an uncanny experience proves positive, negative or neutral for the individuals concerned, their actual reactions and results of the encounter are aspects worthy of examination. The experiences of Green, Huson and customers and staff at haunted inns such as the Eclipse show just how an experience can impact on a witness and may potentially influence their direction in life.

Personal meanings and warnings

That the experience of a ghost may have a personal significance in the life of a witness is a matter that has received relatively little attention in recent decades. In most cases we lack sufficient personal information about the life circumstances of the witness, so the presumption is that seeing or experiencing a ghost generally does not carry any wider meaning for them. However, such a view is not universally shared and especially for certain varieties of apparition that manifest only once.

The best examples of this are those experiences labelled as crisis apparitions, mentioned above, which generally appear just once and are presumed not to return as haunting ghosts. In popular tradition such encounters are considered to be visits by spirits to say farewells or deliver warnings. In some cultures these experiences might be seen as a glimpse of the future, in keeping with the Scottish tradition of second sight.

The appearance of an unknown ghostly woman may be an omen of death or misfortune, the best known being the Irish Banshee, a ghostly woman attached to families who cries or sings before the death of a member of a long-established family. In her exhaustive study *The Banshee* (1992) Dr Patricia Lygsaght records many instances of this tradition, with the Banshee often appearing as an old woman, a point also taken up scholar Patrick Harpur in *Daimonic Reality* (1995) which argues such experiences originate from a separate a dimension which interacts with both our conscious and the unconscious minds and yet is also independent of it, an alternative plane of reality. Such a realm or dimension is highly speculative but there is no doubting that the tradition of ghostly females However, the lore ranges far beyond Ireland, with warning ghosts and step out and scream out in diverse locations.[4]

For instance a mid-19th century English travel writer M.E. Walcott recorded in his *Guide to the Essex, Norfolk and Suffolk Coasts* (1870) a story collected concerning Gunton Hall near Lowestoft in Suffolk. Its owner Lord Suffield told a physician Dr Woodward that servants reported they had heard the cry of the 'White Lady'. His Lordship had heard a piercing scream himself from outside the hall. On going to the widow he saw a shadowy form resembling a woman crossing the lawn. This occurred on the night before Lady Suffield died. The East of England is as geographically as far as one can be from the celtic centre of Ireland, yet the core phenomena remain the same.[5]

Stories of the White Lady as an omen of impending death or calamity fascinated the German writer Johannes von Butlar. His book *Journey to Infinity* (1976) lists several examples, including one which reportedly took place in Britain on a still summer in 1970, during school holidays when a Mr Richard was with his son at the country home of his friends Dick and Moira Aldridge at East Grinstead in Sussex. It was a relaxed evening, and after a late supper they were sitting around a fireplace and 'conversation had become desultory' in a post-prandial reverie. Suddenly there can came a sudden wind sufficient to blow open the French windows and, as the gust swept through the room, Dick stood up and went outside to the terrace.

Oddly not a leaf outside was stirring. Puzzled he remarked "Well, perhaps there is a thunderstorm brewing" and closed the windows again. Valerie his wife had gone on talking quietly with Moira. The story continued, "Dick and I sipped our drinks without saying anything. Once again, the doors burst open. This time we all sat up. Dick went outside once more and returned looking puzzled. 'I don't understand it; it's absolutely calm, there isn't a breath of air.' He could think of no explanation of what had happened. Again he shut the windows".

It was now approaching half past one and Mr Richard decided it was time to leave. Standing up and he began to say farewells when the window blew open with 'a howling blast' and then, 'outside we saw a shadowy white figure that faded slowly as the wind died away'.

Everyone saw this, except for Dick who had his back to the window. The next day Mr Richard received a telephone call from Dick who stated that his next-door neighbour a Mr Dellinger had died at about a quarter to one after a long illness.

The author was scant on sources for this story but it matched a long-standing tradition of such encounters recorded in German where the appearance of a woman in white serves as a warning and the transmission of information, perhaps from the future. This raises the question of whether the apparition exists independently or is being generated by the unconscious mind which is somehow aware of events yet to come or its own future state and content.[6]

Witness trauma

Reactions vary enormously in relation to sightings of phantom ladies. Persons with a high tolerance of ambiguity might very well respond with awe or wonder, or perhaps even indifference. What is interesting is that the direct impact some cases the encounter with a phantom woman, over and above what might be ordinarily expected from seeing the figure of a woman.

Unsurprisingly, when an event appears to coincide with a traumatic life event for a witness this will make an impact. Indeed, it runs contrary to the general and justifiable social and cultural perception as men being far more threatening and violent than women. A number of stories emphasise the traumatic personal impact and the sense of terror felt by the witness.

An unusual first-hand account from around 1667 involving multiple female apparitions entitled *Of divers strange Appearances of Spirits in a Nobleman's House in the West* appears in Richard Bovet's *Pandaemonium, or, The devil's cloyster*. The man was staying in a stately house which had formally been a nunnery. He admitted he had previously heard from servants in the house "….of the noises, stirs, and Apparitions that frequently disturbed the House'. Because there were many visitors he was sharing a room, known as 'my Ladies Chamber', with a steward, a Mr. C. He was awake on a bright moonlit night, '….enough to read a hand-written by even without candles'. Suddenly the writer noticed entering through the locked door, 'five Appearances of very fine and lovely Women…. of excellent stature' all veiled and with trailing dresses, passing around the bed. One approached the bed and appeared to strike him with a blow that felt very soft. The writer responded by asking "in the name of the Blessed Trinity what business they had there" but his entreaty received no reply. He then called out to Mr. C. next to him stating "Sir, do you see what fair Guests we have come to visit us?" whereupon the figures vanished. Receiving no reply he found Mr C. "in some kind of Agony and was "forced to grasp him on the breast with my right hand (which was next him underneath the Bed-cloaths) before I could obtain speech of him; then he told me that he had seen the fair Guests I spoke of". Eventually, Mr C. recovered sufficiently to 'being extremely affrighted at the sight of a dreadful Monster, which assuming a shape betwixt that of a Lion, and a Bear attempted to mount the bed." It was a long time before he could compose himself to sleep again. It transpired that Mr C. was used to haunting phenomena in the house experienced on previous occasions, acknowledging that he had never been so terrified, despite experiencing ghosts before.[7]

A century and half later in around 1800, a young boy living with his family at Blenkinsopp Castle was found traumatised 'sitting trembling on his pillow, terror-struck and bathed in perspiration' and crying out 'The White Lady! The White Lady!' and reported visits of a frightening apparition. The parents allowed the boy to sleep with them whereupon apparently, the apparition no longer visited him. Nonetheless the boy remained so frightened that he wouldn't enter any part of the castle alone, even during the day. In 1830 a man reputedly died after going to confront a White Lady at Worstead Church, Norfolk, on Christmas Eve after boasting that if he saw her he would give her a kiss. He was later found in a corner of the ringing chamber "his limbs shaking, his eyes rolling and his lips gibbering". Briefly reviving he declared "I've seen her! There! There!" and died shortly afterwards.[8]

These reactions could be attributed to adult and childhood nightmares or dismissed as folklore. But better attested cases show the traumatic impact an encounter or believed encounter with a White Lady can engender. A spectral woman who appeared at the badly haunted home of the Proctor family at Willington Mill, Tyneside in the 1840s severely scared one of a team of ghost hunters who sat up for her. The Proctor family were Quakers and well-off financially and there was no obvious reason why their house should have been afflicted by a wide range of phenomena experienced by the family and outsiders. Details were recorded in the diary of Joseph Proctor and later shared with the Society for Psychical Research. The Proctor children were the chief ghost-seers despite all attempts to keep details of sightings from them. It also featured a ghostly woman who 'had eyeholes, but no eyes' and a cat and monkey, though these animals were more amusing than disturbing. More troubling was the appearance of a lady in pale or grey clothing.

The case provides one of the few credible accounts of a ghost hunter actually seeing an apparition during an investigation, when a group of local men mounted an overnight watch. One of them, seated in a chair, saw the figure of a woman in grey advancing upon him. He leapt up with a shriek and in doing so passed right through the oncoming figure. Fainting in horror he collapsed on top of a startled friend who sat in another chair opposite dozing. The shocked witness revived but displayed a state of 'extreme nervous excitement and accompanied with much coldness and faintness for three hours, though not irrational.' An observer noted, 'He had a ghastly look and started at the smallest sound and could not bear to see anything white; he had not been in the least sleepy and was not at all frightened till the moment when the G[host] met his gaze….' and adding 'E. D. has got a shock he will not soon cast off'.⁹

In April 2006 Mr Frogatt of the Low Valley Arms, a pub at Wombwell near Barnsley, South Yorkshire suffered a severe shock when he went downstairs after he thought a burglar was present at about 1.30am on a Tuesday morning. Three large television screens in the pub had been switched on and the burglar alarm had been activated. He began searching the pub and on going into the ladies' toilets he saw standing in them "a woman with no face and silvery grey hair, dressed in a white gown. I stood there for about four or five seconds before I fled in terror".

Waiting outside was Mrs Kathryn Frogatt, 49, who was just behind her husband before he went into the toilets, and on seeing his shocked condition had said she was so concerned about what her husband had experienced she called the police.

"He was in total shock," she said. "He was shaking, he was white and he wouldn't move. He just kept saying 'face, face, it's horrible, it's horrible'. She continued, "I was so worried about what he might have seen I rang the police there and then, sitting on the stairs." On arrival, the police discovered the toilets were flushing themselves and the following day officers issued a press statement about the incident. Because of the shaken condition of Mr Froggatt the police called an ambulance to the scene but Mr Froggatt declined medical help. Recalling his experience Mr Froggatt stated, "It was the ugliest thing I have ever seen…. "I know what I saw and I know there is something here." The powerful effect on Mr Froggatt is consistent with a feature noted by Tyrrell with some apparition sightings that, 'The telepathic impulse does not behave at all gently; on the contrary it crashes in like a thunderbolt'.¹⁰

Distorted facial features

One reason for the disturbed or fearful reaction that some witnesses display is that the face of the apparition is distorted, incomplete or blank. The sudden visualisation of an apparently mutilated face may evoke a range of reactions from shocked sympathy to horror on the part of a witness.

Over 1967-69 a menacing phantom white lady and assorted poltergeist manifestations drove the McGhee family from their home in Spencer Grove, Stoke Newington, Hackney in London. It was seen to emerge from a wardrobe and was described as a woman in white with a distorted face with large dark holes where the eyes should have been. This was collectively witnessed. The haunting built up culminating in unexplained fires, strange noises and poltergeist phenomena afflicting the property for several nightmarish weeks before the family finally fled. The case reached the High Court when Hackney Council refused to reduce their rent and accused the McGhees of negligence for leaving the property empty in the middle of the night. The decision of the Council was overturned by the High Court and the rent reduced to 25p per week. Eventually the house was demolished.¹¹

The Spencer Grove case had some broad similarities with a case from New Zealand in autumn 2020. A bungalow at Pukekhoe near Auckland rented out to five Filipino workers was troubled by the sound of piteous weeping and a menacing female figure with dark spots where her eyes should have been. Scaffolder Darwin Rivera said he had seen the figure of an old woman, wearing what he described as old-fashioned clothing, standing outside the French doors leading from his room. He admitted being scared by the apparition, which he said had long black hair, only black holes for eyes and an "angry" expression. An intriguing detail was that one employee had been on a video call with his wife who angrily accused him of infidelity after seeing a woman in the background. He could see nothing 'and he swore black and blue that there was no one in there'. Lights were also being mysteriously switched on and off.

The newspaper contacted the previous owners of the bungalow who said they too had been disturbed by an other-worldly presence some 24 years earlier, but that nothing had troubled them for two decades before selling up in February 2020. Former owner Mr Kim Tilyard said they had the house blessed but disturbances continued, eventually only ceasing after the family themselves demanded the ghosts departed. His wife Christine Tilyard stated their family learned to live with their spectral housemates and they adopted their own safeguards. Christine Tilyard stated, "We just kept the wardrobe door closed. There's a wardrobe in there that we just never opened. So I'd say they've opened the wardrobe door and whatever is in there has come out."

She raised the possibilities that one of the spirits might be that of her mother, who died earlier in 2020 and lay in the house for a time after her death, declaring, "That's the sort of thing my mum would do." She also recommended a blessing.[12]

With the telepathic transmission of theory of an apparition, it might be postulated that the process could go awry when apparitional details become blurred or distorted by the unconscious imaginative powers of the recipient. Features might be obscured and the right or wrong elements left out or incorporated into the resulting vision. Occasionally an appearance may assume the guise of a headless figure, but such sightings appear to be much rarer today than in the past, if they occurred at all.[13]

In other cases the facial features are concealed or obscured, a result of the position and angle of the observer in relation to it or a veil or other headgear it is wearing concealing them.

It has been considered that elements in such ghostly and traumatic experiences and the exceptionally fearful reactions they can elicit may be a by-product of the functioning (or misfunctioning) of the right-hemispheric temporal lobes within the brain. A rare clinical condition – a real mouthful – 'Prosopometamorphopsia' was first described in 1947 by Joachim Bodamer, based upon a study of the visual distortion of faces suffered by a 24-year-old patient who had been shot in the head. The condition is distinguished from 'prosopagnosia' which is characterised by the inability to recognise faces and may be attributable to structural brain changes or functional disorders e.g. epilepsy, migraine, or physical eye disease.[14]

This was a line of research which interested Andrew Green in the late 1970s but which he was unable to proceed with because of lack of funds but one which experimental psychologists have explored and attempt to clarify, including whether gender differences exaggerate or contribute to greater fears when faced with haunting phenomena. However, as with many areas of brain research no firm conclusions can be reached.[15]

Furthermore, although unusual, these encounters do not always convey terror but occasionally awe or amazement.

On Friday 23rd March 2007 Sacha Christie of Leeds was attending a party organised by some friends for the 30th birthdays of their boyfriends at Featherstone Castle. "I arrived with my friend Sarah at around 7pm and we had a little wander around in the rooms saying hello to everyone who had already arrived and then joined in decorating the rooms for the event. We'd arrived early to help with whatever needed doing."

She continued: "At around 8pm I received a telephone call from the Department of Work and Pensions. Aghast at the time of the call on a weekend I duly proceeded to complain about the time of this call and the inconvenience.

I wandered outside to take myself away from the mêlée and to answer her questions and get rid of her as quickly as possible.

I stood halfway down a staircase pacing up and down and then went to lean against a wall. As I looked up the driveway for one second, I saw a woman wearing a long-sleeved white dress with long dark hair step out of the shadows, her dress billowed out as she took a forward step and as the dress fell backwards it disappeared into the shadows with her. She seemed to have come through the archway on the drive. I stood there in total disbelief. I have been involved in paranormal investigations for over two years now and have never seen a full apparition such as this in all that time, and lo and behold the one time I see an apparition I am on the phone to someone and can do nothing about it!"

Consistent with the obscuring of facial features, notably from the angle of her vantage point Sacha was not able to see the face. "The thing I remember most about her is that she was striding with purpose, not floating or just walking….it was like she had a purpose….she seemed determined if that makes any sense! I knew she was angry."

When the conversation over the telephone ended Sacha rushed back inside into the castle to tell her friend Emma what she had seen: "I said 'Emma, I've just seen a lady in white walking up the driveway…. Is there a story of a woman in white haunting the place?' She pulled a funny face and answered enigmatically 'probably'…. Now all of my friends know what I do so they know that I would be wandering around picking things up and would not have read anything about the place and similarly would not want to be told anything, however she ventured 'do you want me to tell you about it?' having only been there around an hour I said 'No…I am still picking things up…some sort of battle and a procession but I have no idea what it all means yet' at this she pulled an even funnier face, eyes slightly bulging but amused and walked away."

The fact of the conversation taking place was confirmed by her friend Emma in a separate message to me. There was a legendary story known to some of the guests that a bride, along with her retinue had once all been murdered on her wedding day by a jealous lover whom the woman had jilted. The jealous lover was then overcome by remorse and killed himself. No dates or historical corroboration is known, making one wonder if the legend inspired the ghost or if similar sightings inspired the legend. What may be significant about this is that Sacha Christie went on to have further anomalous experiences interpreted as bizarre UFO experiences of seeing lights and apparent objects in the sky.[16]

Sacha is an example of a repeat experiencer, one of a class of people whom Professor Ronald Hutton in his book *Triumph of the Moon* (2000) on contemporary pagan religions maintains have complex experiences of a psychic or spiritual nature, which do not fit comfortably into any existing paradigm in mainstream Western soceity.[17]

These patterns of partly formed apparitions have been noted since the beginnings of psychical research in the 19th century, when early investigators into hallucinatory experiences recorded a "…group of incompletely developed apparitions that, namely, in which the face or head of the figure is indistinct".[18]

An illustrative example was provided for the Society for Psychical Research by a classical scholar Margaret Verrall, later the principal of Newham College in Cambridge of an experience in Brighton. As might be expected of a scholarly lady she provided a detailed description:

> "One evening about the middle or end of September, 1879, as I was washing my hands in a little room at the end of the passage leading to the front door, I heard footsteps, and looking up saw a little old lady coming towards me. She was dressed in a dark dress gathered round the waist in full folds, a grey knitted shawl over her shoulders fastened with a brooch in front, and a cap. I did not see her face, although she was walking towards me. I knew at once that it was a hallucination but was neither startled nor alarmed. The figure disappeared before reaching the room where I was."[19]

Over the next few weeks she saw what she came to call 'my old lady' several times appearing facing her. Gradually, further details emerged, enabling her to identify the brooch fastening the shawl of the figure as one like a circular brooch with a hole in the centre worn by her great-grandmother, a Mrs. Watkins, who had died ten years before. Eventually. she dubbed the apparition 'great-grandmother', but never once saw its face.

Returning to Cambridge in October 1879, she forgot entirely about her Brighton experiences. Then one evening, whilst upstairs and going to her room she heard footsteps coming along the passageway at the top of the house. Looking to the left (instead of turning right into her room) she saw the same old lady approaching. "There was no one else in the passage; the gas was lighted, and I saw the figure plainly." This proved to be the last time the figure appeared.

She recalled: "On the first and last occasions of my seeing the figure, I had heard the sound of footsteps, on the intermediate occasions the impression was only visual. The figure always took its place in the surroundings (i.e., hid the things behind it), and was always in movement coming towards me, the only odd thing about it was that I never saw the face.... there seemed a blank within the cap."[20]

The form never spoke. However, from 1901 Margaret Verrall went on to be a noted spiritualist medium producing automatic writing (where the pen is held by a medium in a trance or semi-trance state and writes out messages). Later she became one of a number of mediums producing a series of significant communications forming part of a collection of communications known as the 'cross-correspondences' which were attributed to a collection of discarnate communicating spirits sending messages in an elaborate code. Her part in these communications continued up until her death in 1916.

The persistence of facelessness or the face being distorted or obscured over so many years makes it hard to posit explanations based purely upon the psychology of individuals and points to some deeper basis. Some answers may lie in an aspect of how the brain recognises and forms images of faces, or alternatively they may lie in the directions postulated by Jungian psychologist Anita Jaffe. In her book *Apparitions and Precognition* (1963) Jaffe ascribes facelessness to a symbolic component generated by unconscious mental processes which relate to future phases of personal development and mental life of individuals as they psychically perceive their own futures.[21] All that currently may be said with any certainty is that haunting experiences involve complex interactions between place and person and that the impact upon individual witnesses may be positive, neutral or wholly negative.

Encounters with Phantom Ladies force us to confront the possibility of a human mind which is unbounded beyond the five recognised senses. It appears to be a mind which enjoys a more fluid and interpenetrative relationship with its own levels, with the minds of others and with the external world, and potentially with the minds of people no longer living who were once connected to specific locations in the historic past.

Notes & References

[1] Green, Andrew *Our Haunted Kingdom* (1973) Wolfe Publications. UK; Fontana edition, 1976; Murdie, Alan (2016) 'Ghost Hunt at the House of Suicides' in *Fortean Times* No.342 July 2016.

[2] Huson, Paul (1977) *How to Test and Develop Your ESP*. Abacus. Chap 10 'Ghost Hunting'.

[3] *Hampshire Chronicle* for 13 January 2022; personal communication Sarah Gerrard 15 October 2022. Alexander, Marc (*Haunted Inns* (1973)Muller pp. 235-239; Guy Playfair *The Haunted Pub Guide* (1985)p. 85.

[4] Lysaght, Patricia (1996) *The Banshee: The Irish Supernatural Death Messneger*. O'Brien Press. Eire; Harpur, Patrick (1994) *Daimonic Reality*. Arkana. UK. Chapter 8.

[5] Walcott, M.E. (1869) *Guide to the Essex, Suffolk and Norfolk Coast*.

[6] Butlar, von Johannes (1976) *Journey to Infinity* Fontana. UK. pp 35-36

[7] Bovet, Richard (1688) *Pandaemonium or The devil's cloyster being a further blow to modern sadduceism, proving the existence of witches and spirits* pp 203-204. London.

[8] Beck, Janet C. *The White Lady of Great Britain and Ireland* Winter, 1970, Vol. 81, No. 4 (Winter, 1970) pp. 292-306; Porter, Enid (1974) *The Folklore of East Anglia*. Batsford citing Suffling, E.R. (c.1882)*History, Legends and Traditions of the Broads District*. Neil Storey floats the possibility that an entry in the Worstead Church burial register for a man named 'Green Potter',65, dated 3 January 1831 might identify the victim. In Storey, Neil (2007) *Norfolk, A Ghost Hunter's Guide*. Countryside Books pp 65-68.

[9] 'The Haunted House at Willington' in *Journal* of the SPR Vol 5 1893 at 331-352.

[10] *Yorkshire Post* 25 April 2006. Murdie, Alan, 'Faceless Ghosts' (2019) *Fortean Times*. No 383. Tyrrell, G.N.M. (1942) n.17 at p.134

[11] Underwood, Peter (1973) *Haunted London*. George G. Harrap & Co Ltd pp 129-132. *McGhee v Hackney LBC* [1969] RVR 342.

[12] *New Zealand Herald* 30 October 2020.

[13] Cowdell, Paul (2011) *Belief in Ghosts in Post-War England*. PhD Thesis, University of Hertfordshire p 40. Murdie, Alan (2000) 'Headless Hauntings?' *Fortean Times* No. 141 Dec 2000 p 47.

[14] Dobbs, David (2007) 'When every face is like another' in *Scientific American* https://blogs.scientificamerican.com/news-blog/when-every-face-is-like-another/ Nov 2007.

[15] Houran, James & Lange, Rense (1997) 'Tolerance of Ambiguity and Fear of the Paranormal in Self-Identified Percipients of Haunting & RSPK Phenomena in Journal of the Society for Psychical Research Vol 62 No. 848 pp 36-40Huot, B., Makarec, K., & Persinger, M. A. (1989). Temporal lobes signs and Jungian dimensions of personality. *Perceptual and Motor Skills, 69* (3,Pt1) pp. 841–842. https://doi.org/10.2466/pms.1989.69.3.841

[16] Christie, Sacha personal communication to Alan Murdie 17 October 2007; Murdie, Alan (2007) Ghostwatch in *Fortean Times* Nov. 2007.

[17] Hutton, Ronald (2000) *Triumph of the Moon*. Oxford: OUP pp. 269-271.

[18] Sidgwick, Henry (1894) *Report on the Census of Hallucinations* in *Proceedings* of the Society for Psychical Research Vol 10 pp. 25-422 at p. 120.

[19] Verrall, Helen (1894) *Report on the Census of Hallucinations in Proceedings of the Society for Psychical Research* Vol 10 at pp. 120–121.

[20] Verrall, n.19 ibid.

[21] Jaffe, Anita (1963) *Apparitions and Precognition.* New York. University Books pp. 133-137

CHAPTER THREE

INVESTIGATING GHOSTS

From the foregoing, it will be realised that the Phantom Ladies in one form or another are not distant and unapproachable symbols, but actual, dynamic and immediate presences which can be encountered by witnesses within both domestic homes and in more public settings. A number of the sites covered in the gazetteer section of this book continue to generate remarkable reports and claims of direct experiences of female ghosts into the 21st century, thus holding out opportunities for further investigation and study.

Andrew Green was an active ghost hunter for more than 50 years, from 1944 up until to his last major investigation at the Royal Albert Hall in 1996. In the process he did much to promote psychical research as a serious activity to the wider public. Now – partly as a result – in the 21st century, ghost hunting as a pastime is enjoying its greatest popularity since the heyday of Victorian spiritualism (when ghost hunting was conducted in séance rooms with the ghosts coming to you rather than going out looking for them at haunted locations). Just as Andrew Green intended when this book was first published in 1977 it is hoped that the sites listed will receive examination and study, now from a new generation of paranormal researchers.

So, just how should one go about this? Before the reader launches into a practical investigation at any haunted site it is important to grasp a number of basic points from the outset and set aside a number of mistaken assumptions about exactly what serious ghost hunting entails, as well as highlighting some of the pitfalls the would-be ghost hunter should avoid if intent on doing anything more than enjoying a series of thrills and chills in the dark.

A ghost hunter or paranormal investigator is engaging in a complex assessment of psycho-physical aspects of an alleged haunted location place and in some cases the people occupying it. Such a task is one to which a wide range of existing skills, knowledge and expertise can be applied. This includes accepting negative evidence i.e. evidence pointing to the fact that a place may not be haunted and looking at the totality of evidence, not just one strand or aspect of it.

Worth recalling is the opinion of veteran psychical researcher Professor Donald J. West (1924-2020) who warned: "It is a human failing among investigators that each one thinks himself the right man to look into a spontaneous case. The task is in practice a delicate one, requiring not only skill in understanding and handling different temperaments, but also a critical judgment of evidence".[1]

The motivations and psychology of just why people wish to engage in paranormal research is an interesting question in itself but, if it is to be scientifically meaningful in any way, it needs as rational and objective an approach as possible. West sought to emphasise the importance of not being hide-bound or dogmatically tied to one's personal beliefs and instead following the evidence wherever it pointed.

Unfortunately, despite ever-more sophisticated gadgetry being deployed by some researchers, many investigations end up attempting to communicate with 'the dead' rather than discovering the mechanics of the phenomena and understanding the experiences that have triggered an investigation in the first place.

Certainly, ghost hunting can be thrilling fun if one has the nerve for it; even Donald West himself conceded he found it in terms of psychical research '… in many ways the most instructive and certainly the most exciting'.[2] But at the same time it should be realised that ghost hunting – which for some means the possibility of contacting the dead should not be treated as a game but a serious attempt to explore and understand aspects of human experience that have perplexed humankind throughout history

One of the biggest obstacles to progress – and there is no avoiding this – is that by their very nature ghost hunts take place in uncontrolled environments where laboratory and clinical conditions cannot be applied. A further problem is that with no set or agreed standards, each investigator remains free to pursue their own course, applying whatever methods or techniques they prefer, even though some have absolutely no scientific basis at all. Simply engaging in research to try and confirm pre-existing beliefs does not always sit easily with any scientific evaluation of evidence. All too often, because of pre-existing notions investigators end up fooling themselves (and others) into believing they have obtained proof of a ghostly presence when everything recorded is perfectly explicable on normal grounds and contains no proof of any haunting at all.

Consequently, it is strongly recommended that anyone interested in conducting practical ghost investigations in a scientific manner studies two publications issued by the Society for Psychical Research which update earlier guides and practices dating back to when Phantom Ladies originally appeared.

Most useful are *Guidance Notes for Investigators of Spontaneous Cases, Apparitions, Hauntings, Poltergeists and Similar Phenomena New Edition* (2018) edited by Steve Parsons (replacing its previous *Notes on Investigating Spontaneous Cases*) and the accompanying guide *Using Equipment: Guidance Notes for Investigators of Apparitions, Haunting, Poltergeists and Similar Phenomena* (2021).[3]

Both works seek to encourage scientifically structured and sound investigative approach for field investigators seeking to obtain meaningful results. For a wider overview, Andrew Green's own book *Ghost Hunting: A Practical Guide* (1973 and updated in 2016) is also recommended, especially for newcomers to the field in the 21st century to help them understand how we developed many contemporary approaches.[4]

Choosing a site and initial enquiries

As will be apparent from the gazetteer entries in Part One of *Phantom Ladies*, there is no shortage of haunted sites, and the list should in no way be considered exhaustive. Although Andrew Green had personally followed up a number of cases, obviously not even the most peripatetic and energetic ghost hunter could cover all locations in the depth required. Potentially all may merit detailed scrutiny and re-examination and one of the purposes of this book is to encourage such efforts.

Naturally, it cannot be guaranteed how many will prove to be haunted and quite possibly it may transpire that some are not and never were. Whatever the case it is important to build upon and expand what has been established before, even if this means superseding and correcting the data.

Preliminaries

What is practical will depend upon your resources and the degree of energy and the degree of commitment you wish to bring to research. So, if after selecting a site, you think a haunting merits re-investigation the next step is to find out more about the current position. Such initial enquiries are a vital preliminary stage.

All too often it is forgotten by many ghost hunters in the 21st century that the bulk of investigative work concerns gathering data from multiple sources, checking its reliability and assessing its weight and discerning patterns. This is an aspect of ghost hunting closer to a form of detective work.

The idea that ghost hunting revolves solely around trying to capture ghosts on camera or recording them with other instruments is a mistake many beginning ghost hunting make in their early enthusiasm. Contrary to impressions given by many television shows, the patient gathering of information is actually what takes up the bulk of the time of any serious investigator.

At the beginning this means ascertaining experiences of witnesses and learning about the state and history of the premises, long before any overnight vigils or practical investigations are launched. With sites listed in *Phantom Ladies* this means checking up on the facts so far as is possible, particularly in the years since this book was first published.

With premises open to the public or accessible during reasonable hours (e.g commercial premises and hotels and pubs) there will usually be opportunities to make direct enquiries on the spot by way of a personal visit. Through this one may learn much from staff, occupiers and neighbours including important information not published either on-line or available from printed sources. A great deal of useful material, including accounts of any recent manifestations can be gleaned this way. Indeed, such initial enquiries can often save the effort of a full investigation when it becomes apparent that claims of any haunting are suspect.

Searches of the internet and public records can also turn up important information. In Great Britain a wealth of documentary material survives from past periods, to be found in libraries, museums and research institutes of different kinds (many of these collections are being digitalised). Some larger stately homes, churches and public institutions also maintain their own archives, as do some newspapers. Much fresh information is likely to be found within or accumulated since *Phantom Ladies* was first published in 1977.

Such enquiries can solve a case at an early stage. A good example is provided by John Fraser who investigated claims of a haunting at Ightham Mote, an ancient manor house in Kent. Numerous books stated the old house was haunted by Dame Dorothy Selby who was bricked up alive in a secret room within by Guy Fawkes for her part in betraying the Gunpowder Plot to blow up Parliament in November 1605.

Many authors uncritically repeated the Guy Fawkes murder story claiming Dame Selby's became an "immured skeleton" discovered many years later in the house and that an exorcism (unsuccessful) had followed finding her bones. Fraser went to Ightham Mote, checked records and visited the local church. He swiftly established Dame Selby had long survived Guy Fawkes and ultimately died on 15 March 1641, some 36 years after Fawkes was executed. Her tomb and monument was to be found inside the local church where previous writers would have found it had they bothered to check.[5]

Equally, whilst a story can be undermined during this initial search phase, one may also turn up fresh information which reveals a genuine haunting. For example, the legend of the Grey Lady of Bury St Edmunds in Suffolk collapsed following enquiries at the West Suffolk Records Office based in the town. But further searches in the archives turned up a wealth of sightings of a female apparition and other ghosts in the town, mostly since the 1960s (see pp. 82-83).[6]

Public appeals

As an alternative some researchers launch public appeals by way of social media or via the letters page of a local newspaper circulating in an area (which can also prompt help from journalists). Such appeals sometimes generate large volumes of replies from people with first or second-hand knowledge of hauntings. However, care should be taking before accepting the accuracy of any information supplied which will need further enquiries and checking.

Private premises and domestic dwellings

Obviously, such approaches are not appropriate with premises that are in private hands. 'Private property, please respect' is an important principle and cold calling to gather information is rarely welcome.

Consideration, discretion, forethought and sensitivity should be the watchwords, with avoiding trying to make any out of 'out of the blue' enquiry.

Indeed, it may be taken as a general presumption most occupiers *will not welcome unsolicited callers*; and consideration should be given to whether any investigation should be undertaken at all, particularly if an occupier is known or suspected to be in a potentially vulnerable category (e.g. elderly, disabled or recently bereaved). The last thing that some new owners or residents may wish to learn is that their home is reputedly haunted. Remember there are plenty of other sites which may equally deserve attention.

Where possible approaches may sometimes be achieved via a personal contact, introduction or recommendation from someone known to the occupier or resident. Alternatively, you might proceed by way of a polite letter, e-mail of enquiry or contact via social media. Tact and discretion are important and most occupiers will want an assurance of confidentiality and not wish the situation to be publicised. However, if the occupier of private property has drawn attention to a haunting in the press or on social media themselves you will be in a better position to initiate contact, or as a result of the occupier contacting you directly for help.

If – and only if – you have obtained a positive invitation to visit from an occupier should you proceed, respecting any conditions imposed. Also be prepared for permissions to be revoked and summarily withdrawn. Additionally, the owners or controllers of some sites may to want to impose a charge for conducting an investigation on their premises. They are within their rights to do so.

Witnesses

Talking directly with witnesses and getting them to describe the manifestations they have experienced provides our best source of information on the nature of ghosts. Any number of a range of skills can be brought to the task of assessing such testimony.

Witnesses should be encouraged to share as much information as possible, including their own ideas about the phenomena. When meeting a witness the investigator should be able to determine whether the person is credible and seek to discover if any corroboration exists for what is being related. Again the process of interviewing the witness to a paranormal experience may result in solving or part-solving a case from what you learn.

Wherever possible an effort should be made to trace and speak to any original eyewitnesses, provided they indicate a willingness to be interviewed. Obviously, as regards tracing most, if not all, original witnesses mentioned in *Phantom Ladies* this is likely to prove impossible with the passage of time. Though well within the range of living memory, the majority of persons mentioned in the text are likely to have died themselves in the natural course of things, whilst others will have moved away. Even if traceable, some may well not want to be troubled or might even have forgotten![7]

However, it is not beyond the bounds of possibility that individuals who knew the witness or family concerned may remain contactable. Sometimes younger family members provide information or records are discovered in some form. In some cases details may have been shared with new occupiers who followed them.

Consequently, a re-investigation may focus on finding more recent witnesses and in some cases one may be alerted to these by mentions in the press or media (including social media) or by an appeal launched by yourself.

It is unfortunate that many sceptics are prejudiced against eye-witness testimony. Since first-person experience is a basic form of evidence, listening to witness testimony is more scientific than ignoring or dismissing it out of hand, and it helps establish whether a case is worth pursuing. Yet there is no doubt that people experience apparitions; what is to be discovered is what lies behind these experiences.

The assumption is not that evidence from a witness is infallible and may be expected to be accurate in all respects, but whether overall it provides prima facie case justifying further investigation.

Factors affecting the reliability of witnesses

Once you have gathered a statement from a witness it is necessary to assess its contents. Thought should be given to whether it has been derived from another person, influenced by another witness or even just copied from some source, even a fictional story or folktale. As Green observed in the context of the haunting of Robertsbridge Library in Sussex, 'One of the initial problems of gauging whether a haunting is genuine or not is, as far as I am concerned, to assess the type of witness and the circumstances involved.'[8]

From learning what has happened direct from the witness it should be possible to form at least an opinion of the reliability and credibility of the testimony as well as gathering details of the manifestations experienced. Naturally, one should not take claims purely on trust or automatically assume there is really anything paranormal happening despite the sincerity of the witness; one should consider if any normal explanations can be postulated, whether ordinary causation can be eliminated and the possibility that a witness may be mistaken.

Some cases of hauntings in domestic premises turn out to be purely of psychological interest or to have a natural cause. The ghost hunters should be alert to cases where the alleged phenomena arises in the context of a medical problem or condition which may increase the tendency to hallucinate or impair waking consciousness. To exclude doubtful cases it may often be important to discover from a witness, as discretely and politely as possible, about their state of health, if they have recently been in hospital or if a witness has been prescribed some form of medication. Obviously, the quality of evidence may be impugned if the witness is taking drugs (whether legal or illegal) or if there are mental health issues. It may also become apparent that a small minority of people are purely attention-seekers or fantasy prone individuals. However, it is best not to diagnose the witness yourself but to bear what you may learn in mind in any assessment.

Facts about the lives of witnesses affecting their credibility may also emerge long after the events concerned. This was the case with a number of original witnesses in the alleged haunting of Borley Rectory in Essex between 1863-1939 which led to the genuineness of haunting being significantly called into question.[9]

At the same time it should not be considered that disclosure of a medical condition or the taking of medication automatically excludes credible testimony from a witness. Indeed, the growing field of clinical parapsychology examines the possibility that certain types of medical conditions may be conducive to particular types of psychic experience. Stress appears to be a significant factor in some domestic hauntings of the poltergeist variety. Two leading SPR investigators Maurice Grosse and Mary Rose Barrington took the view that amongst members stress, such as illness in a household was always a factor in poltergeist cases. The same view has been shared by psychiatrists who have interested themselves in psi phenomena.[10]

However, these sorts of cases are less likely to be relevant in the cases and types of sites listed in *Phantom Ladies* as Green took the decision to exclude cases of the typically short-term poltergeist variety in which personal stress is often a factor.

When it comes to seeking to corroborate a story, evidentially merely to have told someone else about a sighting is not corroboration of its truth (otherwise you would only have to repeat a story twenty-five times to obtain twenty-five corroborations).[11]

Also, consider as Green observed, 'In certain cases I think it unwise to dismiss a case merely because there is only one known person who saw the apparition. There may well be others who are reluctant to divulge that they too saw a ghost, or have moved away from the district'.[12]

Ideally, what should be obtained is evidence which is independent of the witness either via instrumentation or from other witnesses. Other people may confirm hearing about the experience soon after it occurred, perhaps noticing the surprise or shocked demeanour of a witness (which at least confirms a witness is at least consistent in some respect) but it is not a corroboration. However, often only a single witness is involved in a sighting and no other corroboration is available. Second-hand information and hearsay should be treated with caution because versions of experiences may become rapidly distorted or exaggerated to the point where it may be disregarded.

Once a number of quite independent accounts are obtained which show similarities between them then a prima facie evidential case for a haunting can be made. For this it is necessary to look closely at what is being said by the witness in their own words as much as possible.

Descriptions of phenomena

It will be found that peoples' reactions to ghost experiences varies enormously between individuals along with their willingness to share or recall details. Some will give a detailed account of what has happened and, if an apparition has been seen, some may even provide a sketch drawing if invited. In interviewing witnesses of ghostly phenomena, Andrew Green would emphasise to often distressed witnesses that their experiences should not be viewed as bewildering, frightening or uncanny but rather understood as a natural phenomenon shared by many thousands of normal people over the years.

As full a description of the appearance of any apparition is welcome, though it may be that fewer sightings seem to be as clear or as vivid as in past generations. Some apparitions appear life like and are mistaken as living people, some are semi-formed or transparent and some only amorphous shapes or shadows.

In cases where the apparition is described as a woman or female but only appeared indistinct or is vaguely described (for example, if described as 'shadowy') one should ask why it was considered female. On occasion a witness has been able to sense identity rather than be able to list clear distinguishing features of the ghost they see and some researchers have noticed that claims of these types of blurry apparition have increased in recent decades.[13]

"What clothes were the apparition wearing?" is a good question, for if an account is sufficiently detailed it may be possible to establish the period involved. Often though if a witness describes the clothing of the phantom as 'old-fashioned' more information is needed as to how they judge fashions and styles. 'Old' for some witnesses may convey a period of time ranging from the medieval period to the 1980s.[14]

In cases where the apparition is described as being a long-haired woman in a 17th or 18th century property this point should be checked further since hairstyles are not necessarily an invariable guide to gender. Hair lengths of the historical period and the fashion for lengthy male wigs may need to be considered.

In rare cases, the figure may be identified. If reckoned to be a historical personage, archival research may be worth undertaking to see if an image survives which can be compared with the description. The length of time of any sighting and how the figure appeared and disappeared are all relevant questions, as is the behaviour which any figure displayed.

Also worth finding out is whether the witness had any previous experience of psychic phenomena before, and whether the most recent incident resembles it in any way? Green considered that if you see one ghost, you may well go on to see two or three more in the course of a lifetime.

In cases of noisy phenomena it may be possible to get a better description than "footsteps" from enquiry. Were they heavy, regular or light; did they sound like running, creeping or shuffling? Did they sound human, or did they resemble an animal's padding steps? Identifying as far as possible where the steps began and stopped is important, given the scope for noises to arise from purely ordinary causes.

Consistencies occurring in separate testimonies are very interesting; it is from such patterns within the data, or 'signals in the noise' that clues can emerge from which theories might be developed. One should not be disheartened by the fact that this seems a huge challenge, for mainstream psychology grapples with precisely this problem with many aspects of consciousness, as do many the boundaries of many other sciences and enquiries where theories do not yet cover all the observed data.

Site investigation

If one is satisfied that a haunting is worth further investigating and permission can be gained to hold a vigil then attention shifts to seeing how this may best be conducted. Before holding the investigation proper, a thorough examination of the property and its wider surroundings should be undertaken to obtain as full an understanding as possible of the physical aspects of the location. Many ghosts and haunting manifestations turn out to have entirely normal explanations. Numerous cases are recorded where ghostly sounds are traced to entirely natural causes, such as defective premises adversely affected by extreme weather events. An inspection may point to a purely normal causation such as the misperception of natural stimuli (particularly noises in the night).[15]

Otherwise, without understanding the physical location, researchers can be prone to making identical errors as witnesses in terms of misperceiving natural events. In 1999-2000 I was involved with a number of investigations at Charlton House in Eltham, Surrey. One particular first floor room at the rear of the property possessed a window said to rattle mysteriously, a physical event often attributed to the ghost. Several ghost hunters testified to being in the room when this occurred. The rattling proved real but close examination of the floor found it was a vibrational effect traceable to pressure on a particular floorboard which transferred itself through the antique timbers to the window frame. Once investigators avoided stepping on the floorboard in question the 'phenomenon' ceased.

Spells of torrential rain following periods of drought may cause inexplicable sounds within properties old and new, resulting in creaks, knocks and groaning sounds which may surprise a new occupier. Green advised ghost hunters to be on the look-out for signs of damp, defective plumbing, faulty central heating systems and to carefully inspect skirting boards, floorboards, lofts, basements, airing cupboards and lean-tos for signs of disrepair and previous water damage. Other warning features are cracks in cavity walls, inadequate insulation and soundproofing and traces of botched repairs by previous residents. Obviously, the more neglected or dilapidated a property, the greater the scope for structural deficiencies generating strange sounds.

An increase in reports of uncanny noises proving to have a physical origin was reported in the United States according to John E.L. Tunney, the former host of the TV show *Ghost Stalkers,* principally as a side-effect of the covid pandemic. In autumn 2021 he told the *New York Times* of a dramatic increase in ghost reports reaching him, up from an average four or five each month in 2019 to as many as five to 10 a week during 2020-21 which he attributed to heightened states of anxiety, and people spending more time at home during the pandemic, exposing them to ordinary noises they had never noticed before, such as wood expanding. Many ghost hunters consider that people who move into a property for the first time may fall victim to 'new house syndrome', initially mistaking unfamiliar but perfectly normal sounds as manifestations.[16]

The possibility of pranksters lurking on the site or intrusion by trespassers—whether deliberate or accidental—or persons present and engaging in some otherwise innocent and ordinary activity need to be guarded against. With the rise of interest in the paranormal some consideration should be given to the choosing of date, particularly Hallowe'en, holiday and Christmas time and anniversary days for alleged hauntings, as one may from time to time discover one's efforts clash with attempts by other individuals or groups to investigate the same site, particularly if it is open to the public at any time. In some cases the 'ghostly effects' may be the result of infestation by animals – insects, squirrels, rats, mice and birds being the most common culprits.

Holding a site investigation and using equipment

Ghost hunting is best undertaken in groups or pairs of reliable and responsible people who are well-briefed with what is being tested, but preferably without a detailed knowledge in advance of the phenomena concerned or alleged. When it comes to investigating haunted premises out of hours or in the dark, care and a sensible approach as with any nocturnal activity should be foremost. Weather, comfort, safety and security and access have to be considered by all participants. A large stately home raises different challenges to a suburban semi-detached house or a bungalow to a site in the open air in a wood or on a hill top.

Cases involving hauntings by phantom ladies basically involve the same set ups for vigils as those involving any other alleged haunted location and equipment can be as complex or as simple as any group or team wishes to deploy. Many groups deploy some kind of equipment on investigations, but not properly appreciating the function and limitations of many of items or gadgets deployed, or even whether there is any point to some of them.

It is essential that anyone deploying equipment knows how to use it, otherwise there is really no point in taking it. Altogether, just how anomalous readings from instruments might fit in with any particular theory about haunting experiences provides a major challenge in itself and there are many difficult areas and almost no certainties. The use of equipment may back up witness reports, the essential thing being that the use of any device or instrument is relevant to what has been reported. In this regard the reader is recommended to thoroughly study the technical manuals, test the experiment with dry-runs and also learn the basic science and units of measurement.

Equipment can provide tangible and measurable evidence by way of recordings that may provide some corroboration of anomalous physical effects linked with ghostly manifestations. Alternatively, equipment may help establish a purely natural or physical basis for the haunting and no ghost at all. Ideally, the use of instrumentation as to what the witnesses has already reported or provide some insight on the nature of the experience, for example to see if a natural cause may be identified or eliminated.

Many items deployed by today's ghost hunters have an unproven value to paranormal study. For instance, neither negative ion detectors (NID) or electromagnetic field (EMF) meters have been demonstrated as being useful and scientific investigative tools beyond pure conjecture and supposition.

Measuring instruments only record physical characteristics of the environment such as temperature, air pressure, sound waves and electromagnetic flux – none of these is proven to be conclusively linked with the occurrence of any paranormal phenomenon.

Consequently, caution should be applied to any extravagant claims over any gadgetry. The capabilities and limitations of the device or instrument concerned and sources of error should be thoroughly understood. It should be remembered that the role of equipment is to detect physical and environmental anomalies—there are currently no 'ghost detecting' devices in existence. There is no such thing known, tested or patented as a 'spirit detector' which reacts in the presence of spirit entities (it not being proved that spirits exist to any scientific standard). Those who uncritically accept such claims and believe that these do exist are best described as extraordinarily gullible or stupid and are being conned out of their money if they have invested in any such devices.

Other more basic items, such as audio recording devices and thermometers, remain important for objectively recording sounds and variations in temperature. With thermometers it should be possible to capture extreme and inexplicable ambient temperature changes if they occur. However, to do this in a scientific manner requires taking control readings at a site as a preliminary, with naturally arising changes in temperature being factored into any assessment. It proves little to be able to show that an unheated derelict building in the north of England in November is turning cold![17]

Anything relating to electrical problems – flickering lights, inexplicable power failures or surges or even claims of electric shock should be investigated cautiously. The opinion and assistance of a qualified electrician or engineer should be sought as a backup or before embarking on any investigation into the wiring and power supply systems. Researchers should avoid endorsing any claims that ghosts are electrical or electromagnetic in nature or that they create such anomalies. In the case of persons apparently reacting to uncanny feelings, the possibility should be explored that they are actually reacting to electromagnetic fields generated by electromagnetic pollution from power lines or the supply of electricity itself to the premises.

Altogether, equipment has its uses on ghost investigations but should not be overemphasised and careful checks should be made at each stage.

Photography and film

Given that eye-witness testimony may be mistaken, it has been a long-standing hope that instrumentation would provide proof independent of the human eye and mind. As long ago as 1905, one Ernest Law declared he had been looking for the Grey Lady at Hampton Court for some 35 years that, 'I wish a snap shootist would bring his kodak down here and get a photo of her – it is much needed by historians'.[18]

We are still waiting. Strange images were obtained at Hampton Court in 2003 and again 2015 but neither has stood up to analysis. As with many digital images expert analysis frequently reveals a technical cause or glitch.[19]

If apparitions were capable of being recorded on film or by digitalised processes, it might establish that a ghost forms part of the visible light spectrum. This would mean that light emitted as photons would have an actual physical effect upon photographic chemicals in the past and today in a digital form, implying the emission of light radiation today. Large numbers of such images are in circulation, the common factor being the photographer did not see anything at the time.

Regrettably many who hope they have caught proof of a ghost on camera are destined to be disappointed. Whilst a photograph might suggest that something strange or anomalous is happening, it should not be taken as definitive proof in itself. The photographic evidence for ghosts is nowhere near as strong as was once considered. Consequently, an odd photograph is simply the stimulus for further study and investigation. At the very minimum details of the type of camera and its usage should be preserved; some cases have been solved by technical analysis of the film processing (often to the marked disappointment of the photographer!). This point was made more than a quarter of a century ago, by Troy Taylor in the United States, author of *The Ghost Hunter's Guidebook* (1998) who declared "Digital photos: or ghost hunting at its worst!" and stated, "no matter what some people claim, digital cameras cannot be used to capture irrefutable evidence of the paranormal." In particular, digital photography is notorious for generating artefacts by way of their flash facility reflecting on fine particles in the air, creating luminous blobs and blotches invisible to observers when the photograph was taken.[20]

When first noticed these were dubbed 'orbs'. From the mid-1990s and onwards (and still today) many ghost hunters took orbs as signatures of some kind of manifestation. Analysis at the time and subsequent experiments utilising 3-D cameras demonstrate that orbs are merely dust particles lit by the flash facility, like microscopic particles visible to the naked eye illuminated in sunbeams. Thumping cushions or pillows or doing some dusting are likely to raise some for photographic purposes and comparison![21]

In the long term, the value of cameras and photographic evidence in many situations is increasingly being called into question. However, the persistence of marks and photographic anomalies in photographic images pictures taken at haunted sites may suggest some unusual effect which cannot easily be ascribed to a natural causation or the probable lack of skill of the photographer. Possibly, such effects might actually be cases of equipment breakdown which are reported at haunted premises.

Mediums and sensitives

The best detecting device remains the human body. It should be remembered that our sensitivity is far greater than our conscious selves may recognise and subliminal perceptions may account for some impressions from a site.

Some groups go further and employ the services of a medium or clairvoyant although much will depend on the faith that one has in their abilities, and a belief in spiritualist doctrines. Their use has been common in TV programmes devoted to ghost hunting, with film makers regularly involving the use of self-proclaimed psychics and mediums, few of whom have been subject to any independent scrutiny or testing. Unfortunately, many readings are too vague and general in content to be considered evidential, failing to provide any verifiable information. Consequently, their claims are often justly treated with scepticism and frequently ridiculed by much of the viewing public and most critics and some have even been exposed as charlatans. Others reject psychics simply because different sensitives provide different opinions, with readings often diverging widely. It is the inconsistency of differing psychic interpretations which also undermines accuracy though no competent or honest psychic will ever claim a 100% success rate.

That a person claims to be a psychic does not mean s/he is one; equally the possibility that a person does have extrasensory powers or psi abilities should not be dismissed lightly. These abilities – if that is what they are – should not be considered infallible or even reliable for much of the time. Such a conclusion is backed up by more than a century of research showing that psychic impressions and communications are never 100% accurate and indeed can often be wholly unreliable and that many psychics score only at chance level or at most slightly above it in trials. Consequently claims made by a medium about the history of a site should not be automatically accepted without checking and determining whether a medium is likely to have obtained the information from any ordinary source. Even if veridical information (i.e. details which are factually true and accurate) does emerge it may still have no bearing on the phenomena being observed or mean a ghost is responsible.

Verifying information can be a problem, as one may struggle to rule out all possible sources. This is where comparisons between the statements made by a medium and other undisclosed witness testimony may be useful.

Green largely eschewed spiritualistic approaches but on occasions was prepared to work with selected mediums and sensitives such as Eddie Pratt of Caterham, a clairvoyant friend who visited some properties and recorded impressions. On occasion Green felt that Pratt succeeded in obtaining accurate information in ways that were beyond the ordinary senses but he did not attribute this to spiritual agencies.

Similarly, caution must be exercised with respect to claims made for dowsing with pendulums or divining rods wielded by participants and also with the use of Ouija boards. There is much interesting evidence that supports dowsing for water and minerals and even lost objects but there is no firm evidence to show it relates to detecting ghosts or any that spirits communicate through divining rods. The rod itself is capable of detecting nothing in itself; it needs the hands of a sensitive operator to move and show a reaction.

Thus, ghost hunters should avoid uncritically accepting uncorroborated claims and findings not backed by any methodology. Yet there is still space for qualitive approaches in ghost hunting as a factor for consideration, for example, where impressions may be gained from sensitives and mediums and compared with accounts from previous visitors and witness testimony. For example at Samlesbury Hall in Lancashire, Andrew Green noted 'Descriptions given by numerous witnesses always feature the same woman, sometimes gliding down the pathway to stand near the wall and also seen moving silently up one of the stairways in Samlesbury Hall itself'. Such similarities also appeared in separate testimonies recorded at the Cage at St Osyth in Essex, reputedly haunted by a witch named Ursula Kempe who was executed in 1582. Scrutiny of separate individual accounts obtained on different occasions indicated witnesses describing the same phenomena, personal reactions or impressions at particular points, findings, reported by John Fraser in 2019.[22]

Beyond this, there may be scope for examining a pattern I have noticed over the years in the conduct of vigils that male investigators are more fixed on taking readings with instruments compared with some female colleagues who may move towards an intuitive approach. This should not be dismissed. Whether women or men are more sensitive to these phenomena and whether there is a foundation for the belief in female 'intuition' is a question yet to be scientifically determined. Attempts to distinguish between male and females as subjects in psi testing for telepathy and clairvoyance have generally found no major differences between the scores and performances between them but it may be different with 'haunts' involving significant psi phenomena which can exceed anything routinely recorded in laboratories. American parapsychologist Gertrude Schmeidler devised a standardised way of approaching a qualitative assessment at haunted premises in the United States in 1966 which is set out herein as an Appendix and may provide an approach.[23]

An alternative to human sensitivity was once utilised by Professor Bob Morris, who later headed the Koestler Chair of Parapsychology at Edinburgh University taken at a haunted property in the United States in 1971. Then at Duke University in the USA, he visited a reputedly haunted house in Kentucky containing a room where a murder had been committed. Tests took place using different animals, a dog, a cat, a white rat and a rattlesnake. The dog came just two feet into the room before snarling at its owner and backing out of the door. It refused to re-enter, despite cajoling by its owner. The cat was carried into the room and at the same point leapt up on to her owner and then jumped to the floor and orientated itself towards an empty chair. For the next while the cat "spent several minutes hissing and spitting at the empty chair" until removed from the room. The rat showed no discernible changes in reaction but the rattlesnake immediately assumed an attack posture focusing on the same chair. None of the animals reacted in a similar way in any other room in the house.[24]

The existence of striking similarities in evidence from widely separated witnesses can itself be considered evidential if there has been no previous sharing or exposure to the information. From this the research can take almost any direction to explore any hypothesis the investigator wishes to explore.

It is appreciated the foregoing details and advice will not suit every situation and will certainly not suit everyone. However, it is hoped that this will encourage scientifically credible approaches to spontaneous paranormal phenomena so as to yield meaningful results.

Historic cases
Even with seemingly historical cases and legendary stories it may sometimes be possible to obtain new information through research, where archives collected by bodies such as the Society for Psychical Research may sometimes establish a basis that once existed for a story long ago.

One story not included in 1977 by Andrew Green which seemed purely legendary was that the ruins of Woodhouse Lea House near Rosslyn in Lothian, Scotland were frequented by a ghostly lady, the 17th century wife of a Scottish laird who fell victim to marauders and died after being ejected from her home on a freezing winter's night and left to die naked in the snow. Her ghost appears very late in the year.

Supposedly the house became so haunted that it was eventually torn down in the 19th century and a new house built some distance away. Visiting the original site of Woodhouse Lea in early September 2021 I found the mounds and ruins had succumbed to vegetation, but local people still spoke of a haunted archway having endured up until 10 years before.

More significantly, it turns out that the stories of a haunting may have enjoyed some foundation, from tantalising clues in a record held by the Society for Psychical Research. In the late 19th century an account was received from a woman who heard unexplained footsteps in the old building before it was dismantled. Further archival research at the National Library of Scotland turned up an admittedly fragmentary mention of a soldier encountering an apparition whilst on guard duty one night at a nearby encampment during the First World War and the American ghost hunter Hans Holzer collected further local stories in 1974.[25]

Such results may inspire readers to investigate their own local stories of female ghosts which Green had omitted from *Phantom Ladies* as it was believed to be folkloric. For example a white lady was said to walk at Rushbrooke Hall near Bury St Edmunds, supposedly 'Agnes de Rushbrooke' who was murdered by a jealous husband and her body thrown in the moat. Following up the story I discovered in the archives of the SPR a lengthy letter written in 1888 detailing haunting phenomena at Rushbrooke when it was rented by the Vansittart family. Unfortunately there was no follow up by the Society at the time. Abandoned after a fire in 1961, the hall became derelict before being pulled down entirely in 1973.[26]

Thus research may either displace a legend or turn up interesting hints suggesting an account was rooted in actual experiences in the past. Yet it becomes apparent that there are limits to what can be investigated. In the course of editing this book it became clear that there was a subset of Phantom Ladies conforming to traditional motif of a White Lady ghost which because of its characteristics poses major practical difficulties, at least as regards conventional ghost hunting approaches. It is to this enigmatic class of experiences that the final chapter is devoted.

Finally, it is important (as Andrew Green always emphasised) that the welfare of any household living in a haunted property must be remembered at all times and, indeed, should be paramount in terms of how investigators conduct themselves. Hauntings can cause stress and anxiety amongst those encountering ghostly manifestations and investigators should always seek to reduce such negative impacts with human welfare always coming first and ahead of the interests of researchers.

Notes & References

[1] West, Donald (1954) *Psychical Research Today.* Penguin. UK pp. 42-43.

[2] West, Donald (1946) 'The Investigation of Spontaneous Cases' *Proceedings* of the Society for Psychical Research Vol 64 1946-1949 pp.264-299.

[3] Issued by the Society for Psychical Research, 8 Vernon Mews, London W11

[4]. Green, Andrew (1973) *Ghost Hunting: A Practical Guide*. Garnstone Press;(1976) Mayflower Books paperback edn; (2016) 2nd edition edited by Alan Murdie, Arima Books. UK.

[5] Fraser, John (2010) *Ghost Hunting A Survivor's Guide*. The History Press. pp. 140-141.

[6] Murdie, Alan (2007) *Haunted Bury St Edmunds*. Tempus. pp. 78-79.

[7] *The Census of Hallucinations* (1894) *Proceedings* of the Society for Psychical Research Vol 10 25-422 at 66 shows a fall off of experiences being recalled with time particularly for minor ones.

[8] Green, Andrew (1977) *Phantom Ladies* p.93.

[9] See Dingwall, Eric, Goldney Mollie & Hall, Trevor *The Haunting of Borley Rectory* (1956) Duckworth. Ltd; JSPR 45, 115-124. Hall, T. H. (1978) *Search for Harry Price*. London: Duckworth. Hastings, R. J. (1969) *An Examination of the Borley Report'. Proceedings of the SPR 55,* 65-175. Hastings R. J. (1970) *Reply to the authors of the 'Borley Report' Journal of the SPR 45,* 230-237. Randall, J. L. (2000) 'Harry Price: the case for the Defence'. JSPR 64, 159-176.

[10] McHarg, James (1982) 'The Paranormal and the Recognition of Personal Distress' in *Journal of the SPR,* vol. 51 pp. 200-209.

[11] *R v Whitehead* [1929] 1 KB 99 *"In order that evidence may amount to corroboration it must be extraneous to the witness who is to be corroborated. A girl cannot corroborate herself, otherwise it is only necessary for her to repeat her story some twenty-five times in order to get twenty-five corroborations of it"* at 102.

[12] See note 8

[13] Hallson, Peter (1986) Correspondence, *Journal* of the Society for Psychical Research Vol. 53, No. 803 pp. 331-332.

[14] Green Andrew (2016) *Ghost Hunting A Practical Guide* 2nd Edn p.97.

[15] Green, A ibid. n. 14 Chapter 5

[16] *New York Times* 28 Oct 2021.

[17] See n.3

[18] See n.3 ibid

[19] Harper, Charles (1907) *Haunted Houses*. Chapman & Hall Ltd. Pp.16-29 at p.19

[20] Murdie, Alan in Ghostwatch (2015)'Ghostwatch' in *Fortean Times* No 326 15-18.

[21] Taylor, Troy (1999) *The Ghost Hunter's Guidebook*. Whitechapel Productions press. Illinois pp.105-108

[22] Carr, Philip (2009) 'DVD film Riddle of the Orbs' and personal communication; Parsons, Steve (2010) 'Orbs!...Some Definitive Evidence That They Are Not Paranormal' in *Anomaly* the Journal of Association of the Scientific Study of Anomalous Phenomena (ASSAP) Vol 44 November 2010. Steve Parsons concludes Regarding the study images that "...all 630 that we obtained in the survey were readily explained using the stereo photography technique. That is 0% paranormal but 100% explainable."

[23] Green, *Phantom Ladies* p.44; Fraser, John (2019) Lecture at Ghost Hunting Workshop Day hosted by the Society Psychical Research and the Ghost Club 23rd March 2019; Schmeidler, Gertrude (1966) 'Quantitative Investigation of a "Haunted House" (1966) *Journal* of the American Society for Psychical Research Vol LV April 1966 pp.133-149.

[24] Morris, Robert (1971) 'An experimental approach to the survival problem' in *Theta* No. 34:33

[25] Holzer, Hans (1976) *Great British Ghost Hunt*. W.H.Allen.UK. pp 161-16

[26] Murdie, Alan (2008) *Haunted Edinburgh*. Tempus Books. Archive of Alasdair Alpin MacGregor held at National Library of Scotland. Manuscript Collection MacGregor Acc. 6215

CHAPTER FOUR

White Ladies and Phantom Ladies – one and the same? Or different altogether?

On 18th August 2022 Helen Barrell was with her father and stepmother travelling through the gentle countryside which lies between the Suffolk villages of Pin Mill and East Bergholt in the south east of the county. Helen is a historian and was interested in photographing memorials at a number of local village churchyards. Their route took them through Holbrook, a place her father was keen for her to see as he had attended school there. Travelling on the Harkstead Road, at a spot known as Fir Tree Hill, they came to a fork in the road with Back Hill splitting off from it towards the village of Holbrook when "something rather strange happened".

Just before they were about to drive through a part of the road where overhanging trees span the route Helen Barrell recalled "I saw a flash of white right in front of the car. It was like a bright flash, really, that from my point of view was moving from left to right. My dad saw it too and hit the brakes. But then we realised there was nothing there, and he carried on driving."

Her father suggested the cause was "a change of the light" but Helen isn't convinced, saying, "I don't know how it can be, bearing in mind we were just about to enter a tunnel of trees, where the light is subdued but we had not yet done so".

She added "It reminded me of the many, many stories people have told about white ladies etc crossing the road, and people braking suddenly, then realising there was nothing there." Her stepmother did not see anything.[1]

Whilst it is entirely possible that some kind of strange optical effect was at work that afternoon in rural Suffolk caused by light passing through vegetation in some way, Helen Barrell's view of White Lady apparitions are relevant ones to our inquiry.

Just this type of experience had occurred in daylight just over twenty miles away and some 14 years earlier on 13 May 2008, when Valerie Pomfret and her sister were travelling to the village of Great Maplestead in Essex on the A131.

Just rounding the corner which leads to the famous Norman round church of St Giles opposite Maplestead Hall, Valerie was suddenly shaken by 'a strange sensation of being in a different place and time'. Suddenly, she saw a young girl with two long blond plaits down to her waist crossing the road in front of her and stepping directly in the path of her car. The unexpected appearance of the girl caused her to brake sharply.

Again there is mention of obscuring of facial features with the apparition: "Although I could not see her face, her head was turned towards me as though she was looking straight at me. In an instant she disappeared onto what at the time seemed to be a footpath, so I slowed down thinking she might have a dog with her".

Her sister asked her why she had braked, and she explained that she had seen what she took to be a girl crossing the road. As with Helen Barrell's sighting, Valerie too was travelling with the aim of visiting an antique church. On arrival at the church she wondered if there might be a grave of a girl or young woman matching the description of the female on the road but a brief search of the churchyard and grave inscriptions did not reveal anything that seemed relevant.[2]

As *Phantom Ladies* demonstrates, there are no shortage of female ghosts connected with particular premises and occasionally connected to the life events and circumstances of witnesses. Yet also amongst the diverse reports of hauntings there stands out a particular and recurrent type of apparition, a class that is identifiable as a 'White Lady' which seems to manifest in rural rather than urban and domestic settings and does little more than appear and disappear, often on a road.

These White Ladies present as anonymous apparitions in a set and emblematic form. Widely recorded in tradition, they are frequently seen standing beside or on or even crossing a road or materialising at remote and isolated spots. These one-off sightings are difficult to encompass within psi-based theories of apparitions or even as 'spirits of the dead' being seemingly purposeless or bereft of meaning. They are also the most problematic to investigate, because of their unpredictable nature, not to mention the practical difficulties of mounting investigations at remote locales or on roads carrying traffic. Yet it is at these spots where she seems to step out of folklore to briefly impinge on human consciousness, seemingly randomly as regards time and place.

These cases are often classified as 'spectral pedestrians' and are often reported on many open roads and highways across Great Britain but obviously busy roads are impossible to investigate in the same way as enclosed premises because of the hazards that would be entailed for both investigators and road users.

For example, on 12th December 2010 between 8.15pm to 8.25 p.m., Mr Derek McCall was driving alone on the A75 / B721 road in southern Scotland at 60 m.p.h. listening to the radio, when he became aware of the figure of an elderly woman appearing at the roadside, who then wandered into the road in front of him. McCall braked at once but could not avoid a collision. Just at that point when a terrible accident was inevitable the figure vanished. McCall checked his rear-view mirror, but there was nothing to be seen in the road behind. Ms Kathleen Cronie, a friend of Mr McCall recalled how ashen he looked when he came to pick her up that night, in a statement obtained by a psychologist Dr Peter McCue.[3]

An interesting aspect of Derek McCall's sighting is that he was at that time part of a group called 'Mostly Ghostly' who had been in the same area of the A75/B721 and had been discussing ghosts and mysterious sightings just the previous night. along the route. An obvious possibility is that Mr McCall was a victim of autosuggestion 24 hours later or had experienced a nocturnal hallucination, (with his subconscious mind taking such stories more seriously than his waking mind). Such an explanation might further be applied other cases of lone drivers on lonely roads late at night, with the hallucination of spectral pedestrian the by-product of the sub-conscious of a fatigued driver.

But similar sightings emerged on the 15-mile stretch starting from Gretna in the east and ending several miles west-north-west of Annan and conceivably reaching as far as Dumfries and were reported by those who were not ghost hunters.

Explanations like fatigue may account for some night-time encounters but a high percentage of daylight experiences go against any 'tired brain' hypothesis as an all-encompassing cause, as do examples of the White Ladies seen by more than one witness at a time. It is the widespread nature of the experience, both in space and time that forms the puzzle. Incidents like this can make the percipients concerned and some researchers think that in some way, a ghostly encounter was staged for their benefit. One might also wonder about Andrew Green's arrival at a pub near Bedford in 1973 and meeting with a local man who had claimed to have seen an apparition on the Wilden Road the previous week.[4]

In fact the road-crossing lady pre-dates motor vehicles. She is not always dressed in white, grey or black and occasionally other colours are mentioned. What is consistent is the seemingly random appearances and behaviour by apparitions which cross the path of a witness. An apparition seen in Kent in May 1912 by a Mr F.L. Luck and a Mr Fuller near Paddock Wood who were cycling on the road from Staplehurst, evidently resembled an old lady in a brown skirt and bonnet, who was 'reminiscent of Queen Victoria'. The figure appeared at a spot close to a stream and was seen to move into a hedge and then vanish. On reaching the spot, the witnesses noticed that the hedge was clearly so dense it would have been impenetrable for anyone to have passed through naturally. On closer inspection they found traces of an abandoned old gate which could no longer be usable because the growth of the hedge was too thick. She looked solid but had vanished inexplicably.

This and other sightings were collected by Sir Ernest Bennett for his book *Apparitions and Haunted Houses* (1939) with one proving even more dramatic.[5]

On one cold October day, in either 1920 or 1921, a Mrs W. from Somerset was driving in a horse-drawn trap with her sister up Wembdon Hill in Bridgwater. The mare pulling their trap started to slow down and exhibited strange reactions when suddenly "the strangest apparition glided down a steep path, crossed the road, and disappeared through a gate on the left…she was wearing a high-waisted muslin dress, and a white silk shawl over her head, and as she passed through the gate, she seemed to stare straight at me with a horrible look on her face."

Mrs W's sister also recalled the sighting stating that the figure disappeared through a closed gate, and 'floated over the road at about one foot from the ground'. She stated, 'The dress of the figure was so peculiar and so flimsy on such a cold day, that I think the idea of it being anybody dressed up can safely be ruled out.' She described the figure as a "tall figure of a young woman, in a pink dress, of Victorian period, probably with trailing skirts, with a lot of cream lace on and a lace wrap over her head…but before disappearing through a gate, she turned her head and looked at me. I can never forget that look, it was one of intense agony and the skin and eyes looked like grey dust".

She continued "The gate was closed, and as I got a side view of it, I saw the figure only just as long as the angle would allow". After the sighting ended their horse bolted and could not be brought under control for nearly half a mile. There was a story that a local man had seen a similar figure around twenty years earlier as well as a local legend that stated that the road was the site where a man murdered by his wife was buried but there was no corroboration for either of these claims.[6]

Clear similarities existed to another sighting recalled (having occurred some 50 years earlier) by a Mrs Charlotte Goodhall in an account given to the Society for Psychical Research in 1890. It occurred one summer's evening in Bedfordshire when still quite light, on the broad plateau of a high hill, between Willesden and Ravensden, on the road to the town of Bedford, either in 1873 or 1874. The road was unusually wide, with deep margins of grass on both sides. Mrs Goodhall was being driven by her daughter in a low pony carriage, "…when I suddenly saw a figure, dressed in black from head to foot advancing; it appeared to glide along. I said to my daughter, ' Oh, do look at that strange figure!' It passed on the left side of the carriage, on the grass, within two yards of us and as it did so, it turned its face directly our way, and of all the fiendish faces it was the most horrible you can imagine; its garments seemed to trail behind it. My daughter looked back after it as it passed us; she says it turned its face over its shoulder and looked towards us. I myself turned round immediately but it was gone. I told people in the county what we had seen but could never learn any history beyond the saying of the people, that part of the road was supposed to be haunted. The figure passed about three-quarters of a yard beyond the roadway. I was in good health and quite happy, aged about 50. [The figure had] no likeness to any one I ever had seen or have seen since."

Her daughter confirmed the experience and described the encounter as making a deep impression on them.

Such accounts could be multiplied, presenting the challenge of spontaneous experience encountered many years and many miles apart. Whilst single accounts may be prone to being dismissed as anecdotal by sceptics– without solving them – taken together they are a collection of data which has evidential weight and are capable of being considered probative in a judicial context.

The wide separation of these accounts and the emergence of similar patterns within them is enough to suggest a real phenomenon, indeed, were this to occur in the context of legal case, law enforcers might start building up a file about some long-standing, anti-social female human jaywalker putting road users at risk on various highways. And we would have to make her inter-generational as well, a family passing down the practice! They are sufficiently impressive with communities to have them stamp their presence on the names of locations where they appear. There are White Lady Lanes and White Lady Roads in different parts of the country e.g. a bridleway that runs through Ladywood Lane at Badwell Ashe and Great Ashfield in Suffolk which saw a spate of sightings of a strange light in the late 1960s.[7]

Thus, we are left with a large and still-growing body of sightings of female apparitions in different places, appearing spontaneously and seemingly capable of being differentiated from many domestic and localised hauntings where their sense of identity and individuality is more focused and attuned to the environment of the house. an individual identity and conditions in the household.

A distinct class?

At this point it may be asked why should these phantoms be distinguished from others in this book? Part of the answer lies in their consistency. These seemingly chance encounters with female apparitions which take place in the open air and at sites where no-one corporeal is generally residing all show a tendency of the figure to be clad in white, pale or monochrome coloured clothing.

White generally predominates as the colour of her clothes, sometimes varying to grey or black. In this she is distinguishable from the emblematic phantom ladies attire who frequent stately homes, manor houses and many castles. Known by the colour of their dress and, as *Phantom Ladies* demonstrates, throughout the UK there are examples of Green Ladies, Blue Ladies, Red Ladies, Pink Ladies and Ladies in Yellow. Most probably these are derived as a result of the impact of the rich hues in the portraiture of the 18th century which brought vivid bright colours into consciousness of a less visually sophisticated audience. As one commentator has said, 'Every good ghost story of the late eighteenth century featured sinister paintings'.[8]

The presence of such a striking portrait on premises may encourage such identifications, and such a nick name is likely to become attached to manifestations

Their appearance is generally defined in terms of their clothing, setting them apart from ordinary human females.

A second characteristic is that the apparition is usually perceived as a ghost which endlessly repeats the same kind of actions, typically appearing in the path of travellers. The appearance is relatively brief, the route fixed and invariably involves a figure coming in and out of vision and then going on to conceal itself but the story itself is a vague one which cannot be corroborated historically.

A third characteristic is that these apparitions seem to be symbolic and repetitive and yet display behaviour going beyond an 'ordinary' ghost. The phantom White Lady is an anonymous presence in the landscape on lonely roads and rural lanes, around ruins, bridges and rivers or even in the air, apparently defying gravity, all of which is suggestive of superhuman power and performances.

As was observed in an article in the journal *Folklore* in 1970 'The White Lady of Great Britain and Ireland' in 1970 she is an ethereal figure who usually haunts the spot where a group of individuals have died violently, 'While she appears in several guises, the form of a ghost is her most common one, a returning dead woman, who has met her untimely demise usually at the hands of a murderer'.

However the story remains a vague one with attempts to ascertain facts and background presenting the same difficulties as other hauntings but often exacerbated by the fact remote spots often have little in the way of recorded and documented history. Folkloric back-stories are unsupported by any facts, unprovable and often nonsensical. For example, in Dorset, a White Lady appears on the high road passing from Wimborne to Cranbourne through the woods on the St Giles estate. Magnificent fir trees stand by the roadside giving the spot a gloomy atmosphere and the form which haunts the place is described as a female figure dressed in white and wearing a hood over her face. 'She paces to and fro, but as soon as one sees her, she makes a wild rush through the hedge. Afterwards a crashing sound like a wagon and horses going fast through the area continues for some minutes. The popular belief is a murder was committed there in bygone years.'[9]

A Mr C. Randall was a child during the First World War, when his family lived in the village of Shudy Camps in Cambridgeshire. One November night he and his brother went on an errand. Walking past the Park they heard a blood-curdling scream, and then saw a headless figure dressed in white emerge from under an oak tree, walk through a hedge and sit down on the road verge a few feet from them. At this point they realised the figure was a woman.

They were transfixed by the apparition, but it disappeared a few seconds after sitting down, whereupon they took to their heels and ran. Reaching home their mother said, "You look as if you have seen a ghost!" The family made enquiries afterwards, learning that the ghost only appeared in November and was said to be a member of the Dayrell family, Lords of the Manor in the eighteenth and nineteenth century, although there is no record of any of them being beheaded (the possibility of a hoax might seem likely, save for the way the spectre vanished).[10]

Of course, it is not a requirement that folklore needs to always make sense, and in addressing the phenomenon one needs to exclude certain categories of stories and encounters where corroboration is weak, in the sense that no first-hand witnesses can be adduced.

In examining reports it is necessary to filter out those which are second hand or third hand or carry the hallmarks of popular modern folktales, 'friend-of-a-friend' or urban legend (save that these are rural). The best known of these is the phantom hitchhiker who thumbs or begs lifts across Britain and North America usually only to vanish before the end of the journey. Though popular and widespread such stories lack first-hand witnesses and verifiable names and dates.

But some are truly extraordinary being collectively sighted or seen on successive occasions by different witnesses which points to some kind of reality. White Lady encounters suggest or imply momentarily straying into another realm and level of existence, a momentary immersion in this realm where space and time limitations do not apply.

The following remarkable report was collected by the compilers of *Phantasms of the Living* (1886) in the 19th century from an army officer named Norton but goes beyond the crisis type apparitions with which the SPR were concerned:

"About Christmas time 1875 or 1876, being officer on duty, I was seated at the mess table of the 5th Lancers, in the West Cavalry Barracks at Aldershot. There were 10 or 12 other officers present, amongst them a Mr John Atkinson….

"At about 8.45pm Atkinson suddenly glared at the window to his right, attracting the notice of Russell, who seizing his arm, said "Good gracious, Doctor what's the matter with you?" This caused me to look in the direction in which I saw Atkinson looking, viz, at the window opposite and there I saw (for the curtains were looped up, although the room was lighted by a powerful central gaslight in the roof and by candles on the table) a young woman, in what appeared a soiled or somewhat worn bridal dress, walk or glide slowly past the window from east to west. She was about at the centre of the window when I observed her, and outside the window."

That the form was spectral was clear to all those present, the most significant detail emerges from Norton's account: "No person could have actually been in the position where she appeared as the window is 30 feet above the ground". Amazingly, Norton claims that "The occurrence made little if any impression upon me, though it impressed others who were in the room."

Mr Atkinson wrote "The appearance of a woman which I saw pass the mess-room window at Aldershot seemed to be outside, and it passed east to west. The mess room is on the first floor, so the woman would have been walking in the air."

He added, "There has been a very nice story made out of it – like most other ghost stories founded on an optical illusion."

The psychical researcher Edmund Gurney dismissed suggestions that the apparition represented an omen, instead considering it a collective hallucination. The SPR also received an account from another surviving witness, a Montmorency Beaumont who remarked, "I did hear that the incident had been related in some story in a magazine but I never saw it, and I cannot say that I have ever allowed myself great importance to it."[11]

It seems the experience may have inspired stories carried in the sensationalist *Illustrated Police News* that a supernatural being dubbed 'Spring Heeled Jack' was behind terrifying sentries at the camp. But perhaps at the core of the story is the testimony of officers who saw a *female* apparition some thirty feet in the air. So it was a case of a Spring Heeled Jill….

Interestingly, if one undertakes a further search of the Aldershot Barracks and English Heritage website one learns that close to the barracks is an Anglo-Saxon tumulus called "Cockadobby Hill" at a roundabout on the A3011. Colloquially the name Cockadobby means 'Hill of the Goblins' an interesting coincidence for it suggests supernatural tradition stretching back a thousand years or more at one location, an uncanny spot and lair for the supernatural.[12]

One writer who encountered varieties of female haunting in both domestic and rural environments was the academic and writer John Cuthbert Lawson (1874-1935) a distinguished classicist and Fellow of Pembroke College, Cambridge. He was one of a number of occupiers with university backgrounds taking the lease of the ancient Abbey House on Newmarket Road in Cambridge (rated the most haunted domestic house in the city) where he had personal experience of manifestations and had even seen its 'Grey Lady', a haunting that was spread over decades.

Lawson interested himself in of how much of the religion of the ancients survived among the customs and superstitions of the modern Greek peasantry, becoming convinced that echoes of archaic beliefs and practices were still detectable. His book *Modern Greek Folklore and Ancient Greek Religion* (1910) contains a wealth of first-hand observations and anecdotes from two years fieldwork in which he came to acknowledges the existence of real supernatural forces on certain Greek islands.

Lawson himself witnessed a flitting life-like apparition of a nymph in an olive grove during one foray which he could scarcely believe: "Nothing is more amazing in the peasantry of modern Greece than their familiarity with these various beings….Once however I did see a nymph – or what my guide took for one – moving about in an olive-grove near Sparta; and I must confess that had I possessed an initial faith in the existence of nymphs and in the danger of looking upon them, so lifelike was the apparition that I might have sworn as firmly as did my guide that it was a nymph that we had seen, and might have required as strong a dose as he at the next inn to restore my nerves… it is certainly strange that often in Greece not one man only but several together will see an apparition at the same moment, and even agree afterwards as to what they saw."

It is clear that Lawson felt his experience resembled a being closer to a supernatural 'non-human entity' from mythology than anything representing the ghost of a once living Greek woman. He went on to write his landmark book on folklore and its links with classical beliefs after this sighting and boldly included it. Interestingly, psychical researchers have concentrated on his Abbey House ghost at Cambridge but appeared to have passed over his nymph encounter, perhaps because of its religious connotations.[13]

The White Lady: a religious motif?
Published in the year before *Phantom Ladies* appeared was a book *Alone of All Her Sex*: *The Myth and Cult of the Virgin Mary* (1976) by feminist author Marina Warner. In it the author discusses the image and beliefs surrounding the Virgin Mary, spanning the centuries and tracing how these had evolved in parallel with changing Christian doctrines. Her book argued that the Virgin Mary conceived by Christian congregations and the faithful, shifted in culture over the millennia, proposing that the Virgin Mary was an unstable cultural construct comprised of human forms and patterns presented in the language of dreams, symbols and visual art.

Effectively, the cultural and psychosocial model sees the figure of the Virgin Mary as an entirely human construct – indeed, as a feminist, Warner sees it as being 'man-made' in the literal sense – composed of images and metaphors with no inherent or ultimate meaning. Giving little attention to historic visions and apparitions of the Mary her thesis concluded by predicting that the Virgin Mary would ultimately vanish as a figure in which people actively believed and the image would thereby be 'emptied of real powers to heal and to harm' remaining only as a purely abstract symbol.[14]

Warner's approach typifies sceptical and sociological approaches to paranormal and spiritual phenomena, with cultural scholars often seeking to unify all types of anomalous psychic experiences as a social phenomenon generated by society itself. Wedded to materialist philosophies these propose that experiences are a product that is created and shaped by the cultural beliefs of the community. People who live in the social environment are seeing what their cultures tell them to see. This views the White Lady phenomena as a 'psychosocial hallucination' created by the society in which such beliefs flourish, but it is dependent upon the persons knowing the story beforehand.

A folkloric origin for some stories linking both the Virgin Mary and White Lady has been proposed in Christian countries. In some cases, white ladies are referred to by locals by a name which was formerly used at a shrine of a saint or dedicated to the Blessed Virgin Mary before their destruction in the 16th century Protestant Reformation. Such connections are proposed for some English sites, the stories being faint and garbled memories of pre-Reformation Marian devotion. For instance at Uttoxeter, Staffordshire a site once known 'Maiden's Well' or 'Marden's Wall' was once known as Mary's Well by the 19th century was shunned after dark for being haunted by the ghost of a young woman.[15]

Another example concerned a well near Waddow Hall on the banks of the Ribble river in Yorkshire notoriously haunted by 'Peg o' Nell', an active and dangerous spirit blamed for causing drownings. The legend had grown up that Peg in life had been a servant against whom her master or mistress nursed some grievance, angrily wishing Peg might fall in and break her neck. Unfortunately, this curse proved effective as duly Peg fell into the well and expired. After death she returned as a vengeful ghost plaguing the locality, with the well dubbed 'Peg o' Nell's Well' in fearful tribute. Antiquarians speculated that the legend was inspired by the presence of a "headless, now almost shapeless, figure" identified as an icon originally from Whalley or Salley Abbey nearby perhaps once representing the Virgin Mary or St Margaret of Antioch and once placed near the well.[16]

However, such convenient cultural explanations reach their limits when they intersect with actual experience, particularly those recounted by those who had no knowledge of the existence of any ghost tradition at the time. An example is Andrew Green's own encounter, one evening in 1971, of 'human sized and shaped darkness' when driving along Nan Tuck Lane in Sussex. This was months before he learned the story of poor little Nan Tuck and her summary execution for witchcraft, though no record of this is known except for the folklore.[17]

Furthermore it may be remarked that Warner's stated belief that the Virgin Mary as a living symbol would evaporate in the modern world has been falsified, with many Roman Catholic nations showing a marked upsurge in veneration of the Blessed Mary, a devotion encouraged by Pope John Paul II. Pilgrims continue to flock to sites such as Lourdes in France, Knock in Ireland and Fatima in Portugal. Claimed manifestations of her apparition have continued, most famously at Medjugorje in the former Yugoslavia in 1981 along with others unsanctioned by the Vatican at various locations, which become the site of unofficial cults where individuals claim intense religious experiences and visionary encounters. For example, in Ireland in the autumn of 1985 there was a now-largely forgotten wave of extraordinary claims of moving and trembling statues of the Virgin and increasingly bizarre apparitions.[18]

When faced with sightings from sincere witnesses it is axiomatic that psychosocial theories then have to postulate that the stories are capable of generating hallucinations produced within the minds of believers (the alternative being that such stories must generate large numbers of people with an inordinate love of lying who tell such tall tales).

Precisely how does a story go on to generate a hallucination? It is conceivable that someone who is suffering stress alone on a dark night and feeling vulnerable might misperceive or even succumb to imagination but why should it take the form of a woman in white (surely a less threatening form than many that could be imagined) especially if there was no pre-existing story known to the percipient? Even more problematic is that sightings occur in the comparatively safe countryside of Great Britain and Southern Ireland which today enjoy a relatively low homicide rate compared with many other nations, (albeit in relatively remote areas), as well as at times when the witness is in company.

Even more difficult to account for are actual encounters on the part of those without any religious belief or any connection with the district, strangers to the area or those that occur in other countries and cultures and their occurrence to atheists or in non-Christian context.

The experience appears to involve interactions between individuals and their environment which transcend the ordinary constraints of space and time. White Ladies may be compared to the images of people seen in dreams, including those we may know or who have known but which are not those actual persons but representations or simulacrums of them, a fleeting connection with some apparitional drama.

One hypothesis, involving some considerable stretching of the 'idea pattern' theory advanced by G.N.M Tyrrell is that perceivable idea patterns might also exist in the collective minds of a community. He wondered whether, with collectively perceived apparitions and those of high strangeness, popular tradition might supply the information out of which 'collective 'idea-patterns' could form. This would mean a sighting involving a telepathic tapping of the potentially shared subconscious of the wider community, resulting in certain sensitive individuals experiencing in appropriate localities visions of legendary beings, e.g. the Great God Pan, faeries, the Blessed Virgin Mary, and so forth. This proposal might thus provide the explanation for Lawson's experience in rural Greece.[19]

However, the mechanism for this remains wholly obscure, if indeed it takes place at all. The possibility that the hypothetical 'community' in modern times may have had no knowledge of such traditions either. In this regard both the theories of social scientists and psychical researchers remain untestable and as nebulous as the phantoms themselves. The absence of clear explanations, and a general theoretical reluctance to even to explore the topic by most parapsychologists has meant the field has been left to esoteric and occult speculation. Certain esoteric writers link visions of white ladies with apparitions of the Virgin Mary, as do some ufologists in drawing parallels between aerial visions of the Blessed Virgin at shrines by faithful crowds, (a connection made most strongly concerning the later visions received at Fatima in Portugal in October 1917 and with UFO experiences which began occurring thirty years later in 1947).[20]

The principal points of comparison both involve lights in the sky, multi-witnessed events, supposed encounters with powerful celestial beings and occasional physical traces. Such all-encompassing perspectives maintain the theory that anomalous experiences exist on a spectrum and that boundaries between them are porous or even artificial. Thus, whether the witness perceives a White Lady, the Virgin Mary or a UFO entity becomes very much a matter of local interpretation; rather than the phenomenon being understood as an expression of some wider alien or cosmic intelligence, a hypothesis advanced by Dr Peter McCue.[21]

At the same time other writers who note overall similarities also identify marked distinctions between these types of experience. Patrick Harpur points out that whilst both classes of encounter may involve shining figures and glowing lights, a significant point of departure between apparitions hailed as the Blessed Virgin Mary and those classed as White Ladies is that the former convey 'spiritual messages' to the visionaries in keeping with Catholic theology whilst the phantom ladies in diaphanous clothes and veils are usually mute, transmit no messages and do not inspire religious feelings.[22]

Examining the accounts of witnesses of White Lady ghosts, none seem to have thought they were encountering the Virgin Mary, (save for a private interpretation of the Brown Lady of Raynham Hall by the Marchioness of Townshend in 1936).[23] Those who encounter them do not, as a rule, go on to pursue lives as religious devotees or recluses but express surprise, puzzlement, awe or terror. No clear meaning is conveyed with their appearance to observers in the 20th century and 21st century. But what is also lacking is data on how the lives of the witness may have changed afterwards in response. What is needed here is more analysis of the experiences and their context.

The international dimension

Stories of spectral white ladies are extremely widespread. They are told in other parts of Europe as in France with its 'Dame Blanche' and in Germany with its 'Weisse Frauen'. They are encountered in the rural Palantinate haunting lonely spots and the sites of ruined castles. Central and South America are replete with stories of wandering phantom women, such as 'La Llorona' a ghostly woman who screams and cries, haunts coastal districts and lonely and dangerous spots inland.[24]

In Colombia in spring 2009 Carolina Manosca, aged 27, was riding in a car with her family after dark on a country road near Cali, the second largest city in the south west country. Being closer to the equator it gets darker earlier than in Europe or North America and the family were just returning after a social outing together. Carolina noticed the figure of a woman standing on the verge who crossed the road in front of them and then vanished. Later in her home in the city, she twice saw the figure of what she took to be the woman walking up the stairs, and her younger sister saw the same form also ascending the staircase. In all these sightings the facial features were never visible.[25]

Near the town of Campo Viera, in the north-eastern corner of Argentina, is a bridge along National Highway 14, spanning a stream known as 'the Yaza'. It is reportedly the scene of a ghostly woman in white materializing on the road just ahead of drivers.

Sightings have been logged officially since 2013, when a truck driver told police that he had run into a woman crossing the bridge. But when police attended the scene no trace was found of a victim or any accident. A short while after an engineer from Zona Centro claimed a similar experience, whilst in 2016 two different motorists reported separate sightings on the same day. All drivers concerned were convinced they had run down a real woman who had suddenly crossed in front of their vehicles.

Constructed in the 1970s, the Yaza bridge has acquired an unenviable reputation as an accident black spot with a history of crashes and collisions. The same period until 1983 saw numerous human rights abuses and it is claimed that the bodies of dissidents killed in the period were dumped from the bridge, or even buried in the concrete used in its construction.

One story avers that the lady in white was a political activist who was murdered; another that she was a local schoolteacher who became pregnant out of wedlock and committed suicide.

A similar story is told along the Aranilla river in the Tucuman province of Argentina, where a phantom woman who supposedly drowned her children manifests. One sighting on the nearby road to Teniente Berdina was by a teenage motorcyclist who claimed the figure was wearing clothes which they described as white garments that appeared like vapour 'that seemed to move in the wind and levitate in the air'. No face was visible, all being obscured by a mass of black hair. As at Yaza, the apparition is blamed for causing drivers to swerve into the bridge or collide with other vehicles. Essentially, it is the same pattern as claimed at Alconbury in Cambridgeshire in England (mentioned in connection with the entry on the White Lady of Harston).[26]

Japan also has legends of a phantom lady in white, known as the Yuki-Oona or Snow Lady. Seen in remote places, she is viewed as the personification of death in a storm or blizzard. The figure of Yuki-Oona is well known in Japan, with a concentration of folktales in Honshu, revived and preserved for posterity by the Irish writer Lafcadio Hearn (1850-1904) in his landmark study of Japanese ghosts now considered a folklore classic.[27]

White Lady Symbolism

The idea of the White Lady as a personification or symbol of tragedy is embedded in UK folklore. The Welsh tales of the 'Dynes Mewn Gwyn' (woman in white) have been cited as a kind of 'spectral monument commemorating some foul deed' prevalent at the site of a tragedy. This was postulated in the case of, in Powys, Wales a lady trailing a pure white garment falling in graceful folds along a stretch of road between Cann Office and Llanerfyl village. The cause was taken as being that 'several of the work-men were killed here when the road was being constructed.' Since it might be presumed that some of the men had wives or mothers who might mourn them, why not more figures?[28]

In Scotland, similar stories circulated around the Glenfinnan Railway viaduct near Fort William (often used by filmmakers for railway scenes featuring steam trains) constructed between 1897-1901 where a number of labourers died.

A third example, dating from the mid-1960s, concerns the reported sightings of a phantom woman or women in the vicinity of Blue Bell Hill in Kent. This was the scene of a tragic fatal road accident on 19 November 1965 which killed 24-year-old Suzanne Browne on the eve of her wedding, along with two girl friends who were due to be bridesmaids. Since the tragic accident there have been numerous stories in circulation of the hill being haunted by female forms.[29] In Yorkshire the White Lady had an association with appearing at Hallowe'en adding a connection to the dead.

Conceivably, the White Lady is a tragic symbol of both individual and collective trauma, perhaps signifying universalities of emotional suffering arising from death and lives cut short, such as the grief of a mother at the loss of a child. At Patong in Thailand, stories circulated of a foreign female ghost walking along the shoreline at night calling for her child in the aftermath of the 2004 Boxing Day tsunami that claimed the lives of many Thais and foreign tourists. The same motif of the wailing or shrieking woman looking for her child is a ubiquitous and archetypal form of ghost known from the Norfolk coast in the east of England to Latin America.[30]

A landscape generated apparition?

Across the world it is certain types of landscapes and environments that seem to attract the White Lady. This leads to speculation whether apparition might be a factor in evoking or triggering the experience.

Bridges, like all crossing places over moving bodies of water, can prove treacherous especially when situated above rivers with fast flowing currents. Aside from the peril associated with falling into water, crossing an isolated a bridge in the countryside at night may prove an unsettling experience as routes of escape are curtailed if any threat or danger is encountered. The literature of psychoanalysis recognises in neurotic cases a specific fear of bridges (termed 'gephyrophobia' from the Greek ''gephyra" for bridge). Worldwide, certain bridges appear to possess an attraction for suicides and white lady ghosts. But why does the ghost not appear as male which might be all the more frightening?

Possibly there are clues in the landscape, in place names, traditions and associations that point to something palpable and powerful in the land itself which resonates in human consciousness. In ancient cultures in Great Britain and Ireland, sites were often associated with a female power, named after women or dedicated to them. In Scotland the Bronze Age Callanish Stone circle set within the Paird Hills on the Isle of Lewis was reputedly haunted by the 'Shining One' which materialised on 1 May each year. The contours of the land and visible horizon suggest the profile of a sleeping woman, known as the Sleeping Beauty, or in Gaelic 'Cailliach na Mointeach' (the old woman of the moors).[31]

The same association with the feminine arises with lakes and pools, springs and wells where water flowing through small channels and openings in the ground evoked memories of birth and woman life-giving powers.

Seeing feminine forms in the mountains, hills and waters might be dismissed by the sceptical favourite of pareidolia, the experience of illusory patterns being created by the brain. But it is clear that apparitional experiences involve far more detail and go far further and more deeply than simply perceiving the vague suggestion of a feminine shape or form. To witnesses, materialised apparitions seem like vitalized and aminated projections conveying tragic, frightening, menacing and wonderous things. They suggest a glimpse of another world or dimension entirely, transcending time and space.

Such numinous locations provide the backdrop for greater awareness of what anthropologist Mircea Eliade calls 'hierophany', which can be defined as an awareness physical manifestations or revelations of the sacred and of being divinely 'haunted'.[32] It takes us into the realms of mystical speculation and the ideas of feminine archetypes in a collective unconscious mind, postulated by Swiss psychologist Carl Jung and his followers such as Anita Jaffe. Such a sense may be encountered at sites where ancient rituals and symbols once abounded and the ground has been trodden by thousands of pilgrims.

Today, when observers and travellers stray over or into them, there seems to be a merging of times and experience, both linear and the cyclical (for example Valerie Pomfret's impression of being 'shaken by a strange sensation of being in a different place and time'). The experience of mysticism may include encounters with an external presence they identify as feminine. Jung considered it not infrequent that the archetype appears in the form of a spirit in dreams or fantasy-products, or even comports itself like a ghost.[33]

Whether White Lady encounters involve some female principle encoded within the wider natural environment or are perceptions of a deep-rooted aspect within the human psyche is not a question that is easy to answer. Such experiences undermine materialist concepts and notions of subjectivity, with their insistence on solid divisions between subject and object and place and person. One should not be shut off from the idea of an external force, power or discarnate consciousness, a manifestation of something beyond being at work

A Cosmic Principle?

Stories of such encounters permeate the mythology and legends of the world, with an apparition being the manifestation of an entity or the expression of a female deity, and there are many who claim such encounters today.

It may be recalled that belief in a deeper female presence within nature is expressed not only in shapes and images but in abstractions. Ethnographic studies of shamanism and spirit ceremonies reveal a belief in communication, not only with entities in a female form but with a principle inherent in psychoactive plants and psychedelics, evoking hallucinatory visions that are commonly personified as female. A further tradition in the Middle Ages was that the Holy Spirit was female, conveying a divine sense of nurturing, love and healing offering the balance associated with femininity.[34]

Throughout history different cultures have believed in an active spiritual essence present in nature or the Cosmos, itself perceived as possessing essentially female in characteristics and which manifests in a variety of forms.

The fact that White Lady apparitions are so persistent, can be collectively sighted and show recurring patterns should encourage further study and analysis. They raise far wider questions concerning interactions between place and human consciousness than most psychical researchers have considered thus far. Altogether, White Ladies are a class of apparitional sightings which challenge the largely mechanistic approach and interpretation of ghost sightings of 'Phantom Ladies' advanced originally by Andrew Green and others in psychical research.

In contemplating such questions, we have moved a long way from the consideration of seemingly straightforward apparition reports and haunted houses with which this book began and primarily concerns itself.

Clearly, a great many theories could be enumerated at very little effort, and every one might serve us as the basis for a very nice new myth, religion, or pseudo-scientific fad in paranormal research. Andrew Green himself was an atheist and did not hold any religious beliefs and would not have gone beyond the psychical research perspective to consider visionary sightings or folkloric explanations. Nonetheless, having reached this stage of our knowledge, and with potentially numerous meanings to be found in these encounters, the possibility that the phenomena is potentially revelatory is surely deserving further exploration, rather than being simply dismissed. If it means psychical researchers and ghost hunters themselves have to widen their horizons, so be it. Further research is needed.

Notes & References

[1] Personal communication from Helen Barrell, 18 September 2022.

[2] Pomfret, Valerie (2008) Ghost Club Newsletter. Spring 2008.

[3] McCue, Peter Correspondence "The A75 roadadditional reports of apparitions *Paranormal Review* No. 66 April 2013 pp. 33-34

[4] Green, Andrew (1977) *Phantom Ladies*, pp.9-10

[5] Bennett, Ernest (1939) *Apparitions and Haunted Houses* Faber and Faber pp. 287-289

[6] Bennett,n.5 ibid 299-301

[7] *Journal of Paraphysics* (1969) 'Classified Directory'. Issued by Downton Paraphysical Laboratory.

[8] Crawford, Joseph (2011) *Raising Milton's Ghost John Milton and the Sublime of Terror in the Early Romantic Period'*. Chapter 2 21-50 https://www.bloomsburycollections.com/book/raising-miltons-ghost-john-milton-and-the-sublime-of-terror-in-the-early-romantic-period/ch2-milton-s-ghost.

[9] *Beck, Janet C. The White Lady of Great Britain and Ireland* Winter, 1970, Vol. 81, No. 4 (Winter, 1970), pp. 292-306;

[10] Information from Mr Robert Halliday of Bury St Edmunds.

[11] Gurney, Edmund, Myers, F and Podmore, F (1886) *Phantasms of the Living* Vol 2 pp. 206-207.

[12] Historic England site inventory List Entry Number: 1392200 (Bowl Barrow)

[13] Gauld, A. (1972) 'The haunting of Abbey House, Cambridge' *Journal of the SPR 46*, 109-123; Lawson, *Modern Greek Folklore and Ancient Greek Religion*

[14] Warner, Marina (1976) *Alone of All Her Sex: The Myth and Cult of the Virgin Mary.* Weidenfield and Nicolson. London p337.

[15] Hope, Robert Charles (1893) *The Legendary Lore of the Holy Wells of England.* Elliot Stock Publ. London. pp. 155-156

[16] Roby, John (1872) *Traditions of Lancashire* vol 2206-215; 'Ribble Valley Legend of Servant's Curse and Headless Statue'; *Lancashire Telegraph* 16 Feb 2020.

[17] Green, Andrew (1977) *Phantom Ladies* p.71

[18] 'Irish people still claim sightings of Virgin Mary in sky in 1985 were legitimate' *Irish Mirror* 15 April 2019.

[19] Tyrrell, G.N.M. (1953) *Apparitions.* Duckworth pp. 147.

[20] Vallee, Jacques (1966) *Passport to Magonia:* From Folklore to Flying Saucers. Regnery Publishing. pp. 160-161

[21] Explored extensively in McCue, Peter (2012) *Zones of Strangeness: An Examination of Paranormal and UFO Hotspots.* Author HouseUK.

[22] Harpur, Patrick (1995) *Daimonic Reality.* Arkana. UK. Chapter 8 'Ladies' pp. 102-119.

[23] Murdie Alan (2006) The Best Ghost Photograph Ever Taken? Re-assessing the Brown Lady of Raynham Hall' lecture 30 International Conference of the Society for Psychical Research, Liverpool Hope University. 5 September 2006; SPR Research File/Psychic Photograph 2/14 Compiled by Mr C.V.C Herbert 14 January 1937.

[24] Harpur. Patrick (1995) note 21; Magin, Kauert & Ulrich, Magin (2022) *Spuk Orte in der Pfalz. Von Irrlichtern, Geisterhunden und Weißen Frauen.* Agiro-Verlag, Neustadt *(title translation: 'Haunted Places in the Palatinate: Of will-o'-the-wisps, ghost dogs and white ladies').*

[25] Carolina Manosca, personal comm. to Alan Murdie 12 Nov 2010.

[26] Murdie, Alan (2017) 'White Ladies and Haunted Bridges' Ghostwatch column, *Fortean Times* Sept 2017; *Misiones* (on-line version) http://misionesonline.net/2017/03/21/misiones-aseguran-fantasma-una-mujer-provoca-accidentes-automovilisticos-puente/ 16 & 21 March 2017).

[27] Hearn, Lafcadio (2019) *Japanese Ghost Stories.* Penguin Classics 1st Edition

[28] Beck, Janet C. (1970) 'The White Lady of Great Britain and Ireland Winter' in *Folklore* 1970, Vol. 81, No. 4 (Winter, 1970), pp. 292-306.

[29] MacGregor, Alasdair Alpin archive Manuscript CollectionAcc. 6215 Nat. Library of Scotland; Tudor, Sean (2017) *The Ghosts of Blue Bell Hill and other Road Ghosts.* White Ladies Press.

[30] Porter, Enid (1974) *The Folklore of East Anglia.* Batsford. p79; Murdie, Alan (2017) Fortean Times n.26 ibid.

[31] Bord, Janet and Colin (1972) *Mysterious Britain.* Garnstone Press. p27; Ponting, Gerald & Ponting, Margaret (1984) *The stones around Callanish: a guide to the minor megalithic sites of the Callanish area*; Curtis, Margaret & Curtis, Ronald (1994 [2008]) *Callanish: stones, moon & sacred landscape.* p52

[32] Mircea Eliade (1954) *Cosmos and History: The Myth of the Eternal Return*, translated W. Trask (Princeton, NJ: Princeton University Press.

[33] Jung, Carl Gustav (1923) *Collected Works: Structure & Dynamics of the Psyche* Vol 8 405.

[34] Adams, Cameron (2011) 'Psychedelics, Spirits and the Sacred Feminine: Communion as a Cultural Critique' in Vol.2 No.3. April 2011 pp 49-52; Redgrove, Peter (1986) *The Black Goddess and the Sixth Sense.* Paladin. Chap 3 p.116.

APPENDIX

Testing the atmosphere of a haunted house and finding out the parts of the premises where the phenomena seem most common is an important part of any investigation.

An approach taken by American parapsychologist Gertrude Schmeidler in 1966 to haunted premises is simple to conduct a test to sample the emotional atmosphere of a site and the explore sense of a presence which people may be reporting. (Quantitative Investigation of a "Haunted House" (1966) *Journal of the American Society for Psychical Research* Vol LV April 1966 133-149).

With premises a floor plan should be provided to each person taking part. Participants go round and note an impression and mark the approximate area on the map. This is an attempt to determine emotional quality from this kind of subjective scanning of a location.

Examples of words to be used include:

active	demanding	irritable	trusting
dignified	despondent	jolly	vindictive
affectionate	determined	leisurely	warm
aggressive alert	emotional	mature	weak
aloof	fearful	meek	
anxious	forgiving	mischievous	
arrogant	friendly	noisy	
bitter	gentle	obliging	
calm	greedy	patient	
comforting	headstrong/impulsive	peaceable	
changeable	helpful	rigid	
cold	humorous	shy	
complaining	immature	stern	
confused	impatient	strong	
cruel	impulsive	submissive	
contented	independent	tolerant	

Participants mark on the plan any areas where they feel a particular emotional sensation seems concentrated.

The results are then compared to see if there is any commonality feelings of a particular area. This process may help eliminate natural causes as well as potentially revealing the site of any paranormal presence.

Whilst it is possible that participants may be picking up the emotional qualities of the group, the concentration of particular feelings in any specific area may narrow down the focus for the phenomena. Once established these can provide a place to focus experimental efforts, physical tests and the siting of equipment to see if any anomalies register.

INDEX

Avon
Bath, 18

Banshee, 148

Bedfordshire
Chicksands Priory, 15, 16, 135
Wilden, 16, 179
Luton, 17

Boleyn, Anne, ghost of
Rochford Hall, Essex; 32
Hampton Court, London, 68, 69, 169
Tower of London, 19, 60, 68

Brown Lady, 71, 133, 187
Raynham Hall, Norfolk at, 71, 133, 187

Buckinghamshire
Claydon House, Middle Claydon, Winslow, 17

Cambridgeshire
Alconbury, 18, 188
Cambridge, 18, 139, 154, 183, 184 (192)
Harston, 39, 100, 106
Sawston Hall, 18
Shudy Camps, 182

Castles
Berry Pomeroy, Devon, 24, 25, 133
Blenkinsopp Castle, Northumbria, 150
Castle Rushen, Isle of Man, 41, 136
Chilham, Kent, 43
Corfe Castle, Dorset, 27
Craster Castle, Alnwick, 74
Crathes Castle, Grampian, 118
Featherstone Castle, Yorks, 153
Glamis Castle, Tayside, 121
Hastings Castle, Sussex, 92
Langley Castle, Northumbria, 75
Manor Bier, Pembroke, 123
Maxstoke Castle, Birmingham, 102
Meggernie Castle, Tayside, 122
Muchalls Castle, Grampian, 13, 118, 119

Pevensey Castle, Sussex, 13, 92, 93
Sudeley Castle, Gloucestershire, 32, 130

Cheshire
Gawsworth Hall, Macclesfield, 19

Churches,
Chardstock, Devon, 25
St. Botolph's Church, Boston, Lincs, 58
Church of St. Lawrence, Ludlow, Salop, 13, 77
St. Michael and All Angels, Milton Common, Oxon, 76
St. Nicholas Church, Curdworth, Birmingham, 13, 104, 105
St. Nicholas Church, Pluckley, Kent, 54, 135
St. Mary the Virgin, Bletchingley, Surrey, 83, 132
St. Mary's Church, Reigate, 86
Worstead, Norfolk, 150

Cornwall
Penfound Manor, Penstock; Penzance, 19
Cumbria, Levens Hall, 22
Lorton Hall, 20, 21, 131

Derbyshire
Denleen Separates Ltd, Ilkeston, 23
Shardlow, 23

Devon
Chambercombe Manor, Ilfracombe, 26
Clothes Shop, Exeter, 25
Chardstock Church, Chardstock, 25
Plymouth, 11, 27, 133
Shute School, Axminster, 24

Dorset
Corfe Castle, 27
Longham, 28
Angel Inn, Lyme Regis, 29
Royal Lion Hotel, Lyme Regis, 28
Wimborne, 28, 182

Essex,
Woolston Hall Country Club, Chigwell, 31, 136
Valence House, Dagenham, 31

Gloucestershire
Sudeley Castle, Winchcombe, 32, 130
Swan Pool, Redbrook, 33, 130

Grampian,
Muchalls Castle, Stonehaven, 13, 118, 119

Greater Manchester
Chadderton, 34, 35, 133
Hall-i'-th'-Wood, 34

Green Lady or Ladies (UK) at:
Aston, West Midlands,100; Crathes Castle, Grampian 118; Thorpe Hall, Lincs 146; Inverawe House, 120- 121; Taynuilt, Strathclyde 120;Longleat House, Wilts, 111;

Grey Lady and Ladies (UK)
Garrick Theatre, Avon 15; Claydon Hall, Bucks,17;Abbey House, Cambridge, 184; Sawston Hall, Cambs; 18; Levens Hall, Cumbria, 22; Lorton Hall, Cumbria,20-21; Shute School, Axminster, Devon; 24 Chardstock, Devon, 25; Shardlow, Derbyshire, 23; Castle Rushen, Isle of Man; Ringwood, Hants,39; Hampton Court, London,169; Old Palace, Croydon, London, 67; Wandsworth Prison, London, 64: Oxney Bottom, Kent,52; Craster Tower, Northumbria, 74; Milton Common, Oxon, 76; Bury St Edmunds, Suffolk, 81, 82, 162; Blithfield Hall, Rugeley, Staffs, 80; Glamis Castle, Tayside,121.

Hampshire
Wherwell Priory, Andover, 35
Bramshill, 11, 36, 37, 38, 132
Havant, 36, 130
Marwell Hall, 39
Ringwood, Winchester, 146, 147

Hertfordshire
St Albans, 40

Hotels
Deans Place Hotel, Alfriston, Sussex, 88
Ettington Park Country Club, Warwickshire 99, 135
Garricks Head, Bath, Avon 15
George Hotel, Dorchester-on-Thames, Oxon, 75
Hoar Cross Hall, Staffs, 78
Lion Hotel, Llandinam, 28
Lord Crewe Arms, Durham,30
Royal Circus Hotel, Edinburgh, 119
Samuel Pepys, Northants, 74
Talbot Hotel, Oundle, Northants 73

Isle of Man
Castletown, 41

Kent
Bridge Place Country Club(former), 42
Broadstairs 11, 43
Chilham, 43
Cranbrook, 11, 44
Fawkham Green, 46
Grace Hill, 46
Margate, 47
New Romney, 11, 50
Oxney Bottom, 52
Plaxtol, 52, 53
Pluckley, 54, 135
Staplehurst, 179

Lancashire
Creston, 55
Preston, 55, 56

Leicestershire
Brooksby, Melton Mowbray, 56
Shepstone,

Lincolnshire
St. Botolph's Church, Boston, 58
Deeping St. Nicholas, 59
Doddington, 59
Thorpe Hall, 146
Lights, ghostly
Badwell Ashe-Great Ashfield, Suffolk 181; Old Soar Manor,Sussex , 52, 53; Penzance, Cornwall; 20 Spencer Grove, London;151

Lights, interference with,
Chadderton, Greater Manchester 35, 133;
Theatre Royal, Margate, 47-50

London
Aylward Street, E.1. 60
Brentford, Boston Manor House, TW8, 65
Clapham, Bingo Hall, SW4, 62
Clapham Common, The Plough Inn, S.W.4. 63
Croydon, The Old Palace, 67
Croydon, Roundshaw Estate, SM6, 65 -67
Enfield, The Old Horseshoes Pub, EN2, 67
Hackney, Spencer Grove, N16, 151
Paddington, Sarah Siddons School, W2 , 64
St James' Park, Birdcage Walk, S.W.1, 62
Tower of London, EC1, 60, 68

Wandsworth Prison, S.W. 18, 64
Whitehall, Admiralty House, SW1, 61

Northern Ireland
Spring Hill, Londonderry, 117

Merseyside
Bebington Hall, 70
Speke Hall, 70

Music, phantom
Old Soar House, 52, 53
Sussex Royal Lion Hotel, Dorset , 28
Sawston Hall, Cambs, 18

Norfolk
Magdalene Street, Norwich, 72
Raynham Hall, 71, 187
Raynham Hall, ghost photograph, 133
Shrieking Pits, Aylmerton, Sheringham, 72
Worstead Church, 150

Northamptonshire,
Higham Ferrers, 73
Oundle, 73
Slipton, 74

Northumbria
Blenkinsopp Castle, 150
Craster Tower, Alnwick 74, 132, 133
Langley Castle, 75

Oxfordshire
Dorchester-on-Thames, 75
Milton Common, 76

Red Lady or Red Ladies
Pluckley, Kent 54; Ludlow, Salop, 77; Crowcombe, Sussex 78

Somerset
Bridgewater, 179

Staffordshire
Burslem, 78, 79
Hoar Cross Hall, 78
Rugeley 79, 80
Uttoxeter, 185

Suffolk
Badwell Ashe, 181
Bury St Edmunds, 81, 82, 162, 173
Great Ashfield, 181
Gunton, nr Lowestoft, 148
Pin Mill to East Bergholt, 177

Surrey
Bletchingley, Surrey, 83, 132
Guildford, 5
Kenley, 85, 135
Reigate, St Mary's Church, 86
Wray Farm, Reigate, 87, 132

Sussex
Alfriston, 88
Brighton, 88, 154
Buxted, 9, 89
Crowborough, 90
Hastings, 13, 88, 90, 91, 92
Pevensey, 92, 93
Robertsbridge, 4, 11, 90, 93, 94, 164
Ticehurst, 95, 132

Telepathy, 2, 3, 134, 135, 137, 138, 139, 151, 152, 172, 186

Tyne and Wear
Washington, 97
Willington Mill, 150

Virgin Mary, apparition of, 71, 184-187

Warwickshire
Hillborough Manor, Bidford on Avon, 97, 98
Stratford On Avon, 99

West Midlands
Aston, Birmingham, 100, 104
Black Patch Park, Smethwick, 106
Brookfields, Birmingham, 101
Curdworth, Birmingham, 104, 105
Erdington, Birmingham, 103, 107, 134
Knowle, 105
Long Acre, Birmingham, 104
Maxstoke Castle, Coleshill, 102
Warley Abbey Grounds, Smethwick, 106
Walmley, Sutton Coldfield, 107
West Bromwich, 108

Witton Lakes, Upper Witton, 103

White Lady or Ladies (UK)
Chicksands Priory, Beds 15,16; Skefco, Luton, Beds, 17; Deeping, Lincs 5; Royal Hotel, Edinburgh, Lothian, 119; Alconbury, Cambs, 18, 188; Harston, Cambs;18; Longham, Dorset, 28; Rochford Hall, Essex, 32; Havant, Hants,38; Samlesbury Hall, Lancs 56, 171; Worstead, Norfolk, 150; Blenkinsopp Castle, Northumbria 150; Langley Castle, Northumbria, 75; The George Hotel, Dorchester on Thames, Oxon 75; Rushbrooke Hall, Suffolk,173; Reigate, Surrey,86,132; Glamis Castle, Tayside, 121; Brookfields, West Midlands,101; Grimshaw Hall, Knowle, West Midlands,105; Witton, Erdington, West Midlands 103, 104; Maddington, Wilts, 110; Kidderminster, Worcs; Barnsley,Yorks,40; Featherstone Castle, Yorks 153; and Chapter Four, generally.

White Lady or Ladies (outside the UK)
Argentina, in: Campo Vierra, 188; Aranilla river, Tucaman,188; Colombia, in, 187 Egypt, in: Zeitoun, Cairo; France, in: Lourdes 186; Germany, in: 139;Greece, as nymph 184; Japan, in, 188; Thailand, in: Patong, 189

Wiltshire
Littlecote House, 109
Longleat House, 111
Stanton St. Bernard, 110

Worcestershire
Kidderminster, 40

Yorkshire
Haworth, 116
Keighley, 116
Ripley Castle, 112
Settle, Tosside, 113
Sheriff Hutton, 113
Staithes, 114
Wombwell near Barnsley, 151
York, Castlegate, 116
York, Theatre Royal, 114, 115

Scotland

Central Region
Stirling, 117

Lothian
Edinburgh, 119 - 121, 172
Woodhouse Lea, 172, 173

Tayside
Glamis Castle, Glamis, 121
Meggernie Castle, 122

Wales
Anglesey, 123 (11)
Llanerchymedd, 123
Penrhos, 123

Dyfed, 123
Manor Bier, Pembroke, 123

Powys
Llandinam, 125
Llanerfyl village, 189
Red Bridge, 124

www.ingramcontent.com/pod-product-compliance
Lightning Source LLC
Chambersburg PA
CBHW071200160426
43196CB00011B/2137